Praise for *Action Learning in Action*

"Michael Marquardt is the guru of action learning and how to best make it work. *Action Learning in Action* offers down-to-earth techniques for maximizing both personal and organizational learning. Read it before your competitors do!"

> Howard Schuman, Managing Director,
> East-West Capital Resources

"Michael Marquardt has the ability to cut through to the essence in providing practical examples. *Action Learning in Action* is a must-read for those interested in positioning organizations for success in the new millennium."

> Robert L. Dilworth, Ed.D.,
> Professor, Virginia Commonwealth University

"Michael Marquardt has given us the key action learning tool that has been missing to this point—a clear, very readable 'what it is' and 'how to do it' resource for dealing with the ever increasing complexity of today's business environment. Like the concept of action learning itself, you can't overestimate the power of this book."

> Stephen M. Soffe, Public Sector Manager

"For those of us who call ourselves practitioners and human performance technologists charged by our organization with the mission of improving team effectiveness and engineering worthy team competence and performance, this book is an essential resource on how to prepare high-performing teams for ongoing accomplishments."

> Emmanuel Justima, Director of Human Resources,
> TD Manufacturing

"Michael Marquardt is one of the best writers in our field. In this book he explores five valuable applications available to anyone or any organization that employs action learning. A powerful, practical guide."

> Angus Reynolds, Workforce Education and
> Development Program Coordinator,
> Southern Illinois University

Action Learning in Action

Action Learning in Action

Transforming Problems and People for World-Class Organizational Learning

Michael J. Marquardt

Author of BUILDING THE LEARNING ORGANIZATION

Foreword by Reg Revans

DAVIES-BLACK PUBLISHING
Palo Alto, California

Published by Davies-Black Publishing, an imprint of Consulting Psychologists Press, Inc., 3803 East Bayshore Road, Palo Alto, CA 94303; 800-624-1765.

Copublished with American Society for Training & Development

Special discounts on bulk quantities of Davies-Black books are available to corporations, professional associations, and other organizations. For details, contact the Director of Book Sales at Davies-Black Publishing, an imprint of Consulting Psychologists Press, Inc., 3803 East Bayshore Road, Palo Alto, CA 94303; 650-691-9123; Fax 650-988-0673.

03 02 01 00 99   10 9 8 7 6 5 4 3 2 1
Printed in the United States of America

Library of Congress Cataloging-in-Publication Data
    Marquardt, Michael J.
    Action learning in action : transforming problems and people for
    world-class organizational learning / Michael J. Marquardt ;
    foreword by Reg Revans. — 1st ed.
        p. cm.
    Includes bibliographical references and index.
    ISBN 0-89106-124-X
      1. Organizational learning. 2. Active learning I. Title.
    HD58.82.M3698   1999
    658.3'124—dc21   98-51048
                                                        CIP

FIRST EDITION
First printing 1999

Contents

Foreword

We live in a changing world, and, in order to understand the changes more deeply, we have a mounting responsibility to understand our very selves. There is nothing at all novel about this obligation of self-understanding and self-development. However, the steadily mounting specialization of our complex systems is preventing many of us from discriminating between cleverness and integrity, between smartness and truth.

A recent article in *The Independent* entitled "In America, the Truth Is Sacrosanct—Well, Almost" describes how many people in the United States are becoming embarrassingly conscious of the differences between business efficiency, as measured by economic experts, and traditional honesty, as long expressed by moral philosophers.

When Abraham Lincoln said "that government of the people, by the people, for the people shall not perish from the earth," he was proclaiming a form of social responsibility that is a key element of action learning. For democracy, as for learning, to flourish, the people must be involved in identifying what needs to be done, what stops them from doing it, and what they can do about it.

Action learning was first organized in the coal mining industry during World War II. Since many of the colliery managers had overseas customers, the concept of understanding oneself as well as one's technology became an international concern. It eventually led to the conviction that for English managers to understand their own problems and their own staffs, they should learn to perceive clearly how those from another culture and a different industry were able to develop realistic interpretations of their current difficulties. Recognition of one's own personal status was thus collectively identified.

As throughout the rest of the world, here in Birmingham, England, things are changing. But, unlike in many other neighborhoods, things are changing for the benefit of all the community and not exclusively for the profits of the privileged. Action learning has been adopted by

Birmingham's Forward Engineering Group Training Scheme. Already it is clear, according to its chairman, that action learning's "honest, forthright approach has not only inspired a critical appraisal of our policies, but also enabled us to identify what we are trying to do, what's stopping us from doing it, and what we might do about it." The managers of many different businesses all volunteer to cooperate, to barter among themselves not their cleverness but their weaknesses, and, finally, to hold semipublic meetings for local people trying to understand Lincoln's inspiration of "of, by, and for the people."

The spontaneous commitment to action learning in Birmingham in the 1960s was similar to the public presentation by a dozen Egyptian businesses, in the 1970s, of their cooperative reviews of each other's problems and progress. The chairman opened the Cairo Conference with these words:

> We are all in the same boat. This makes the findings about each other very important and very relevant. I want to say, and in public, that all of us, whatsoever our positions, have a great deal to learn with and from each other. So much of importance, both basic and long term, goes wrong under our very noses that we must have others to notice it. We ourselves are too mechanically absorbed in our programmed routines and in our daily problems.

The history of mankind supports the commonsense ideas of action learning—the importance of posing fresh questions and taking action on ideas. The following few examples show how action learning was implicit even in the teachings and writings of the ancient philosophers:

> One may learn by doing the thing; for though you think you know it, you may have no certainty until you try.
> —Sophocles, *Trachiniae*

> To do a little good is better than to write difficult books. The perfect man in nothing if he does not diffuse benefits on others, if he does not console the lonely.
> —Buddha, *Benares Deer Park*

> But be doers of the word, and not only hearers of it, binding yourself with false ideas.
> —*Epistle of James*

> It is not enough to know what is good; you must be able to do it.
> —George Bernard Shaw, *Back to Methuselah*

The wisdom inherent in action learning is even more important in dealing with the rapid changes in today's world. And action learning can be used anywhere in the world. It is my hope that this book can bring the wisdom of action learning to all cultures and all kinds of people.

Reg Revans, father of action learning
and author of *The ABC of Action Learning* and
The Origins and Growth of Action Learning
June 1998

Preface

Action learning is a deceptively simple yet amazingly intricate problem-solving strategy that has the capacity to create powerful individual and organizationwide changes. It is built on a number of organizational, sociological, epistemological, and psychological systems that energize and synergize each other in the process of transforming problems and people. The potent resources inherent in action learning offer tremendous opportunities for individuals, teams, and organizations to grow and develop.

Yet, despite its power, simplicity, and cost-effectiveness, action learning is still rarely utilized within American organizations. Although action learning was developed and successfully applied over sixty years ago, most of us are still unfamiliar with the concept, much less the practice, of action learning. Perhaps its very simplicity is the cause of this—if something is not complex, then how can it solve the complex issues facing complex organizations in today's complex world? Or maybe we Americans tend to focus on quick, short-term efficiency rather than long-term effectiveness, on urgent activities rather than important actions. Or perhaps the cause is our tendency not to trust turning over our problems and important projects to our less wise, less experienced workers. Or maybe we want simple, easy answers rather than systematic changes that challenge our basic assumptions and modi operandi.

Another reason for action learning's limited use is perhaps our confusion about what action learning truly is. Action learning, as publicized in the U.S., barely resembles the classic action learning as developed by Reg Revans and others earlier in this century. Thus, when the watered-down version leads to poor results, we discard it rather than seeking to discover what it really is and to fully apply action learning, with all of its rich elements.

Why This Book?

It is the challenge of this book to provide a comprehensive overview of the true principles and successful practices of action learning as it has emerged on a worldwide basis. The book will describe what action learning is, how and why it works, and what benefits accrue to organizations that employ it. This book also includes a step-by-step guide to implementing action learning programs in your organization.

A key focus of the book will be an exploration of the five valuable applications available to anyone or any organization employing action learning: improving problem-solving, developing a learning organization, building effective teams, training leaders, and helping people achieve personal and professional growth and development. Numerous case studies of companies that are successfully applying action learning to their most challenging and perplexing problems, and at the same time using it to develop individuals, leaders, teams, and organizations, will also be provided.

Levels of Presenting Action Learning

There are a number of levels at which action learning will be presented in this book:

Idea or paradigm level—a way of looking at the world

Theory level—a means of explaining or predicting events; for example, theories involving scientific method, organizational change, or experiential learning

Technique level—a method of doing something

One cannot appreciate the potential or practice the power of action learning without, in fact, seeing the world and other people in a new and different way—a way that represents a new paradigm of thinking. And, as we shall see, action learning is indeed built on solid theory from the fields of education, management, psychology, and sociology.

In this book, however, we will be focusing primarily on the pragmatic, concrete level of technique and practices. There will be numerous guidelines, strategies, and illustrations of how action learning works. Examples will be presented of how action learning has solved problems and changed people and organizations.

Writing a book on action learning presents a challenge, since the concepts of action learning cannot be packaged and presented neatly and simply. There are too many forms and variations, some of which are yet to emerge. Although action learning contains some essential principles and elements, it is flexible and adaptable enough to work magnificently in a multitude of settings and situations.

Readers should recognize, therefore, that when an author attempts to describe action learning, that description is akin to an artist's rendition of a landscape—the landscape is much more than the painting. It is important to recognize that action learning, to be truly understood, needs to be experienced.

Overview of the Book

Part 1 provides an overview of action learning—what it is, where it came from, and how it works. In Chapter 1 the context and history of action learning will be explored, and the question "Why is action learning required in today's world of rapid change and chaos?" will be answered. Chapter 2 will describe the action learning process and principles—the six crucial components that complement and synergize each other to create successful problem solving as well as individual, team, and organizationwide development. Chapter 3 describes the types of action learning programs, the possible roles of participants, and the life cycle of an action learning group. It also provides a description of the actual workings and processes of an action learning meeting.

Part 2 explores the five key powerful synchronous ways in which action learning can be applied: problem solving (Chapter 4), creating a learning organization (Chapter 5), team building (Chapter 6), leadership development (Chapter 7), and personal and career growth (Chapter 8). Many organizational stories are provided to illustrate and demonstrate how action learning can achieve these benefits. Global companies are now seeking to use action learning in their offices throughout the world, and in more and more parts of the world organizations and communities are also beginning to use action learning. Chapter 9 examines how action learning may need to be modified in work with multicultural or cross-cultural environments.

The final section of the book, Part 3, provides a comprehensive, practical guide for establishing an action learning program in an organization. Chapter 10 provides a step-by-step guide on how to establish action learning programs in your organization, and Chapter 11 examines the various options to be considered as one begins undertaking an organizational action learning program. Chapter 12 looks at the important role played by the facilitator. How to handle potential pitfalls that may arise in action learning programs is covered in Chapter 13, and Chapter 14 provides a framework and approach for assessing the ongoing status and success of individual action learning meetings, as well as the company's overall action learning program.

Enjoy a New and Powerful Way of Learning and Action!

As a veteran, worldwide searcher of new ideas and successful practices, I am fortunate to have discovered action learning, with its power and diverse applications both for the workplace and for the community. Action learning represents a wonderful resource and tool for all of us as we journey into the twenty-first century. It is my hope that this book leaves you with a similar degree of enthusiasm, excitement, and awe toward action learning.

Michael J. Marquardt

Acknowledgments

I have been privileged and honored by the many people who have been so inspirational and supportive in helping me write this book.

First, the people who introduced me to action learning itself—Reg Revans, the pioneer and dedicated advocate; Lex Dilworth of Virginia Commonwealth University, who provided me the opportunity for experiencing action learning at its birthplace in England; Judy O'Neil, Joel Montgomery, Laura Bierema, and Verna Wilis, who, as leaders of action learning in the United States, encouraged me to share action learning with others.

Second, I would like to thank the authors of the guest essays, who, starting in Chapter 4, share their experiences of action learning with readers and who provide a different and welcome style and approach to the subject: Rebecca Kraft, Terry Carter, Laura Frey Horn, Shankar Sankaran, Isabel Rimanoczy, Jim O'Hern, Darlene Van Tiem, Suresh Vatsyayann, Carter McNamara, Eleanor Howard, Robert Dilworth, Teresa Carlson, Trish Gorely, Doune Macdonald, Robyn Burgess-Limerick, and Stephanie Hanrahan. I especially want to thank my students in action learning courses at George Washington University, both in the United States and in Asia; I have learned more about action learning from them than they have from me.

Then there are those who helped make this book a reality—Melinda Adams Merino, acquisitions editor at Davies-Black Publishing, who believed the time was ripe for a book on action learning in the United States; Cat Sharpe, who encouraged and promoted my booklet on action learning for the American Society for Training and Development (ASTD); and Nancy Olsen, VP for publications at ASTD, who has been a wonderful supporter of this and other writings of mine.

Finally, I would like to thank my family for their love and patience, as well as for their warm encouragement in allowing their husband and dad to write when they wanted to play. Thanks, Eveline, Chris, Stephanie, Catherine, and Emily.

About the Author

Michael J. Marquardt, Ed.D., is professor of human resource development and program director of overseas programs at George Washington University. He also serves as president of Global Learning Associates, a premier consulting firm assisting corporations around the world to become successful global learning organizations.

Marquardt has held a number of senior management, training, and marketing positions with organizations such as Grolier, World Center for Development and Training, International Coffee Organization, Overseas Education Fund, TradeTec, and U.S. Office of Personnel Management. He has trained over 25,000 managers in eighty-five countries, consulting with such clients as Marriott, DuPont, Pentax, Motorola, Peace Corps, COMSAT, Rover, United Nations Development Program, Xerox, Arthur Andersen, National Semiconductor, Warner-Lambert, TRW, Citicorp, and Singapore Airlines, as well as the governments of Indonesia, Malaysia, Jamaica, Honduras, and Swaziland.

He is author or coauthor of more than forty publications in the field of management and organization development, including *Building the Learning Organization* (selected as Book of the Year by the Academy of Human Resource Development), *Global Human Resource Development,* and *Corporate Culture: International HRD Perspectives.* Marquardt has been a keynote speaker at international conferences in Australia, Japan, England, Malaysia, South Africa, Sweden, Singapore, and India as well as throughout North America. His achievements and leadership have been recognized through numerous awards, including the International Practitioner of the Year Award from the American Society for Training and Development. He presently serves as a senior advisor for the United Nations Staff College in the areas of policy, technology, and learning systems. He is a Fellow of the Academy of

Human Resource Development and a cofounder of the Asian Learning Organization Network.

Marquardt received his doctoral degree in human resource development from George Washington University and his master's and bachelor's degrees from Maryknoll College. He has also done graduate work at Harvard University, Columbia University, and the University of Virginia. He enjoys sailing, skiing, music, and traveling with his wife and their four children.

Action Learning: What It Is and Why It Works

Action learning is a powerful problem-solving process as well as a program that has an amazing capacity to simultaneously effect powerful individual and organizationwide changes. In Part 1 we will provide an overview of action learning—what it is, where it came from, and how and why it works. Chapter 1 explores the context and history of action learning, illustrating why action learning is so important in today's world of rapid change and chaos. Chapter 2 describes the process that makes action learning unique, that is, the six key components that complement and synergize each other and thus allow for successful problem solving as well as individual, team, and organizationwide development. Chapter 3 examines types of action learning programs and describes the workings of an action learning group meeting. Let's begin the adventure.

Emergence of Action Learning in a World of Change

Change is all around us. Technology and globalization have transformed both our lives and the world in which we work. Organizations and individuals must continually adapt if they seek to participate in creative and meaningful ways with their changing environment.

Corporations that change too slowly will not survive for long in the twenty-first century. But how do they find time to learn and develop long-range capabilities for change when day-to-day crises must be met? Simply put, today's organizations are too busy fighting alligators to find time to drain the swamp.

The answer lies in finding ways to fight (act) and drain (learn) simultaneously. Learning and acting must become concurrent, since too many demands and too little time prohibit an exclusive focus on one or the other. The days when workers, especially leaders, could be absent from their offices for extended periods of training are over.

For many organizations around the world, *action learning* has quietly become one of the most powerful action-oriented, problem-solving tools, as well as their key approach to individual, team, and organization development. Organizations as diverse as Exxon, General Electric, TRW, Motorola, Arthur Andersen, General Motors, the U.S. Army,

Marriott, and British Airways now use action learning for solving problems, developing global executives, identifying strategic competitive advantages, reducing operating costs, creating performance management systems, and becoming learning organizations.

Respected academic and corporate centers of learning in Europe, Asia, and North America are beginning to tout the action learning method as the most robust and effective form of professional and corporate development. Harvard University's executive development programs, for example, have moved from the case study method to programs incorporating action learning. Michael Porter, Harvard's renowned business professor and author, bases his courses on the premise that "education is not truly valuable unless it is translated into action."

What Is Action Learning?

Simply described, *action learning* is both a process and a powerful program that involves a small group of people solving real problems while at the same time focusing on what they are learning and how their learning can benefit each group member and the organization as a whole.

Action learning contains a well-tested framework that enables people to effectively and efficiently learn and to simultaneously handle difficult, real-life situations. It is built on the application of new questions to existing knowledge as well as on reflection about actions taken during and after the problem-solving sessions.

Perhaps action learning's greatest value is its capacity for equipping individuals, teams, and organizations to more effectively respond to change. *Learning* is what makes action learning strategic rather than tactical. Fresh thinking and new learning are needed if we are to avoid responding to today's problems with yesterday's solutions while tomorrow's challenges engulf us (Dilworth, 1998).

Among the benefits of action learning are:

▲ Shared learning throughout various levels of the organization
▲ Greater self-awareness and self-confidence due to new insights and feedback
▲ Ability to ask better questions and be more reflective
▲ Improved communications and teamwork

These benefits are evident as one examines the five ways in which action learning can be applied.

Widespread Applications of Action Learning

Action learning has the unique and inherent capability of being applied simultaneously to the five most important needs facing organizations today:

Problem solving: Action learning programs are brilliant in their ability to find solutions to complex organizational problems—the more difficult the problem, the better suited action learning is to meeting the challenge.

Organizational learning: Action learning is the DNA of organizational learning—action learning teams serve as a model and an impetus for individual, group, and companywide learning.

Team building: Action learning helps develop strong teams and builds skills for individuals to work effectively in future teams.

Leadership development: Action learning has become the premier way for training future and current managers in organizations throughout the world because it prepares and develops leaders to deal with real problems.

Professional growth and career development: High levels of self-awareness, self-development, and continuous learning are gained via action learning.

The manner in which action learning is able to develop and produce each of these critical capacities is explored and illustrated in Chapters 4 through 8.

Components of an Action Learning Program

An action learning program derives its power and benefits from six interactive and interdependent components (see Figure 1.1 on page 6). The strength and success of action learning rely on the effective interaction of these elements.

A Problem

Action learning is built around a problem (project, challenge, issue, or task), the resolution of which is of high importance to an individual, team, and/or organization. The problem should be significant, be within the responsibility of the team, and provide opportunity for learning. Selection of the problem is fundamental to action learning because we learn best when undertaking some action, which can then be reflected upon. The problem gives the group something to focus on

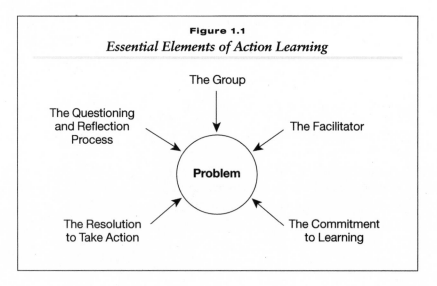

Figure 1.1
Essential Elements of Action Learning

that is real and important, that is relevant, and that means something to them. The problem creates a "hook" on which to test stored-up knowledge.

The Group
The core entity in action learning is the action learning group (also called a *set* or *team*). The group is composed of four to eight individuals who examine an organizational problem that has no easily identifiable solution. Ideally, the makeup of the group is diverse, so as to maximize various perspectives and obtain fresh viewpoints. Depending on the type of action learning problem, groups can be composed of individuals from across functions or departments. In some situations, groups are composed of individuals from other organizations or professions—for example, the company's suppliers or customers.

The Questioning and Reflection Process
By focusing on the right questions rather than the right answers, action learning focuses on what one does not know, as well as on what one does know. Action learning tackles problems through a process that involves first asking questions, to clarify the exact nature of the problem, and then reflecting and identifying possible solutions before taking action.

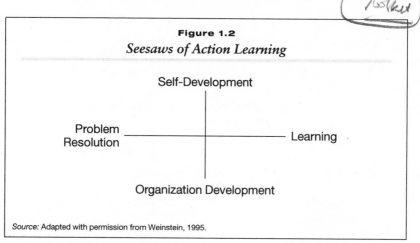

Figure 1.2
Seesaws of Action Learning

Self-Development

Problem
Resolution ———————————————————— Learning

Organization Development

Source: Adapted with permission from Weinstein, 1995.

When you read and are taught, you gain knowledge; when you take action, you gain experience; when you reflect, you gain an understanding of both.
—Anonymous

The Resolution to Take Action

For action learning advocates, there is no real learning unless action is taken, for one is never sure the idea or plan will be effective until it has been implemented. Therefore, members of the action learning group must either have the power to take action themselves or be assured that their recommendations will be implemented, barring any significant change in the environment, or barring the group's obvious lack of essential information. Action enhances learning because it provides a basis and anchor for the critical dimension of reflection (described earlier).

The Commitment to Learning

In action learning the learning is as important as the action. Action learning places equal emphasis on accomplishing the task and on the learning/development of individuals and organizations. Figure 1.2 captures the interplay between solving the problem and learning, as well as between self-development and organization development.

The Facilitator

Facilitation is important in helping the group memebers slow down their process, which will then allow sufficient time for them to reflect on their learning. A facilitator (also referred to as a *set advisor*) may be a working group member (possessing familiarity with the problem being discussed) or an external participant (not necessarily understanding the problem content or organizational context, but possessing facilitation skills for action learning).

The facilitator is very important in helping participants reflect both on what they are learning and on how they are solving problems. He or she helps group members reflect on how they listen, how they may have reframed the problem, how they give each other feedback, how they are planning and working, and how their assumptions may be shaping their beliefs and actions. The facilitator also helps participants focus on what they are achieving, what they are finding difficult, what processes they are employing, and what the implications of these processes are.

In Chapter 2 we will explore in greater depth how to implement each of these six essential components in action learning programs.

What Action Learning Is Not

The term *action learning* has been used by many organizations and individuals to describe programs that have little or no relationship to true action learning. Some of these programs barely resemble action learning, with its six crucial elements, first developed by Reg Revans and others nearly sixty years ago. Thus it is important to know what action learning is not, as well as what it is.

Task Forces and Quality Circles

Task forces and quality circles differ from action learning groups in three significant ways. First, task forces and quality circles tend to focus on the specific problem or task to be addressed rather than on identifying the organizationwide, environmental, systemic elements in which the problem resides, and which must also be affected if lasting change is to take place.

Second, these groups generally do not have the power or the expectation of taking action. That power is left for some higher body to implement, in whole or in part, as may be expedient. Progress on implementing what was developed in the task force is often monitored, either by some manager caught up in organizational power games or by some expert who has a smaller stake in implementation than the original planning group does.

Third, task forces and quality circles are charged with addressing a problem or improving a product or procedure; any learning that occurs is incidental. Action learning groups, on the other hand, are charged with *learning from* the problems they are solving, the assumptions they are challenging, and the actions they are confronting. In addition, action learning groups often address unfamiliar problems rather than problems about which they have expertise, as might be more common in task forces. The focus is on a real work-centered project where action and learning from that action are expected.

Groups such as task forces lose a great deal of potential learning for the following reasons:

▲ There is a separation between work and learning; task forces view learning as something done in preparing for the work of the task group, not as something integral to it.

▲ Learning is seen as taking time away from work rather than as being the most important part of work.

▲ In task teams, members make recommendations but do not themselves act on their solutions. Thus they lose the learning that would have been gained by their testing their recommendations, to see if they will work or how they can be improved. Action learning advocates believe that there can be little true learning without action to test the validity of ideas.

▲ Most critically, task forces do not provide the opportunity for members to learn more about themselves in a way that allows them to modify their behavior in future settings.

Learning and Reflecting on the Job

Encouraging employees to discuss, reflect, and learn while carrying out their day-to-day duties is admirable and valuable, but it is not action learning. Action learning involves a diverse team of people working together on significant problems over a relatively long period of time. It requires time for questioning and reflection, as well as time for sharing learnings. It requires learning and acting on other people's jobs. It entails frank, honest, and supportive feedback on behavior, attitudes, and learning styles. It requires team learning, team reflection, and team growth.

Outdoor Adventures

Outdoor adventures do offer many of the elements of action learning. Teams are confronted with challenges and problems, and members must identify creative ways of solving those problems. Members are involved in situations in which they are vulnerable and have to work together to find the correct answers. There is time allocated for reflection on how actions relate to and apply to the real world of work. Climbing ropes and rappelling down cliffs can indeed help build teamwork and force people into new ways of thinking.

However, the problems are not real work problems. The challenges faced are more often puzzles requiring cleverness and creativity rather than situations with no easy, correct answer that different groups would resolve quite differently.

If the group fails in its outdoor adventure, the members still go on, with little or no impact on their lives. Thus the quality and the relevance of the learning, as well as the value of success, are diminished. Too many participants see outdoor adventure as simply "whoopee in the woods" and not the real world (Froiland, 1994).

Simulation

Simulation, which includes case studies and business games, is a weak equivalent of action learning, since there are no consequences for actions taken. Thus there is much less interest in and commitment to the activity. In addition, case studies or business games appeal to instincts of rivalry and exhibitionism rather than to team building and individual growth.

In simulation activities, the situation to be analyzed is quite theoretical. Participants, therefore, do not bear any responsibility for the solutions they propose to problems. As Revans (1980) notes, "The cases are edited descriptions by unknown authors of inaccessible conditions for which participants cannot be responsible and upon which they cannot deploy their most effective managerial talent, namely, the power of observation." In case studies, participants cannot test the validity of their solution by taking any real-time action to apply it. Without risk, without being able to see the consequences of their own action, there can be little true learning for participants.

Participants in case studies and business games may come to believe that they would follow their ideas in practice, but these ideas may bear little relationship to the real world. True learning and behavioral change require that the participants see the practical outcomes of their

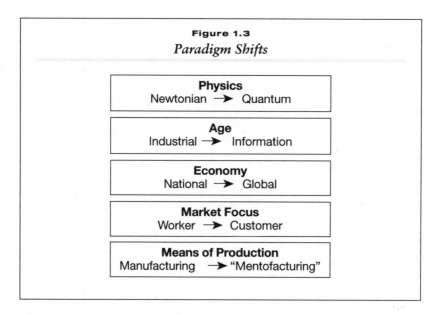

Figure 1.3
Paradigm Shifts

Physics
Newtonian ➤ Quantum

Age
Industrial ➤ Information

Economy
National ➤ Global

Market Focus
Worker ➤ Customer

Means of Production
Manufacturing ➤ "Mentofacturing"

own actions or decisions. They must be able to test their conclusions to see if such actions will work and be convincing to others outside the group, such as leaders in the organization.

Why Action Learning Is Needed in Today's World

There is so much change in today's world that today's solutions will be totally inadequate to tomorrow's challenges. Sociologists and management specialists have identified five dramatic, paradigmatic shifts causing the chaos in today's world and workplace (see Figure 1.3).

Action learning provides a solid resource for organizations' successful response to today's ever changing, ever more competitive environment. It provides a means for organizations to solve complex problems in a systemic way, so they stay solved.

Newtonian to Quantum Physics

For nearly three centuries the world and the workplace have been built upon the principles of Newtonian physics—cause and effect, predictability and certainty, distinct wholes and parts, reality as what is seen. Newtonian physics is a science of quantifiable determinism, linear thinking, and controllable futures.

In the Newtonian mind-set, people engage in complex planning for a world that they believe is predictable. They continually search for better methods of objectively perceiving the world. This mechanistic and reductionist way of thinking and acting still dominates life today. Margaret Wheatley (1992), author of *Leadership and the New Science,* regards this mind-set as "unempowering and disabling for all of us" in today's world.

Quantum physics, introduced by Einstein and others in the 1920s, deals with the world at the subatomic level, examining the intricate patterns out of which seemingly discrete events arise. Quantum physics recognizes that the universe and every object in it are in reality vast empty spaces filled with fields and movements, the basic substance of the universe. Thus relationships between objects and between observers and objects are what determine reality. The quantum universe is composed of an environment rich in relationships; it is a world of chaos and process, not just of objects and things.

In understanding quantum physics, we realize that we cannot make predictions with certainty, that chaos is part of reality. By extension, organizations must change the way they think, the way they attempt to solve problems and deal with such dilemmas as order versus change, autonomy versus control, structure versus flexibility, and planning versus flowing.

Industrial to Information Age

Just as machine technology created the Industrial Age, which began in the late eighteenth century, today's computer technology has created the Information Age.

Alvin Toffler (1990) writes that the advanced global economy cannot run for thirty seconds without the information technology of computers and the other new, rapidly improving complexities of production. Yet today's best computer systems will be considered "primitive" within a few years. We are moving from information exchange to virtual organizations to Internet commerce, which can transform every process of global business, including buying, selling, and information flow.

The world has indeed entered an era of ever increasing technological advancement, with optoelectronics, cyberspace, digital video, local-area networks, groupware, virtual reality, and electronic classrooms. The power of computer technology has also progressed from the mainframe to the desktop to the laptop to the user's hand. More and more companies' operations are increasingly automated, requiring computer-generated automation and customization. The impact on organizational work and on learning has been overwhelming.

All of these technologies have helped create the Information Age. Each has become necessary in managing the "data deluge" present in the fast-changing organizations of today. In a global economy, where being informed, being in touch, and being there first can make all the difference between success and being second-best, technology and information provide an enormous advantage indeed.

The emerging power and applicability of technology have turned the world of work on its head. Because of technology, organizations will become more virtual than physical. People will be more linked to customers in Kuala Lumpur than to co-workers across the hall.

The impact of technology on creating and managing information continues, always in accelerated form. Trying to figure out the capabilities and future directions of our rapidly changing Information Age is impossible. Let's look at just a few of the already existing powers of technology:

▲ Superconducting transmission lines can transmit data up to 100 times faster than today's fiber-optical networks. One line can carry one trillion bits of information a second, enough to send the complete contents of the Library of Congress in two minutes.

▲ Neural networks bring advances in computer intelligence that process commands sequentially. The neural network uses associative "reasoning" to store information in patterned connections and process complex questions through its own logic.

▲ Expert systems, a subset of artificial intelligence, are beginning to solve problems in much the same way as human experts.

▲ Telephones are being manufactured that are small enough to wear as earrings; cellular phones can now respond to e-mail.

One of the most amazing and transforming technological additions to our lives is the Internet. The use of the Internet is one of the fastest-growing phenomena the business world has ever seen, building from a base of fewer than a thousand connected computers in the early 1980s to over ten million host computers today. Internet commerce is projected to grow from a mere $8 billion in 1997 to over $327 billion in 2002 (Tapscott, 1995).

The increased power and capability of technology provide opportunities for expanding knowledge and information (Bates, 1995):

▲ Reduced costs and more flexible use and application of telecommunications through developments such as ISDN, fiber optics, and cellular radio
▲ Miniaturization (tiny cameras; microphones; small, high-resolution display screens)
▲ Increased portability through use of radio communications and miniaturization
▲ Expanded processing power through new microchip development and advanced software
▲ More powerful and user-friendly command and software tools, making it much easier for users to create and communicate their own materials

National to Global Economy

Globalization has caused a converging of economic and social forces, of interests and commitments, of values and tastes, of challenges and opportunities. We can easily communicate with people 10,000 miles away because we share a global language (English) and a global medium for communications (computers and the Internet).

Four main forces have quickly brought us to this global age: technology, travel, trade, and television. These four forces have laid the groundwork of a more collective experience for people everywhere. More and more of us share common tastes in foods (hamburgers, pizza, tacos), fashion (denim jeans), and fun (theme parks, rock music, television). Nearly two billion passengers fly the world's airways each year. People are watching the same movies, reading the same magazines, and dancing the same dances from Boston to Bangkok to Buenos Aires.

Ever more of us speak English—now spoken by more than 1.5 billion people in over 130 countries (often as a second, third, or fourth language). The English language, like all languages, carries with it implicit and explicit cultural and social values (e.g., precision, individualism, active control, clarity). It has become the global language of the airlines, the media, computers, business, and the marketplace.

The signs of the global marketplace are all around us:

▲ U.S. corporations have invested $1 trillion abroad and employ over 100 million overseas workers; over 100,000 U.S. firms are engaged in global ventures valued at over $2 trillion. Over one-third of U.S. economic growth has been due to exports, providing jobs for over 11 million Americans.

▲ Ten percent of U.S. manufacturing is foreign-owned and employs four million Americans; Mitsubishi USA is America's fourth-largest exporter, and Toyota has displaced Chrysler as the third-largest in U.S. auto sales. Foreign investment in the United States has now surpassed the $3-trillion mark.

▲ McDonald's operates more than 12,500 restaurants in seventy countries and is adding 600 new restaurants per year.

▲ Many of the Persian Gulf countries have more foreign-born than native workers. More than 70 percent of the employees of Canon work outside Japan.

▲ Financial markets are open twenty-four hours a day around the world.

▲ Over half of the Ph.D. degrees in engineering, mathematics, and economics awarded by American universities in 1997 went to non-U.S. citizens.

▲ Global standards and regulations for trade and commerce, finance, and products and services have emerged.

▲ More and more companies—InterContinental, Xerox, Motorola, Honda, Samsung, Pentax—are manufacturing and selling chiefly outside their countries of origin.

▲ Coca-Cola earns more money in Japan than in the United States.

▲ Over 70 percent of profits for the $20-billion music industry in the United States is from outside our country. Movies often depend on global viewers for big profits.

The global marketplace has created the need for global corporations. These organizations in turn have created an even more global marketplace. The growing similarity of what customers wish to purchase, including quality and price, has spurred both tremendous opportunities and tremendous pressures for businesses to become global. More and more companies, whether small or large, young or old, recognize that the choice is between becoming global or becoming extinct.

Global organizations are companies that operate as if the entire world were a single entity. They are fully integrated so that all their activities link, leverage, and compete on a worldwide scale (Marquardt and Snyder, 1997). Global firms emphasize global operations over national or multinational operations. They use global sourcing of employees, capital, technology, facilities, and raw materials. They deem cultural sensitivity to employees, customers, and patterns as critical to the success of the organization (Adler, 1996). Globalization of an organization has occurred when the organization has developed a global corporate culture, strategy, structure, and communications process (Rhinesmith, 1996).

Worker-Focused to Customer-Focused Market

In today's marketplace, organizations are looking more and more to the customer to determine how they will set strategies and carry out operations. Customers rather than workers will be the focus of leadership's attention in setting organizational priorities.

On a worldwide scale, customers will continue to push for new standards in quality, variety, customization, convenience, time, and innovation. They will increase the rapidity with which companies are compelled to move beyond domestic markets. Organizations will have no choice but to shop the world for customers, employees, resources, technology, markets, and business partners. The new demands for quality, the constant changes in tastes, the existence of global fads, and short product life cycles are forcing new global partnerships and alliances. Challenges raised by new niche markets, new and emerging industries, deregulation, fights over market share, and aggressive national competitors have created the need for merging global forces in order to survive.

Global communications and marketing have increased consumers' awareness about possible products and services. Global competition has offered customers more varied choices of higher quality. What has been created is a convergence of consumer needs and preferences. Consumers are now able to choose the products and services they want, on the basis of the best: cost (least expensive and most economical), quality (free of defects; meeting and exceeding the customer's expectations), time (available as quickly as possible), service (pleasant and courteous; available immediately on products that are repairable or replaceable), innovation (new products, not yet envisioned by the customer when produced), and customization (tailored to very specific needs).

Manufacturing to "Mentofacturing"

As a result of the four paradigm shifts just described, we live in an environment and an age in which the prime driver of the economy is knowledge. Knowledge is the key raw material for wealth creation and is quickly becoming the fountain of organizational and personal power. Manufacturing work (working with our hands) has been replaced by knowledge work (working with our minds, i.e., *mentofac-*

turing). Brains have replaced brawn as the most important means of increasing productivity and profits.

Mentofacturing is needed to create, understand, and manage the company's knowledge. Knowledge, which is created continuously in every corner of the globe, doubles every three to four years. It has become a company's most valuable asset, absolutely critical for the survival of organizations competing with the world's brightest companies.

Thomas Stewart, in a recent issue of *Fortune* magazine, asserts that "every company depends increasingly on knowledge—patents, process, management skills, technologies, information about customers and suppliers, and old-fashioned experience. . . . This knowledge that exists in an organization can be used to create differential advantage. In other words, it's the sum of everything everybody in your company knows that gives you a competitive edge in the marketplace" (p. 44).

Organizations must employ more and more knowledge workers. Not only senior executives, but employees at all levels must be highly educated, highly skilled knowledge workers. In the new postmanufacturing society, knowledge is not just another resource alongside the traditional factors of production, land, labor, and capital. It is the only meaningful resource in today's workforce. In an economy based on knowledge, the knowledge worker is the single greatest asset, and mentofacturing is the most important activity.

Mentofacturing capacity and products (i.e., valuable knowledge) have become more important for organizations than financial resources, market position, technology, or any other company asset. Better mentofacturing and knowledge will increase the abilities of employees to continuously improve products and services, to adapt structures and systems, to become world-class.

By the year 2000, three-quarters of the jobs in the U.S. economy will involve creating and processing knowledge. Knowledge workers have already discovered that continual learning is not only a prerequisite of employment but also a major form of work. Shoshana Zuboff (1988) writes that the "behaviors that define learning and those that define being productive are one and the same. Learning is at the heart of productive activity. To put it simply, learning is the new form of labor" (p. 395).

Action Learning's Response

Action learning naturally and inherently responds to the suppositions of each and every one of these five paradigm shifts. It has the unique capability, flexibility, and resilience to adapt to and affect them in truly creative and effective ways.

Action learning fits comfortably with the dynamics of quantum physics, since action learning strives to recognize new patterns rather than revert to the old ways of predictability. Action learning examines systems, and it practices holistic thinking rather than piecemeal, fragmented thinking.

Action learning is much better able to handle the abundance of data produced by the Information Age. It enables people to cope with the dizzying speed and complexity of today's world of work. Sets are able to filter out important knowledge from useless data. Action learning recognizes that knowledge and continuous learning are more important than unreflective activity and productivity. It emphasizes the interaction of the human with the technological.

Global teams are better built and work much better when action learning processes are employed. Action learning programs create and manage global projects in culturally diverse settings. Cultural dimensions that are oftentimes hidden or buried in normal group settings are brought out into the open and lead to synergistic success through action learning.

Outsiders (customers, suppliers, community leaders) have always been considered a vital part of action learning teams, since they bring in fresh perspectives and often ask the unasked questions. The systems thinking inherent in action learning recognizes the importance of bringing all stakeholders to any challenge or problem.

Finally, a key element of action learning is mentofacturing, which is as critical as any action planned and undertaken by a group or organization. Proponents of action learning have long recognized that what benefits the organization most in the long term is the building of its learning capacity and knowledge base.

Brief History of Action Learning

Action learning has been helping organizations deal with cataclysmic change for over fifty years. The pioneer who introduced the world to action learning and remains its most prominent leader is Reg Revans. A Cambridge physicist, Revans began his journey in the 1930s when he observed how scientists working at the Cavendish Laboratory shared their problems, questioned each other, and received support from the group. All the scientists had contributions to make, even when they were not experts in a particular field. In this way, they evolved workable solutions, over a period of time, to their own and one another's problems.

In 1945, Revans became the first director of education and training for the newly formed National Coal Board (NCB). He organized managers into small groups of four or five members, meeting with them in the coalfields, never far away from their own pits. From the beginning they worked on coalfield problems, visiting each other's pits and working as consultants to each other. Significantly, at a time when most pit productivity in the U.K. remained static, an increase in output by 30 percent was recorded in those mines that took part in these prototype action learning programs.

In 1955, after he became a professor of industrial administration in the U.K., Revans learned that the Royal Infirmary at the University of Manchester was having difficulty retaining trained staff, particularly nurses. He involved those who were seen as part of the problem in solving the problem. A significant finding was that nurses were discouraged from asking questions and thus from reaching a fuller understanding of their role. Small groups (composed of doctors, nurses, and administrators) worked on nearly forty separate projects, with impressive results.

A few years later, Revans achieved similar successes in Belgium with government officials, business leaders, and academics. As part of an interuniversity project, which involved five universities and twenty-three of the largest Belgian organizations, action learning programs took Belgium from the bottom of the European countries to the top, ahead even of Japan and the United States (Barker, 1998). For his efforts, Revans was knighted to Belgium's Order of Leopold.

In the 1970s and 1980s, Revans carried the concept of action learning to Australia, Malaysia, Hong Kong, Lapland, India, Saudi Arabia, Tibet, South Africa, Singapore, Nigeria, and Egypt. He became president of the International Management Center in Buckingham in 1982, where the first MBA programs based exclusively on action learning were started. In 1995, Revans hosted the first action learning conference in London, which was attended by 100 delegates from every part of the world.

Why Did the *Titanic* Sink?

The story of action learning actually began with the sinking of the *Titanic*. When this luxury ship went down, on April 14, 1912, over 1,400 passengers perished. Angry questions were raised on both sides of the Atlantic. How could the allegedly unsinkable ship go down on its maiden voyage across the North Atlantic? What had gone wrong? Why couldn't the planners and builders have foreseen such a tragedy?

Reg Revans' father was commissioned to investigate. What he discovered was that several of the planners and builders had indeed been concerned, though none of them had ever raised their concerns in the company of their colleagues. Their reasoning was that if no other "expert" seemed unsure about the structure and safety of the ship, then it must have already been concluded that the ship was fine. They were afraid of appearing foolish by asking "dumb" questions.

This story, passed on by his father, so impressed Revans that he began developing a process in which group members would be not only able but encouraged to ask "dumb" questions. Wisdom and common sense, rather than cleverness, were necessary for solving problems. When they could, groups should seek outsiders and nonexperts for fresh perspectives, ask new questions, and challenge basic assumptions. Over seventy-five years later, these fundamental insights still form the roots of action learning. ■

Theoretical Roots of Action Learning

What has made action learning so powerful is its ability to integrate the theories and practices of several disciplines—namely, education, psychology, management, systems thinking, political science, ethics, anthropology, and sociology (see Figure 1.4).

Action learning builds on the education principles of Knowles, Dewey, Kolb, and Mezirow and their emphases on adult learning, utilitarianism and practicality, learning styles, and transformative learning. It captures the psychological insights of Lewin, Jung, and Maslow into motivating, energizing, and liberating the talents of individuals and teams. The management theories of Drucker, Senge, Greenleaf, Wheatley, and Peters are seen in action learning's focus on systems thinking, service and facilitation, and managing chaos. Weick's "sensemaking" and the cultural insights of Hofstede and Kohls form the sociological and anthropological aspects of group work and problem solving. Finally, as can be seen in Revans' foreword to this book, action learning is built on ethical and political theses of democracy, egalitarianism, truthfulness, and caring for one's fellow travelers.

Action learning's ability to harness the powers of these disciplines enables it to be successfully applied to solving problems, developing leaders, and building organizations, teams, and individuals.

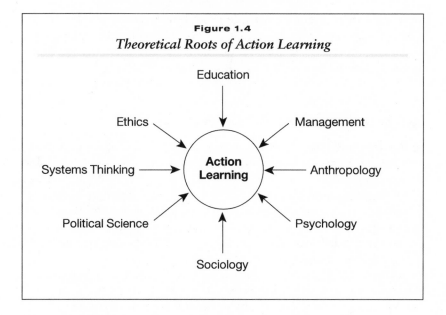

Figure 1.4
Theoretical Roots of Action Learning

Action Learning Since the 1970s

In spite of the early efforts of Revans and a few of his colleagues, action learning generated little worldwide interest until 1975, when Sir Arnold Weinstock encouraged the General Electric Company in Europe to experiment with the action learning approach. Soon thereafter, GE began using action learning in the United States and throughout the world, and it has become a model for corporate action learning programs worldwide (Noel & Charan, 1992).

The use of action learning has proliferated on a global scale, especially in the last five years. Hundreds of organizations, from British Airways to Lucent Technologies, have adopted action learning as the preeminent form for organizationwide learning and leadership development (Marquardt, 1997a; Marsick et al., 1992; Pedler, 1991).

Academic programs using action learning as a key form of learning and executive development have been created in Singapore, Italy, Malaysia, China, Sweden, the United States, and elsewhere. Associations and conferences dedicated to action learning are springing up in all parts of the world. A global conference on action learning via the Internet was held in March 1998 (see Chapter 5). Several U.S. government agencies, as well as ministries in India, Romania, Canada, Australia, and the United Kingdom, have initiated action learning programs. The InterAmerican Bank and other global public institutions now use action learning as a key process in determining loan and technical assistance efforts. All over the world, organizations have begun to feel the power of action learning.

Action Learning: A Key for Survival

Today's turbulent world forces us to learn faster and better in order to survive. Problems are ever more difficult for us to decipher, much less to understand and resolve. Dilworth (1998) has remarked that change "now tends to outdistance our ability to learn." Existing knowledge tends to misdirect rather than facilitate problem resolution. People and organizations need to learn new ways of coping with problems. Only by improving the learning capacity of individuals and organizations can we deal with the dynamics of change.

Revans (1998) observes that the world "is not only changing but doing so in a fashion hard to understand." He points out that the concept of action learning, whereby one identifies improvement not only in technological performance but also in personal self-development and cooperation with colleagues, is sensitive to "many different historical, economic, industrial, social, and political conditions. Thus action learning becomes a simple and direct approach in adapting to the accelerating rate of change." It allows us to build better ships, and to avoid the catastrophes of future *Titanics*.

In this chapter we have considered the power that action learning contributes in enabling us to cope with the chaotic world around us. In Chapter 2 we will examine the six essential elements that make action learning programs work effectively and thus be so valuable to organizations, teams, and individuals.

Six Essential Elements of Effective Action Learning

As presented in Chapter 1, action learning programs are built around six distinct interactive components:

▲ A problem
▲ The group
▲ The questioning and reflection process
▲ The commitment to taking action
▲ The commitment to learning
▲ The facilitator

Action learning, when all its essential elements are incorporated, has tremendous, far-reaching power and strength. The key to attaining the inherent potency of action learning is to fully and properly include all six of these components, each of which complements and leverages the other five. In this chapter we will examine the principles and practicalities present within each of these six elements.

A Problem

Action learning can be employed to address a wide variety of problems—complex problems that touch on different parts of the organization; problems that are not amenable to expert solutions; problems on which decisions have not already been made; and problems that are organizational rather than technical in nature. The focus of an action learning problem may be any of the following:

▲ Organizational or departmental issue
▲ Individual's management issue, quandary, irritation, or responsibility
▲ Individual's developmental issue—qualities, competencies, or behaviors that one seeks to improve

Examples of such problems could include any of the following:

▲ Reducing turnover in the workforce
▲ Improving information systems and reducing paperwork
▲ Increasing sales by a predetermined amount
▲ Resolving a problem between R & D and production
▲ Increasing the use of computers in a company
▲ Reorganizing a department
▲ Closing a production department or line
▲ Improving productivity in a retailing or manufacturing company
▲ Developing a new performance appraisal system

Criteria for Selection

There are several criteria for determining whether the project is appropriate for an action learning group. First, the project chosen by or for the group must be a real organizational problem, task, or issue that needs to be addressed and exists in a real time frame. It should be of genuine significance and not merely a hypothetical problem. This rules out the type of project or task that is pulled out of a hat to give trainees a "realistic" problem to work on. The problem or project is real if it is seen as crucial for the members. In addition, the organization should desire a tangible result by a definite date so as to justify the investment of time and funds.

The project must also be feasible—that is, it must be within the competence of the group to understand the problem and identify possible solutions.

Either the problem should be within the group's sphere of responsibility or the group must be given the authority to do something about the problem. It should be a problem or task that participants care about and that, if solved, will make a difference.

Moreover, the project should be a problem and not a puzzle. A puzzle can be defined as a perplexing question to which an answer or solution already exists but has not been found. A problem, on the other hand, has no existing solution. Different people will come up with different ideas and suggestions as to how to solve it. In other words, there may be a number of possible solutions that might be satisfactory.

Finally, the project should provide learning opportunities for members and should have possible applications to other parts of the organization. If the problem is viewed as just an exercise, or if participants doubt that the solution they construct will be implemented, there is less learning.

It is one of the fundamental tenets of action learning that we learn best when undertaking some action, which we then reflect upon. The main reason for having a problem or project is that it gives the group something to focus on that is real and important, that is relevant, and that means something to them. It creates a "hook" on which to test stored-up knowledge.

Familiarity of Problems and Settings

Most problem solving is done in natural work teams in a familiar work area. We tend to be comfortable with what we know and with the established ways of thinking in these situations. However, when we are called upon to examine a familiar problem in an unfamiliar setting, we are forced to be much more creative, ask much fresher questions, and ascend, according to many action learning practitioners, to the most potent form of action learning.

Action learning programs can be employed in and operate effectively within each of the four quadrants shown in Figure 2.1 on page 26. Examining how to reengineer one's own job would place a group member in quadrant 1. The same problem may be in quadrants 2, 3, or 4, depending on whether the other set members are from the same organization, are in the same job or industry category, or are familiar with what reengineering means.

Proponents of action learning recommend that participants come from a variety of settings and experiences with the problem, since fresh questions are more likely to be asked and to lead to better solutions. Stretching the capabilities of group members also results in more significant learnings.

Figure 2.1
Settings and Problems for Action Learning

		SETTING	
		Familiar	**Unfamiliar**
	Familiar	**1** Example: Own job	**3** Example: London hospitals
PROBLEM	**Unfamiliar**	**2** Example: New job in own organization	**4** Example: Belgium program GE leadership

---

Reg Revans preferred to establish action learning groups in which the participants were in unfamiliar settings or environments. For example, when working with ten London hospitals in the mid-1960s, Revans created groups in which the members were very familiar with the problems, but not with the setting (quadrant 2). All the hospitals were having significant difficulties in resolving problems of morale, turnover, and productivity. Revans established a multifunctional team in each hospital that consisted of a physician, an administrator, a nurse, a person from housekeeping, and someone from the pharmacy. Each team, instead of addressing problems of its own hospital, addressed problems of one of the other hospitals, so that each hospital had an action team other than its own. The results were remarkable: reductions in patient stays, improved worker morale, less staff turnover, and better communications. When the hospital personnel returned to their own hospitals, they were able to see their hospitals' problems in a new light. In addition, they had greater self-confidence because they had been able to help another hospital with similar problems.

Soon thereafter, Revans was asked to work with an interuniversity program in Belgium that included five major universities and twenty-three large Belgian companies. Each company was asked to identify an important, seemingly intractable problem it faced and to volunteer a senior manager to participate in the program. The appointed managers spent up to nine months in another company and then met in action learning teams weekly to support and challenge each other's efforts as participants worked in quadrant 4. Over a ten-year period, hundreds of "unsolvable"problems got solved. General Electric's executive development programs, which will be discussed in Chapter 5, also use the quadrant 4 approach.

Action learning groups where the majority of participants are in quadrant 1 (familiar problem within a familiar setting) generally gain deeper knowledge about the problem, while action learning groups primarily operating in quadrant 4 (unfamiliar problem in an unfamiliar setting) gain broader knowledge and a greater systems perspective.

The Group

As described in Chapter 1, the group, which is composed of four to eight individuals, is the core entity in action learning. Chapter 11 provides some guidelines for choosing group members.

The group size of four to eight members is desirable because research has shown that groups with fewer than four members do not provide enough diversity, creativity, and challenging dynamics, and groups with more than eight members result in too much complexity in addition to limiting each individual's "airtime," an important aspect of action learning.

The group should include people who care about the problem, know something about the problem, and have the power to carry out the recommendations of the group. Revans has referred to these members as those "who can, who care, and who know."

Diversity

Diversity is sought in forming action learning groups so that there is a greater possibility of varying perspectives, as well as the likelihood of a wider array of creative questions, for one of the greatest obstacles in solving intractable organizational problems is seeing them in our old ways, with old eyes. We all have mind-sets that we are not even aware of, and these mind-sets limit the scope of ideas we can generate to solve problems with a fresh perspective. To break out of these self-imposed assumptions, we have to try to begin seeing the problem from a new perspective and with fresh eyes.

Though diversity is sought, it is important that group members be near the same level of perceived competence so that members feel comfortable challenging one another, as appropriate. The dynamics of the group and the diversity of its participants are important keys to success.

Dilworth (1998) points out that the determination of who will be in an action learning group is strategic. It is not something that should be done randomly. By bringing together people from different parts of the organization, you can gain freshness and build organizational integration through the creation of networks that did not exist before. Volunteers are fine, but cliques or groups with similar views are to be avoided.

Learning styles are also an important factor in forming action learning groups. A group composed of all activists and no reflective types may encourage a rush to judgment. Reflectors tend to raise questions and slow things down to focus on the learning taking place. Pragmatists may opt to stay with what is most likely to work, while theorists tend to want to try something new. It is also useful to balance gender, age, and ethnicity in groups, as this adds diversity and richness.

Outside Expertise

Bringing outside expertise into the action learning group is generally not encouraged. It tends to create dependency on external resources, decreases the learning and the growth in confidence of the group members, and neglects the fact that experience with the problem (rather than expertise about the answer) is what is most important in problem solving.

Proponents of action learning believe that ordinary people, working and learning together, are capable of meeting and overcoming most challenges. Most organizational problems do not require technical expertise; rather, they usually require interpreting or making sense of a great deal of confusing information and multiple perspectives.

Dixon (1998) notes that "people can make sense of their world . . . this capacity is greatly enhanced when people work together, rather than individually, so that they can influence each other's perceptions, add to each other's ideas, and press each other to think more carefully about the issues at hand" (p. 46). There are times, however, when calling on outside expertise or resources is desired. It is important that experts not be allowed to thrust themselves upon the group. It is generally best that they be available to the group only for a short period of time or be sought out only between group meetings.

Attributes of Group Members

Experience and research have shown that action learning programs tend to be most effective when the group members exhibit the following attributes:

▲ Commitment to solving the problem
▲ Ability to listen, to question self and others
▲ Willingness to be open and to learn from other group members
▲ Valuing of others and respect for them
▲ Commitment to taking action and achieving success
▲ Awareness of own and others' ability to learn and develop

The Questioning and Reflection Process

Proponents of action learning believe that learning (new knowledge, skills, or values) cannot occur without questions and reflection. The action learning model starts with *programmed knowledge* (i.e., knowledge in current use, in books, in one's mind, in the organization's memory, lectures, case studies, etc.). To this base is added the process of *questioning,* which offers access to what is not yet known, and *reflection,* which involves recalling, thinking about, pulling apart, making sense, and trying to understand. Hence the formula $L = P + Q + R$, where L = learning, P = programmed knowledge, Q = questioning, and R = reflection.

Programmed knowledge (P) is an important source of learning, but it is embedded in the past and is therefore unlikely to match precisely with the unique needs of the new problem or situation. Thus action learning builds upon the experience and knowledge of a group (the group's P) but adds the fresh questioning (Q) and reflective insights (R) that can result in valuable new learning for the individuals, the group, and, ultimately, the organization. The balance between P and Q should be similar to the balance between the yin and yang of Chinese literature and philosophy.

Programmed instruction is traditionally used by people in most problem-solving activities. It allows for incremental, narrowly focused understanding and learning but rarely generates the quantum improvements or spectacular leaps in knowledge necessary in today's rapidly changing environment.

In addition, P-only groups are generally unable to solve problems from a systems perspective. Questioning and reflection, necessary to a holistic overview, make the critical difference in the quality of problem solving. The questioning and reflective aspects of action learning also provide essential ingredients of and opportunities for individual, team, and organizational growth.

By beginning with questioning rather than using past knowledge as the first reference point, the team can start to gauge whether the available information is adequate and relevant to the present needs. As Dilworth (1998) notes, questioning "will also point to areas that will require creation of new knowledge (new P). The key is to start with fresh questions, not with constructs from the past" (p. 35).

For me, the process of insightful questioning clarified problems and issues. I found that the questioning of this "knowledge in use" by no means denigrates its importance or value; however, it does present the opportunity for the introduction of new knowledge, which may contradict established belief. —Pat

---

By focusing on the right questions rather than the right answers, action learning explores what one does not know as well as what one does know. Questioning, unlike most of programmed knowledge, not only enables us to add to the sum of knowledge but also (and more important) provides us with the spur for reorganizing that knowledge. This is one reason why action learning, unlike the many quick fixes available to the busy practitioner, can provide "moments of truth that stick in the memory, and may provide a turning point in one's life and the life of the organization within which the action learning is taking place" (Morris, 1991, p. 74).

Asking Questions

Helpful, insightful, and challenging questions are pivotal in reaching valuable solutions. Asking questions causes people to think, provided questions are asked in a supportive, unpresumptuous, and sharing spirit. Helpful questions are those that open doors in the mind and get people to think more deeply. Such questions test assumptions, explore why people act in the way that they do, and seek an understanding of what prevents them from taking decisive action.

The major difference between asking questions in action learning and asking them in most other settings is that in action learning, questions are not only seeking answers. Rather, they are seeking to go deeper, to understand, to respond to what is being asked, to give it thought. Asking questions is not only a quest for solutions but also an opportunity to explore.

The process and procedure of asking questions rather than immediately providing solutions unfreezes the group and defuses defensiveness. When everything is uncertain and nobody knows what to do next, asking the right questions can spur creative thinking by:

▲ Shaking up underlying assumptions that are present in all of us
▲ Helping to create new connections
▲ Assisting us in developing new mental models relative to how things are or should be
▲ Helping to balance programmed instruction with the questioning
▲ Getting us to an elevated level of discernment and understanding that will cause better reflection and more effective action

---

You look at what's there and say, Why? I dream about what isn't there and ask, Why not?
—George Bernard Shaw

What exactly are the helpful, "right" questions? The right questions are simply those that give the action learning group the information it needs at the time. If a group fails to come up with the right questions for a given project, it fails to get the information needed to solve the problem.

Questions can help to clarify ("Are you saying that . . . ?"), attempt to understand ("Could you explain more?"), open up new avenues ("Have you explored/thought of . . . ?"), unpeel layers ("And then what happened?"), and offer ideas and insights ("Would such and such help?"). Questions can help "unpack" a statement and can challenge as well as offer insights, ideas, and suggestions.

Six foundational questions are often asked. The first three questions can help identify underlying assumptions and expectations:

▲ What is the organization (are we, are you) seeking to accomplish?
▲ What is stopping the organization (us, you) from accomplishing it?
▲ What can the organization (we, you) do about it?

The second three questions help the group focus on the realities of the situation:

▲ Who knows what we are trying to do (i.e., who has the real facts and can put things into proper perspective)?

▲ Who cares about getting the solution implemented (who has a vested interest in getting the problem solved as opposed to merely talking about it)?

▲ Who can get the solution implemented (who has the power; who controls the resources that can make change happen)?

These six questions almost always lead to more questions and, generally, to ever more discriminating inquiries. As one hears oneself respond to questions, certain inconsistencies may become apparent. Alternatively, talking out loud can also lead presenters in developing insights, ideas, or explanations that had not occurred to them when they were going over the issues in their own minds. The very act of talking aloud is creative.

It is not only the responder who benefits from the questioning process. Group members who see their questions being seriously considered gain confidence in their ability to ask effective and relevant questions, a most critical skill in today's turbulent world of change. These new and important capabilities will quickly result in different behaviors at work.

Moreover, as group members are asked questions, they attain a higher level of reflective listening. Reflection is crucial to solving the problem as well as to helping individuals and groups learn. Solid, reflective questions make us more aware of ourselves and of what is happening around us.

The most important revelation for me in my action learning group was about the power of good questions to drive learning. A good question was one that made people think and reflect on their position or problem. In addition, having people who are unfamiliar with the specifics of your business or environment is helpful because many times their questions come from a totally different point of view, which causes you to see the problem differently. I saw the power of an inquiry style over a debate style, where everyone tries to sell his or her favorite idea. Exploring the problem and building off each other's ideas made us more effective in coming to a solution. Reflective questions led to five casual acquaintances entering a room to practice action learning and coming out of the room with a deeper form of friendship.
—Jim

Reflecting

At the heart of action learning is the process of reflection, which is designed to develop questioning insight, or, as Revans notes, "the capacity to ask fresh questions in conditions of ignorance, risk, and confusion, when nobody knows what to do next."

Action learning programs provide the essential time and space needed to stand back and reflect, unfreeze thoughts, rise above every-day problems, and bring things into a common perspective. Reflection generates mutual support as group members listen intently and draw out each other's experiences and practical judgments. This questioning and reflection process also encourages members to view each other as learning resources.

In action learning, members should be open to trying out new ways of doing things, experimenting, reflecting on experiences, considering the results or effects of the experience, and repeating the cycle by trying out newly gained knowledge in different situations.

We had the experience but missed the meaning.—T. S. Eliot

We do not see things as they are, we see them as we are.
—from the Talmud

The Commitment to Taking Action

Action learning recognizes that there is significantly more learning, and a higher level of learning, when action is based on the reflective recom-mendations and decisions of the group. Thus action learning groups should have the expectation and responsibility of carrying out their ideas and recommendations.

Merely producing reports and recommendations for someone else to implement results in diminished commitment, effectiveness, and learning on the part of the members. Being required to implement, however, prevents the group from resembling a think tank or a debat-ing group, which may be intellectually stimulating and emotionally releasing but may have no real-world impact.

Advocates of action learning believe that there is no real learning unless or until action is taken. *Implementation* should be part of the contract between the organization and the action learning group, thus expanding the action learning formula to: L = P + Q + R + I.

Unless the organization, group, or individual puts into effect the action being agreed to, there is no evidence that something different or better has been or can be done. Consequently, there is no indication as to whether any valid learning or worthwhile action has taken place. Only by testing their ideas in practice will group members know whether their ideas are effective and practical, whether any issues have been overlooked and what problems may occur as a result, what to do differently in the future, and how the ideas can be applied to other parts of the organization and other parts of member's lives.

As Dixon (1998, p. 46) notes, the most valuable learning occurs when participants "reflect on their action, not just on their planning." An analogy would involve a tennis novice trying to learn how to serve the ball by making a serving plan but never actually hitting the ball and consequently never knowing where the ball would have landed. The "action in action learning is not about developing a recommendation; it is about taking action" (p. 46).

To encourage action, Pedler (1991) suggests the following questions for participants to reflect on:

▲ How can we/you move forward on this problem/issue?
▲ How would someone you most admire deal with this situation?
▲ Can you think of three options for action?
▲ What are the pros and cons of these actions?
▲ What steps are you going to take before the next meeting?
▲ What have you learned?
▲ What do you most need from us now?

The Commitment to Learning

Solving a problem provides important, immediate, short-term benefits to an organization or individual. The greater, longer-term benefit of action learning, however, is the learning gained by the group members and the application of their learnings on a systemwide basis throughout the organization and/or in other parts of their lives.

It is important to remember that in action learning people are brought together for reasons other than solving an immediate problem or handling a current project. An increase in the knowledge and capacity of individuals, teams, and the organization to better adapt to the rapid change around them is even more important. As Dilworth (1998) notes, the learning that occurs in action learning has greater strategic value for the organization than the immediate tactical advantage of early problem correction.

Therefore, during the action learning process, individuals are expected to take responsibility for their own, the team's, and the organization's learning and development. Time is set aside to talk about personal learnings and about how the team's learnings can be utilized in other parts of the organization.

Individuals, teams, and organizations will learn best and most when they are faced with difficulties that they do not know how to address. Under these circumstances, as Dixon (1998) notes, they are forced to sort through their past experiences for relevant concepts, put ideas together in unique ways, and seek out new information that may relate to the issue—all of which are important aspects of learning.

The action learning process results in powerful, significant, and transformative learning because it inherently embodies a number of key learning principles:

▲ Learning is increased when we are asked questions (or ask ourselves questions).

▲ Learning intensifies when we reflect on what we did in the experience.

▲ Greater learning occurs when we are given time and space to deal with problems and reflect on our decisions, when a sense of urgency exists, when we can see results, when we are allowed to take risks and when we are encouraged and supported in our deliberations.

▲ We can learn critically when we are able to question the assumptions on which our actions are based.

▲ We learn when we receive accurate feedback from others and from the results of our problem-solving actions.

▲ When relying solely on experts, we can become immobilized and fail to seek or trust our own solutions.

▲ Nonhierarchical groups from across organizational departments and functions are often better able to gain new perspectives and therefore augment learning.

▲ Action learning is most effective when learners are examining the organizational system as a whole.

▲ Group responsibility for the task empowers the members and enhances learning.

▲ We are most challenged when we work on unfamiliar problems in unfamiliar settings, where we can unfreeze some of our previous ways of doing things and develop new ways of thinking.

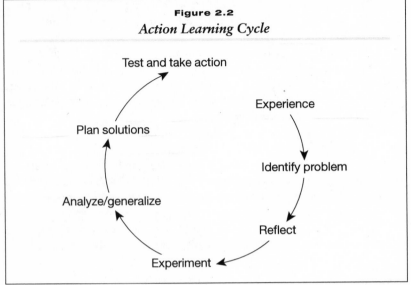

Figure 2.2
Action Learning Cycle

Test and take action

Experience

Plan solutions

Identify problem

Analyze/generalize

Reflect

Experiment

▲ By working cooperatively with others on real issues, the group can move to a higher level of learning relative to application, synthesis, and evaluation.

▲ People learn when they do something, and they learn more as they feel more responsible for their task.

▲ Action learning is built upon the entire learning cycle: learning and creating knowledge through concrete experience, observing and identifying the problem, reflecting on this experience, experimenting, analyzing and forming generalizations from experiments, planning solutions, testing the implications of the generalizations in new experiences, and beginning the process again (see Figure 2.2).

The learner knows more than anyone else what he or she has learned. Action learning teaches not only how to learn effectively but also how to learn about and for oneself. Thus there is a social as well as an intellectual aspect of learning in action learning. We will explore in Chapter 8 how action learning enhances personal and professional learning and development.

In action learning groups, there is learning not only at the individual level but at the team and organizational levels as well. The group as an entity should be able to think and create. It should be able to generate valuable knowledge and possible actions through its analysis of complex issues.

Action learning also involves learning in three dimensions:

Speed of learning—how fast the group is able to move through the learning cycle (i.e., planning, implementing, and reflecting) and complete each iteration

Depth of learning—how well the group is able to learn at the end of each iteration of the cycle by questioning underlying assumptions and improving the capacity to learn in the future

Breadth of learning—how extensively the group is able to transfer the new insights and knowledge derived from each iteration of the learning cycle to other issues and other parts of organizational, team, or individual life.

The Facilitator

Most of us, in our impatience to move on and get out, find it extremely difficult to take time to reflect on what we have learned. Only when given sufficient time and space, however, can we be fully cognizant of what is happening and what learning may have occurred.

The facilitator is very important in helping action learning participants reflect on what is happening and on how they are solving problems. In action learning programs, the facilitator may play a variety of managerial roles in addition to the facilitative role. These functions are complementary and synchronous in that the facilitator never occupies one role exclusively. The managerial or strategic function involves constantly monitoring and appreciating where the group is at any given time; the facilitative role is more tactical. Thus the overall managerial and facilitative roles include the following:

Coordinator—acting as a link; maintaining constant close contact with key people outside the action learning sets to ensure that a complete understanding of the action learning process exists among senior management; advising on problem selection and group membership

Catalyst—moving people out of the anecdotal mode and into the analytical mode of behavior (more prevalent in the early stages of the set)

Observer—concentrating on the group process, as well as on what is being said

Climate setter—setting a group climate within which open, effective communication can occur

Communications enabler—helping members develop the skills of giving and receiving information, opinions, and experience

Learning coach—helping members treat their experience as a source of learning; assisting members in assuming responsibility for their own learning and development

Techniques of Facilitation

The facilitator may use a variety of means to "capture" the learning of the members. Members may be asked to reflect on the nature of their interactions and on the implications of various actions in the learning process. The facilitator may intervene during the problem-solving process or may arrange a time at the end of each meeting for members to reflect on what they have learned.

The job of the facilitator is not to teach but to create an "atmosphere wherein the [members] can learn for and from themselves, to develop confidence in themselves, to reflect and develop new ideas" (Lawlor, 1991, p. 256).

Characteristics of an Effective Facilitator

The facilitator should be trained in and understand how his or her actions can assist the action learning process. He or she should be competent and confident enough to work with the processes that are basic to action learning. These include providing "airspace" for every member, focusing on the task/projects at hand, using a questioning approach, paying attention to listening, giving time for reflection, creating an emphasis on learning, and avoiding judgment.

A list of desired characteristics and attributes of the facilitator would include the following:

▲ Listening skills (ability to keep quiet, avoid putting words in the mouths of others, hear what is not said as well as what is being said)
▲ Ability to stand apart from the action in order to bring the process issues to the surface
▲ Understanding of group processes
▲ Ability to provide feedback
▲ Understanding of basic management theory

▲ Willingness to confront (sparingly) and give feedback
▲ Good judgment as to when to direct the group's attention away from the task and toward learning
▲ Tolerance of ambiguity
▲ Openness and frankness
▲ Patience
▲ Desire to see other people learn
▲ Empathy
▲ Skill in timing interventions (an intervention that comes too early may result in missed understanding; an intervention that comes too late may result in a missed opportunity)
▲ Ability to ask exceptionally good questions that both make people think and make them feel challenged and supported rather than criticized

Building on a Multitude of Complementary Processes

In a sense, action learning provides a surprisingly simple formula for both action (problem solving) and learning at a variety of levels. At the same time, action learning taps into an amazing array of complementary processes that, taken as a whole, are as complex and powerful as any approach known to organizational systems.

It is within this precise yet chaotic interweaving of action learning processes and procedures that the full effectiveness of action learning is attained. Each of the six components discussed in this chapter is valuable and necessary in creating the optimum capacity and potency of action learning. Interwoven as such, the processes and procedures of action learning can catapult individuals, teams, and organizations to a much higher level and frequency of success.

Action Learning Programs

In the preceding chapter, we examined the six components that, together and in systematic support of one another, can lead to highly successful action learning programs. In this chapter, we will describe how an actual action learning group operates. Among the questions we will consider are the following:

▲ What are the different types of action learning programs?
▲ What is the structure of an action learning program?
▲ Are there typical procedures?
▲ What are the roles of the group?

Types of Action Learning Programs

Although there are several varieties of action learning programs, two basic types exist: single-project and open-group action learning programs. Both contain the six essential components of action learning, but they possess distinct and different procedures and processes.

Single-Project Program

In the single-project action learning program, the group members all work on the same problem or problems introduced by the organization. (The organization has established an action learning group or groups to tackle one or more company problems.) The learning group thus serves as the vehicle of organizational challenges.

In-company action learning programs have a sponsor—someone who understands the nature of the program, thinks it is important, and can be influential in making sure the group gains access to necessary resources. The sponsor may appoint himself or herself to be the client or may appoint someone else. The sponsor ensures that the program is given high visibility and acceptance. He or she is seen as the champion of the action learning group.

Precisely who will be members of the group depends on the aims of the program. Members may be chosen by management or they may be volunteers. If the project is a companywide initiative, such as a corporate strategy for creating a new corporate culture, a wide cross section of staff is likely to be involved. If, however, the issue is more focused, such as creating a new staff appraisal system, participants may be selected according to their interest and knowledge.

Single-project programs generally go through the following five phases:

Introductory period—The action learning group explores the questions "What are we trying to do?" "What is preventing us?" and "How can we overcome those obstacles?"

Diagnostic period—The issues of Who knows? Who cares? and Who can? are examined.

Consultation period—Outside resources are interviewed and/or observed.

Implementation period—Action plans are developed, recommended to senior management, and implemented.

Review period—Learnings are shared and project solutions are applied systematically to other parts of the organization.

There are special advantages to a single-project, in-company action learning group:

▲ Networking and interdepartmental contacts
▲ Visibility for the group members
▲ Greater cohesiveness within the organization as people realize the benefits of working together

Open-Group Program

An open group is one in which each individual member brings his or her own project/task/problem to the table. Each person is a client for the other group members. The members support and assist each other for an agreed-upon period of time. Usually all the group members are from different organizations, although the group may consist of people from different units of the same organization.

An open group generally consists of four to eight members who come together on a periodic basis to work and learn. Members act as resources to one another, supporting and challenging each other as they tackle their allotted projects and focus on their learning.

At the beginning of each meeting, an agenda is set to determine the order of presenting and to allocate equal or requested time so that everyone can present. At the first meeting, each person takes some time to describe the issue or problem he or she wishes to tackle. These problems may be tentative and still not fully formed, as long as everyone is clear about what needs doing and what he or she wants to do.

The time is divided among the group members for each to present his or her problem to the rest of the group and to explain what work has been done since the last meeting, what the results were, what new difficulties have arisen, and what further action he or she intends to take. The rest of the group members serve as questioners, consultants, and advisors. At the end of his or her allocated time, the presenter makes a commitment as to what action will be taken prior the next meeting. Subsequent meetings will begin with the sharing of news and the reintegration of the group.

Members may rotate their service in the group advisor role, or the group may seek an external group advisor. After each presentation and/or at the end of all presentations, the group discusses what worked well, what questions were most helpful, what the learnings were, what can be done better next time, and how these learnings are applicable to other situations.

There are some unique advantages to the open group. For example, group members are able to see how different organizations tackle the same issues and problems, recognizing that people in different companies tend to have different perspectives, values, and understanding. Just hearing these is valuable, as it challenges preconceived notions that things have to be a certain way. Members also have more freedom to discuss issues, since people tend to be more open and honest with others who are not working in the same organization. Relationships are less hierarchical, there are fewer political issues to be concerned about, and there is more opportunity to share with peers.

Structure of Action Learning Programs

Time Frame

An action learning group could conceivably achieve its goal (solve a problem and acquire learning) in a fairly short time—a few hours. In order to gain the maximum benefit in terms of intensive learning, as well as a qualitative solving of a more complex problem, however, a greater amount of time—three to twelve months—is generally needed.

During the life of the action learning program, the group may meet on a part-time basis (for example, three hours per week or month for several months) or a full-time basis (eight hours a day for several days or weeks) or on the basis of some combination of part-time and full-time.

In general, it is valuable for participants to meet regularly so that they can report on their actions and progress, share setbacks and new proposals for tackling the problems, and consider their own development, attitudes, and actions. Regular meetings provide the opportunity for members to recognize changes occurring within themselves and/or in the organization and to learn from these changes.

Distribution of Time

Although every action learning program has its own unique dynamic, each gradually alters the relative distribution of the time and energy devoted to the three major activities of an action learning group: reporting problems, clarifying problems, and resolving problems (see Figure 3.1). When the group is first formed, reporting and clarifying will dominate. Clients report on the status of the problem—its nature and background, range of options available, activities, and so on. The other members of the group seek clarification of these points to ensure that they understand the problem, at least from the perspective of the client.

Only after reporting and clarifying are complete can the group move on to its principal purpose, namely, the resolution of problems. Successive meetings should spend less time on reporting and clarifying (as members are more familiar with the problem) and more time on examining and resolving the problem and supporting the actions of the client.

Since most action learning programs face practical time constraints, and since opportunities may exist only for a limited period of time, it is important for the group (with the assistance of the set advisor) to move as rapidly as possible toward problem resolution (Harries, 1991).

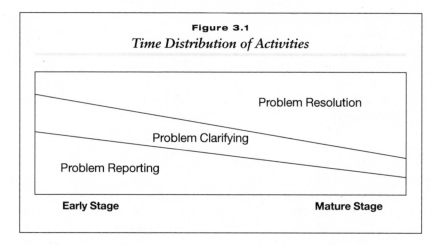

Figure 3.1
Time Distribution of Activities

Problem Resolution

Problem Clarifying

Problem Reporting

Early Stage   Mature Stage

Phases

An action learning program generally goes through three somewhat overlapping phases: understanding the problem, developing alternatives, and constructing a solution and taking action.

Understanding the Problem

A vital element of all action learning programs is the group's effort to understand the problem. Redefining the problem is necessary as the first phase, since the problem as initially presented inevitably reflects assumptions, biases, symptoms, and limited perspectives.

It is thus important that the action learning group have the flexibility and power to redefine the problem after a systematic look at it. Without this flexibility, the group finds itself in an awkward dilemma, needing to choose between solving the real problem and meeting the expectations of the client and/or upper-level management.

Developing Alternatives

The second phase of action learning revolves around developing a variety of possible solutions and actions that the organization or person might be able to take. Key elements of this phase include deciding which actions are relevant to what the organization is trying to accomplish, what the obstacles to these actions are, and how these obstacles can be overcome.

Constructing a Solution and Taking Action

In the third phase of action learning, concrete action and activities are agreed to by the client/presenter. It is important that actions be coordinated in collaboration with those who will be affected by the solutions constructed.

If the action learning group completes the first two phases and has no opportunity to take action, a number of problems may occur. The group may lose focus, make unrealistic recommendations, or lose the reality of implementation. In addition, members will lose the valuable learnings that would have been possible if they had been able to test their proposed solution.

Most of us know from experience that those who are responsible for implementing something always want to be sure that the best possible implementation plan has been developed. They thus seek to study the problem for themselves and determine their own solutions to the problem (which probably will be different from those of the action learning group). And, given that the group realizes that its recommendations are unlikely to be implemented, it will focus on flowery recommendations that may bring recognition to the team and not cause them any political problems.

Procedures

In addition to the six essential elements of action learning as described in Chapter 2 (problem, group, questioning and reflection, action, learning, and facilitation), there are a number of procedures that contribute to the success of action learning programs:

▲ Establishing ground rules
▲ Sharing with and supporting others in the group
▲ Communicating effectively
▲ Planning productively

Establishing Ground Rules and Norms

Action learning groups generally need ground rules to govern members' behavior in and outside of meetings. Some of the typical ground rules involve the following elements:

▲ Confidentiality
▲ Being nonjudgmental
▲ Being frank and honest

▲ Sticking to the agreed schedule or plan
▲ Listening carefully
▲ Being supportive
▲ Giving and receiving feedback in a positive way
▲ Focusing on the problem
▲ Being prepared for each meeting

Sharing With and Supporting Others in the Group

This element includes sharing not only the problem but also one's perspectives, assumptions, frustrations, limitations, ideas, and biases. "Airtime" and an efficient pace allow for reflective questioning and creative insights. The success of the group requires all members to take personal responsibility for sharing the best of what is inside them. Lawlor (1991) notes that many action learning groups have taken several meetings to really "get the open and frank climate which is essential for action learning."

In order for people to share their problems and offer possible solutions based on personal experiences, it is important that there be a commitment of their support for each other. Group members need to demonstrate strong interest and caring in regard to the client's or organization's problem. Without this sense of support, expressions of differing views and perceptions may be seen as merely offensive and aggressive.

Communicating Effectively

Action learning succeeds to the extent that there is intense, high-level, high-quality listening and speaking. There should be free and creative exploration of subtle issues, deep listening, and the suspension of arrogance.

Proponents of action learning encourage a balance between listening and speaking as well as between inquiry and advocacy. Action learning meetings need both discussion and dialogue. Discussion emphasizes analysis, gaining different viewpoints, and breaking problems and issues into manageable parts. Dialogue, on the other hand, focuses on acquiring greater understanding and attaining shared meaning. It requires being able to recognize the patterns of interaction in a group that might promote or undermine sharing, learning, and problem solving. Dialogue is critical for connecting, inventing, and coordinating learning and action.

Questions are the heart of communicating in action learning. The ability to ask helpful and challenging questions is an art as well as a science. The purpose of all questions is to help the client/presenter, as well as the other group members, understand an issue more clearly and thus be better able to reframe it to identify the best solutions. To that end, the best questions are these:

▲ Those that begin with *how, what, where,* and *when* rather than with *why*
▲ Precision questions—What exactly? How exactly? Everyone? Always?
▲ Challenging questions—What's stopping you? What would happen if you . . . ?
▲ Reflective questions—Have you thought of . . . ? Would suggesting . . . be of any use?

In action learning groups, there should be time and space in communications for silence and reflection, for carefully sharing ideas and insights. Developing the skill of critical reflection and reframing allows members to examine the taken-for-granted assumptions that often prevent acting in new and forceful ways.

Planning Productively

Productive planning involves the goal of generating action points to be worked on before the next meeting. Good action points should have a number of important characteristics. They should be:

▲ Specific
▲ Measurable
▲ Able to be achieved—feasible
▲ Real—important, relevant, necessary
▲ Time-bound—able to be completed by a particular date (i.e., before the next meeting)

Unlike other activities in the action learning group, the generating of action points is not determined by group consensus or required total participation. It is up to the client to determine which actions he or she feels comfortable with and capable of undertaking.

If there is no action, then there is no learning. Many an action learning group has lost its enthusiasm for helping and supporting a member if he or she has not taken action between meetings. Action generates feedback as to the real value and effectiveness of the plan. Those group members who attempt to take action generally get the most out of the action learning process.

Group Roles

In action learning groups there are three primary roles, which may be interchanged so that various members play all three roles at various times:

▲ Presenter
▲ Facilitator
▲ Group member

Presenter

A presenter (or client) is the person who has the problem or project on which the action learning group is focusing. The presenter may be representing himself or herself or representing a sponsor, unit, or organization. In an open-group program, each member becomes a presenter for an agreed-upon period of time. In single-project programs, one person or the entire group may be designated as the presenter.

Beaty et al. (1993) suggest that the presenter answer the following questions in preparing for and structuring his or her allotted time:

▲ What have I done since the last group meeting, and what were the outcomes?
▲ Are any action points not completed?
▲ What are my most pressing problems now?
▲ What are the possible next steps?
▲ What could get in the way?
▲ What do I need from this meeting?

There are a number of options for organizing the presentation:

▲ Ask the group to listen while you give a brief presentation, and then ask for comments.
▲ Take questions and comments as you present.
▲ Use a flipchart to illustrate the issues.
▲ Ask for information or suggestions.
▲ Focus on the possible consequences of actions (or inaction) since the last meeting.
▲ Discuss an issue while you listen, and take notes on any useful ideas that emerge.

The other group members are there to help the presenter. They can do this more easily if the presenter lets them know which questions or comments are particularly useful and which are not. It does no one any good to spend time discussing something that is unlikely to generate an action point. It is important for the presenter to be assertive, using phrases like "What I really need is . . ." or "That's interesting, but now I'd like to move to . . . ."

The presenter does not have to defend his or her desire to move on to another point, nor does he or she need to respond to every question. He or she can simply absorb what is being said, using what is useful and ignoring the rest. Defensiveness, needing to win arguments, and needing to be seen as right tend to result in less productive sessions.

The presenter needs to know how to receive, listen, and really hear the questions that are being asked and the comments that are being made. Most of us tend to believe in the sanctity of our ideas and actions and to reject other ways. Some of us may feel it is a weakness to admit that we may need help. However, groups can be truly powerful and helpful only if members allow themselves to be helped. One of the great strengths of the action learning group is its noncompetitive spirit. Believing that other members really want to help allows for mutual exploration of problems (Beaty et al., 1993).

The presenter should develop (with the group's help) and share his or her plans for action before transferring the presenter role to someone else. Action points should be appropriate to the problem and possible within the time allocated.

Facilitator

The facilitator's role, at its simplest, is to help the group work on problems and to help in its learning. The first task may be to brief the members about some of the purposes and principles of action learning and about the facilitator's role in the process. The facilitator should explain how an action learning group works and how each member can most appropriately give support to others.

The facilitator focuses primarily on group processes and learnings. He or she tries to ensure that all group members receive adequate talking time (or "airtime") and encourages supportiveness among the members. The facilitator guides the participants in reflecting on how they solve problems, on their personal learnings, and on how these might apply to other organizational challenges and situations. The facilitator should help group members examine their group behavior—

especially how they listen, give each other feedback, plan actions and solutions, and challenge one another. He or she should be present at the first meeting so that appropriate climate, bonds, and norms are set. The facilitator must remember that he or she is not there to provide solutions, be an expert, control everything, or be a teacher or the chairperson.

Pearce (1991) suggests that a person try to do the following when serving as a facilitator:

▲ Act as genuinely as possible, bringing his or her experience to the group
▲ Try to respond honestly and openly at all times
▲ Focus on group processes and learning
▲ Help members to be honest with themselves
▲ Demonstrate questioning and reflection
▲ Help connect ideas, people, events, and problems to the environment

In Chapter 12, the key roles and effective practices of the facilitator are further developed and explained.

Group Member

Group members play many roles in helping the presenter and each other. For example, a group can be a support network, a resource for information and ideas, a problem-solving forum, or an association of sympathetic, constructive challengers.

The success of the group depends on the personal commitment of each member. Optimum problem solving and learning are gained when members commit themselves to the following:

▲ Regular participation—showing up at every meeting and staying for the entire meeting
▲ Equal participation—allowing adequate time for everyone to express ideas and ask questions
▲ Colleague support—building a supportive environment by listening and caring
▲ Questioning and challenging—posing reflective and challenging questions
▲ Reflection—examining their assumptions and the quality of their own participation
▲ Taking action—carrying out what was promised

An obvious key role of every group member is to be supportive of the presenter. McGill and Beaty (1995) list a number of ways in which members can accomplish this:

Ask questions that are helpful to the presenter: These questions should not be designed to serve one's own purposes, such as providing information for oneself or making one look knowledgeable.

Recognize that each presenter is the world expert on his or her problem: This creates a mind-set that moves from solving the problem to helping the presenter solve his or her problem. Instead of suggesting a solution that would appeal to the presenter, the member helps the presenter come to his or her own conclusions about what to do next: "What do you think would happen if . . .?" rather than "I think you should . . . ."

Cultivate an attitude of empathy: This attitude helps capture how the presenter feels. It provides the best data on how to help the other person. Members do not have to solve the problem; their responsibility is to help the presenter help himself or herself.

Build trust and confidentiality: This enables the presenter to disclose feelings and thoughts to others without judgment. Lack of trust can make the group impotent, since individuals will be unlikely to focus on real and important issues when they feel they will be ridiculed or that others will discuss the issue outside the group. People are able to take risks with new ideas or new actions when they feel supported.

Balance talking, listening, observing, and thinking: This requires a great deal of attention and effort. For example, an observation like "When you said that, you frowned," can generate feedback that helps the presenter uncover important aspects of the problem that could otherwise remain hidden.

Know how to give support and to challenge: At appropriate junctures, this helps the presenter think through the problem and come to a clearer understanding. Sometimes it is important to avoid getting into rescuing when someone is struggling, for that may be a time when the most powerful learning is occurring. Also, allowing the person to resolve the problem can help build his or her confidence.

Recognize issues underlying the problem that has been presented: The presenter is often unable to articulate very clearly the problems and issues that are confronting him or her. Group members collectively can bring many different perspectives to uncovering the problem. They should help the presenter learn more about the problem and the context of the problem, as well as about himself or herself: "What is your role in this problem/project?" "What do you hope for?" "Where do you feel stuck?" "What do you think the problem is?" "Imagine a point in the future—how do you get there?" "What have you learned?"

Group members must provide time for reflection. This allows the presenter to have adequate time to consider comments. Silence may be the most liberating and useful part of action learning for the presenter. Filling in silent time can cause the presenter to lose the thread of his or her thought completely, and the impact of the observation may be lost.

Help the presenter generate his or her own action plan: Asking questions like "What do you want to do?" or "What do you expect to happen if you do that?" helps the presenter generate an action plan.

Group members must be willing to explore both the problems and themselves. They need to believe in the process, resist impatience, reduce defensiveness, embrace change, reflect on their own participation, and innovate in ways that lead to improvement. They should be enthusiastic about learning from experience, interpretation, and sharing. Each member should see himself or herself as someone who can contribute richness and new meaning to the problem or project. Sharing is enhanced where there is respect for another point of view, confidence in another's interpretation, and willingness to commit to action.

From Theory and Principles to Applications and Best Practices

In these first three chapters we have discussed what action learning is and is not, why action learning is so critical in today's changing environment, and the essential components needed to make action learning more effective. We have also examined the two types of action learning programs and the steps and procedures involved in implementing successful action learning programs. In Part 2 we will explore how action learning can be used in solving problems as well as in developing individuals, teams, and organizations.

Organizational Applications of Action Learning

In Part 2 we will explore the five extraordinary, synchronous ways in which action learning can be applied—namely, in solving problems (Chapter 4), creating learning organizations (Chapter 5), building teams (Chapter 6), developing leaders (Chapter 7), and bringing about significant personal and career growth (Chapter 8). Interspersed throughout these chapters will be organizational and individual stories that illustrate and demonstrate how action learning has been effectively applied and practiced. In Chapter 9, we will examine how action learning can be adapted for successful worldwide use.

CHAPTER 4

Problem Solving

We live in a world of rapid change and complexity. Problems are becoming more confusing and more difficult to identify and solve. Moreover, the world is changing in a way that we cannot fully understand. The old days in which one person possessed the information, imagination, and capacity to solve problems is gone—using the talents, perspectives, and brains of a diverse group has become a prerequisite for solving complex problems.

Today's organizations are facing two types of problems: *technical* and *adaptive*.

The necessary knowledge to solve technical problems already exists in a legitimized form or set of procedures. The challenge in solving these problems is to obtain and apply the knowledge in an efficient and rational way. Technical problems have a linear, logical way of being solved, with precedents within or outside the organization.

Adaptive problems, however, involve attitudes, work habits, and other aspects of people's lives. No satisfactory response has yet been developed for these, and no technical expertise is fully adequate. The challenge in solving these problems is to mobilize people so that they are able to make painful but necessary adjustments while learning new ways of working.

Both kinds of problems are suited to action learning. Certainly action learning solves technical problems more efficiently and effectively than any other problem-solving method used by organizations. And action learning may be the only way to successfully deal with adaptive problems. As Reg Revans notes, "the key to action learning is that people start to learn with and from each other only when they discover that no one knows the answer, but all are obliged to find it."

Action learning programs solve problems in much more innovative, systemic ways than other organizational approaches do. Over the last fifty years, action learning programs have been instrumental in creating thousands of new products and services, saving million of dollars, reducing delivery time, improving service quality, and changing dysfunctional organizational cultures. As Reg Revans (1982b) explains:

> When in an epoch of change, when tomorrow is necessarily different from yesterday, new ways of thinking must emerge. New questions need to be asked before solutions are sought. Action learning's primary objective is to learn how to ask appropriate questions under conditions of risk rather than find answers to questions that have already been defined by others. We have to act ourselves into a new way of thinking rather than think ourselves into a new way of acting [p. 65].

Using Systems Thinking

What makes action learning so powerful in solving problems is its inherent ability to employ a systemic, holistic, and comprehensive approach. Asking layers of questions and reflecting on possible responses to those questions forces group members to think beyond symptoms to root causes.

Most leaders agree that systems thinking is crucial to solving complex problems. Simply described, systems thinking is a conceptual framework that helps make full patterns clearer and helps us to see how to change these patterns more effectively. It is a "discipline for seeing the whole," says Senge (1990), "a framework for seeing interrelationships rather than the linear cause-effect chains, for seeing underlying structures rather than events, for seeing patterns of change rather than snapshots" (p. 68).

Systems thinking recognizes that organizations are like giant networks of interconnected nodes. Changes, whether planned or unplanned, in one part of the organization can affect other parts of the organization, with surprising consequences. This type of thinking is difficult for most of us because we are taught to break problems apart, to fragment the world. This appears initially to make complex tasks and subjects more manageable, but we pay a hidden, enormous price— we can no longer see the consequences of our actions, and we lose our intrinsic sense of connection to a larger whole. When we then want to see the big picture, we try to reassemble the fragments and organize all the pieces. The task is futile—similar to trying to reassemble the fragments of a broken mirror.

Problem solving should gain maximum leverage. However, high-leverage changes are usually not obvious to most participants in the environment in which they are operating. Thus we gravitate toward those symptoms that are close in time and space.

Experience of systems thinking and solutions has demonstrated that small, well-focused actions can produce significant, enduring improvements when these actions occur at the right time and in the right place and with sufficient leverage (e.g., changing the direction of a space shuttle at takeoff by a few millimeters). Tackling a difficult problem is often a matter of seeing where the high leverage lies and making a change that leads to lasting, significant improvement.

Action learning fits very easily into systems thinking. As a result, it leads to much better resolution of and systems solutions to the real and most important problems of the organization or individual.

The original problem is very rarely the problem that ends up being addressed. There's something about action learning that allows people to uncover layers to an issue. Too often we apply solutions to surface problems. That's why so many of our problems don't remain solved. When we think we know what the problem is and try to provide a solution (because that is what is expected of us as leaders), we miss an opportunity to examine the issue in all its depth and complexity.
—Terry

With each question, the problems expressed became more clearly defined. Action learning was a much more powerful tool than I realized. In some cases, the problem took on a completely different perspective.
—Bryan

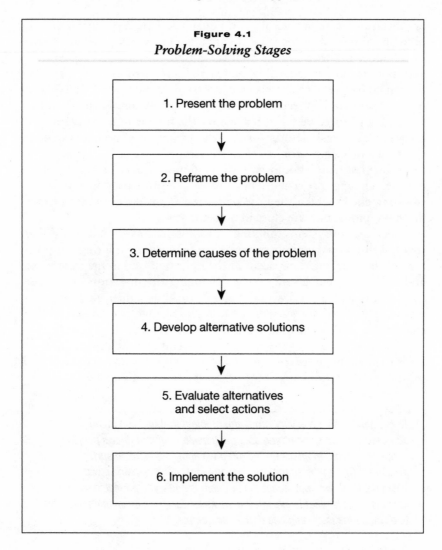

Figure 4.1
Problem-Solving Stages

1. Present the problem

2. Reframe the problem

3. Determine causes of the problem

4. Develop alternative solutions

5. Evaluate alternatives
and select actions

6. Implement the solution

Stages in the Problem-Solving Process

Action learning generally follows a six-stage problem-solving process
(see Figure 4.1). These stages sometimes overlap, and a set may revert
to an earlier stage if the questioning-reflection efforts lead it there.

Present the Problem

It is important that the client prepare and present information about the problem as well as possible. Pedler (1991) suggests that this preparation be made through an examination of the following questions:

▲ How would you describe your problem situation in one sentence?
▲ Why is this problem important, both to you and to your company?
▲ How will you recognize progress on this problem?
▲ Who else would like to see progress on this problem?
▲ What difficulties do you anticipate as you or your organization work through the problem?
▲ What are the benefits, both to you and to the organization, if this problem is reduced or resolved?

Reframe the Problem

Often the presenter or a group member begins the discussion with what Block (1981) calls the *presenting problem*—that is, the problem that is being brought to the group. This problem may be the most obvious problem and/or the one the presenter feels most comfortable in presenting. Focusing on the problem as originally stated usually leads to incorrect problem recognition and formulation. At this stage, questions such as the following are raised:

▲ Why is this problem being presented?
▲ How is the problem being managed?
▲ What are we trying to accomplish?
▲ Is the presenting problem a symptom of a more significant problem?
▲ How can we reframe this problem in a broader context?
▲ Who will be affected if we resolve this problem? How will they be affected?

When the group members question and examine the basic assumptions, organizational or personal frameworks, political and social issues, and so forth, of the presenting problem, they discover a new underlying problem. This is the true problem, which, if solved, will generate the greatest amount of leverage and success and/or eliminate the most important obstacles.

Determine Causes of the Problem

Causes, unlike symptoms, are seldom apparent, and people have to ferret them out. Different individuals, whose views of the problem are invariably affected by their own experiences and responsibilities, may perceive very different causes for the same problem. Using a systems perspective and identifying long-range and long-term causes is important at this stage. Here are some questions that can be asked:

▲ What are the possible sources of the problem?
▲ What changes inside or outside the organization may have contributed to the problem?
▲ What people are most involved with the problem?
▲ Do these people have insights or perspectives that may help clarify the problem?
▲ Why is this problem being created?

Develop Alternative Solutions

The temptation to accept the first alternative often prevents groups from achieving the best solutions to their problems. Developing a number of alternatives allows groups to resist the temptation of trying to solve problems too quickly. Multiple alternatives also increase the likelihood of generating an effective decision.

As in the previous stage, problem solving at this stage requires systems thinking—the capacity to see the whole as well as the parts, the long-range as well as short-range impact of actions taken, possible patterns as well as chaotic possibilities. The expectation of developing multiple alternatives helps develop creativity and imagination in the group.

Some appropriate questions for the group to ask at this point are the following:

▲ What are the possible ways in which this problem could be solved and stay solved?
▲ What is the impact of each of our alternatives?
▲ What is preventing us from solving this problem?
▲ Which of these obstacles are major?

The Pizza Man Delivers $35 Million

One consultant (Bill) used action learning in his consulting work with a client organization. The action learning problem was to come up with new and different approaches for performing support services to operate a government-agency laboratory more efficiently and cost effectively. Many times (before becoming aware of and using the action learning approach) Bill found the discussion becoming bogged down with the same old thinking because everyone present was from the same industry and pretty much the same background. People thought they knew ahead of time what would work and what would not.

To break the logjam of the same old thinking and biases, Bill encouraged outsiders—secretaries, administrative assistants, interns, and so on—to sit in on these strategy meetings and ask questions. Although many of the questions asked were considered naive in nature, they sometimes spawned analytical discussion between the engineers and scientists and a revisiting of ideas that had not been seriously considered.

One day, the group was working late into the evening and decided to send out for pizza. Who better to ask fresh questions than the pizza man? The pizza man agreed to join the group for a couple of hours (the group covered his tips and pay, of course). He clearly had no experience of the issues they were dealing with, but he asked lots of "dumb" questions and made interesting comments that caused the group to question a number of basic assumptions. Ultimately, one of the engineering teams adapted several of his suggestions, which resulted in a potential $35-million savings over the life of the contract the team was working on. ■

Evaluate Alternatives and Select Actions

After a variety of alternative solutions have been identified, the group begins to evaluate each of them. The following questions can be asked at this stage:

▲ How realistic is the solution in terms of the goals and resources of the organization? (An alternative that may seem logical but cannot be implemented is useless.)
▲ How effective will this solution be in solving the problem?
▲ Are there any new problems that might be created by this solution?

Implement the Solution

Problems whose solution is supported by strong, external pressure, that have the necessary resources, and that represent an irresistible opportunity are the ones most likely to be implemented. When, and only when, the solution has been implemented and is being monitored, the group can evaluate its effectiveness. In action learning there is clear recognition that one can learn about the quality of an action only after the action has been reflected upon. Without action and reflection on the action, there is no evidence that something different or better has been or can be done.

Success at National Semiconductor

Working in action learning teams is seen as a key to increasing productivity and creativity at National Semiconductor. When senior managers at National Semiconductor's South Portland plant saw that there was a problem with delivery performance for one of its major customers, AT&T, they decided to do something about it. They created an action learning team to deal with improving the company's performance with respect to customers' requests.

The eight team members comprised representatives from sales, marketing, engineering, manufacturing, and planning, as well as someone from AT&T. Meeting for a couple of days a month, for three months, the team eventually came up with a list of almost forty ideas that resulted in four key action initiatives:

▲ Analyzing the delivery problems in new ways
▲ Increasing the frequency of lead-time updates
▲ Creating critical-device lists
▲ Developing prealert reports

After the initiatives developed by the action learning team were implemented, AT&T recognized National Semiconductor as one of its world-class suppliers. ■

Problems in Problem Solving

Biases

Research by Tversky and Kahneman (1974) shows that most people tend to rely on heuristic principles, or rules of thumb, to simplify the process of problem solving and making decisions. Here are three of the most common heuristics:

Recent and past occurrence—we tend to assume that what is available in memory will be more likely to occur again, and soon, in the future.

Representativeness—we tend to assess the likelihood of an occurrence by trying to match it with a preexisting category (for example, employers may rely on stereotypes to predict an individual's performance).

Anchoring and adjustment—we do not make choices out of thin air; usually we start with some initial value or basic assumption (different values, often unchallenged, lead to different choices).

Each of these three heuristics leads to a number of biases so deeply embedded in the human thinking process that it is difficult to recognize them as illogical. These biases include insensitivity to actual prior probabilities, misconceptions about chance, insufficient judgment, and overconfidence.

Through the questioning, probing, and reflective elements of action learning, problem solving is much more likely to avoid these and other biases. Throughout the action learning process, group members are continuously forced to show that they have considered their own biases.

Preconceptions

In order to avoid preconceptions in problem solving, the owner of the problem must examine his or her own inner processes of decision making before examining the effects of decisions on the external surroundings. Pedler (1991) refers to the dual *public* and *private* nature of all problems. A successful solution will involve internal changes in people as well as external changes in organizations. Problem solving becomes more than error detection and correction; it involves reconstructive learning, reframing, and double-loop learning (Argyris and Schön, 1978).

When people view the same information from several perspectives, they become more open to it. It is important that we as individuals develop mind-sets that are open to alternative solutions to problems. These mind-sets are developed when we accept impressions of information without thinking critically about them.

Solving Problems at General Electric

Probably one of the best-known and most successful of all corporate action learning programs is GE's WorkOut, which began in 1989. Among the key goals of WorkOut are:

▲ Solving critical systemwide problems
▲ Improving responsiveness to customers
▲ Minimizing vertical and horizontal barriers
▲ Ridding the company of needless boundaries and bureaucracy

WorkOut is also seen as an opportunity to provide GE professionals with a broad array of functional experiences in leadership and organizational development.

WorkOuts generally occur over a three-day period and involve a group of 40 to 100 people who meet at a conference center or hotel. Sessions begin with a talk by the CEO or another leader who roughs out a problem agenda for the participants to work on and then leaves. An outside facilitator breaks the participants into action learning groups to tackle various parts of the agenda. Over the next two days, the groups identify solutions and prepare presentations for the third day.

On the third day, the GE executive returns and takes a place in front of the room. One by one, the action learning groups present their proposals. The rules of WorkOut require the executive to make only one of three responses: (a) agree on the spot, (b) say no, or (c) ask for more information—in which case the executive must charter a team to get the information by an agreed-upon date. Executives almost always agree on the spot, since a negative answer would need great reasoning and would destroy the tremendous power and value of the WorkOuts.

WorkOut has not only solved many organization-related problems and improved job performance, it has transformed the climate at GE into a much more productive atmosphere of mutual respect and cooperation. "Us versus them" is increasingly coming to mean GE versus the competition. ■

Solving Problems at AT&T

AT&T's use of action learning occurs under its Gap Group program, in which leaders of each AT&T group seek to identify and overcome the gaps in performance or output faced by the divisions. High-potential managers bring in a key problem from their divisions. They then work with action learning groups of six to seven peers from other divisions over a period of seven days, during which each manager gets one day of "airtime" that is dedicated to working on his or her business problem.

The problem-solving process is quite simple. Each manager presents his or her issue to be examined that day. The group then wrestles with the problem and searches for agreement as to the true nature of the problem. Possible alternatives and solutions are proposed. A facilitator or subject-matter expert guides the action learning process. When the group has agreed on a possible solution, the manager develops an action plan for his or her problem and is accountable for producing results in the time period designated. The action learning group may meet informally after an agreed-upon period of time, to check progress.

Gap Groups are composed of as diverse a membership as possible. "We tried it once the other way," says Joe Dalerneau, executive education director at AT&T, "by having sets formed of people who were, for example, all from sales, and they would always say, `I've tried that' to every suggestion that was raised" (Froiland, 1994). ■

Outside Experts

Revans stresses the importance of action learning group members taking responsibility for solving problems by using the internal resources of the group rather than relying on outside experts. Relying on external expertise often reduces the abilities and confidence of group members. Wisdom rather than cleverness is what is needed in problem solving, and no one knows the problem better than those who are experiencing it.

Isaacs (1993) states that organizations are often overdependent on outside consultants and outside solutions—one of the major learning disabilities in organizations today. Sustained learning in organizations requires the development of internal resources dedicated to self-reflection and systemwide growth.

Encouraging group members to solve their own problems increases their ability to learn and inspires others to do the same—critical elements in a company's becoming a learning organization. Action learning develops highly skilled and effective practitioners who can create and orchestrate effective change and develop new programs, structures, and principles that serve to extend and sustain the learning process over time and over multiple populations.

Solving Organizational and Community Problems

Action learning groups possess a superb ability to examine and reframe the most difficult and complex of problems and to identify the most effective ways of solving those problems. The solving of problems and the resolution of issues within the organization or community are a key focus and a unique capability of action learning. The final two studies reported in this chapter attest to the success of action learning in solving important and highly challenging problems at organizationwide and even communitywide levels.

Action Learning at Bristol-Myers Squibb

Rebecca Kraft, Organizational Consultant

Company Background

Bristol-Myers Squibb Co. (BMS) is a research-based, diversified health and personal care company of 51,000 employees with worldwide sales of $15 billion in 1996. Its products are marketed in 136 countries, with operations in more than 50 countries. The vision of BMS is to extend and enhance human life by providing the highest-quality health and personal care products. The formation of BMS was accomplished through a merger in 1989 of Bristol-Myers and Squibb, making the new company among the largest pharmaceutical companies.

The company's products are in four industry segments:

Pharmaceutical products—prescription medicines (mainly cardiovascular, anticancer, and antiinfection drugs)

Nonprescription health products—infant formulas and other nutritional products, as well as analgesics, cough/cold remedies, and skin care products

Medical devices—orthopedic implants for hip and knee replacements, ostomy and wound care products, surgical instruments, and other medical devices

Toiletries and beauty aids—hair coloring and hair care products, deodorants, antiperspirants, and other toiletries and beauty aids

Action Learning Projects at BMS

Through action learning groups, problems at BMS are being solved in much more innovative and systematic ways than through previous approaches used by the company. Over the last four years a number of exciting and valuable action learning projects have been developed and implemented. Three recent projects are briefly described below.

Project 1

This project focused on exploring marketing synergy between the prescription products division and the over-the-counter consumer products division, as well as marketing approaches related to professional customer relationships and retail customer relationships. The project identified both opportunities and constraints. John Nosek, director of consumer sales and presenter for the action learning project, summarizes his experience with the project as follows:

> The goal of our project was to develop a single BMS corporate customer interface by creating a multifunctional business team selling to key retail and wholesale trade customers. I considered three ideas before pursuing the above project. The project selected includes the characteristics of a "breakthrough" project as defined by Robert Davies. I think this was particularly true in the areas of core competencies (sales force effectiveness) and in the benefits to trade customers (value-added services). I took my knowledge and learnings from participating in the creation of the BMS consumer sales organization and applied those to the action learning project. I maintain that if you approach trade customers with a multifunctional business team representing the three BMS consumer companies, it could also be done corporately—with even greater results of productivity, profitability, and customer focus. I learned significantly more about the BMS pharmaceutical divisions and their sales and customer support approaches to the trade. I did this through established contacts within the company, GLD participants, and my sponsor. I believe the company will ultimately adopt or embrace a variation of the subject outlined in the action learning project, since it provides a sustainable competitive advantage.

Project 2

This project focused on defining the current market dynamics, the market assessment/opportunity, and the recommendation for a multifunctional corporate business team. The stated business challenge was to develop a sales approach to provide competitive advantage as a preeminent customer-focused organization driving growth and productivity. The recommendations included increasing customer support by providing a single point of contact between a customer and the company, regardless of the product being marketed.

Project 3

This action learning project examined the overall business strategy and manufacturing strategy and then considered the question "Does a plant closure fit the firm's current business strategy?" Plant closures generally require significant commitments of cash to fund employee terminations and benefits, disposition of equipment and facilities, inventory buildups, and so forth. The reasons for a plant closure are many: to reduce manufacturing overhead, to eliminate redundant facilities, to consolidate and take advantage of economies of scale or new technologies, to concentrate manufacturing in tax-advantaged areas, or some combination. (For example, an existing network of plants may have been established when significant trade barriers between countries forced firms to produce locally, to avoid tariff and non-tariff trade barriers.) This action learning team examined the current model for analyzing plant closures and then developed recommendations for a new risk-based decision model for analyzing plant closures.

Impact of Action Learning at BMS

At Bristol-Myers Squibb, employees have quickly learned the concept of action learning and applied it to real-time business problems. Working in action learning teams is clearly seen as a key tool for increased productivity and creativity at BMS. The learning environment has produced solid results for participants such as Kirsten Detrick, director of the Worldwide Medicines Group, whose project focused on the development and implementation of a reduced-price strategy on Nuprin. The project included project measurements (such as an evaluation of the number of accounts that implemented the strategy), effect on the brand, and sales results by class of trade. The company adopted Detrick's recommendations, and she successfully implemented her action learning project.

Solving Health Problem in the Cook Islands

Suresh Vatsyayann

My posting as a United Nations volunteer in Atiu, in the Cook Islands, was from 1986 to 1988. I discovered rapidly that there was a rather alarming lack of general public health awareness in the community at large. Several domestic and public areas fell below the World Health Organization's minimum standards. In addition, I felt concern that there appeared to be developing a semipermanent need for expatriate officers like myself. I was alarmed to note that the community saw this as inevitable and thus had little motivation to achieve a full understanding of public health, its rationale, and its practices.

Soon after my arrival, a partnership was established among administrators, teachers, and informal and formal leaders of the island, as well as the staff attached to the health department at Atiu. We soon commenced an extensive action learning and research program to tackle the island's health situation. The action learning teams began with the belief and assumption that the community should have the power to pursue its own health agenda.

We set out to assemble evidence that could lead to an understanding of the health, disease, demographic, and behavior patterns; physical geography; housing; external environment; and educational and economic development standards of the community that had bearing on the health situation on Atiu.

Our intention from the outset was also to utilize the research project as a means of in-service, on-the-spot manpower training for the partners to acquire and analyze data and act to bring about change for the betterment of the community. We believed the acquisition of such knowledge and skills to be a very important first step in the encouragement of sound and healthy practice at home and in the community, a step toward positive health development. Finally, we envisaged the project as having wider implications for the Cook Islands medical service as a whole, given that the situation on Atiu presents a set of health problems and situations fairly typical of other islands.

Benefits of the Action Learning Program

The action learning program afforded an opportunity for increasing public health awareness among people, especially among leaders strategically placed to assist in disseminating the information to the public at large.

One product of the action learning program was a structured series of public health videotapes that were shown nationally in centers where public health propaganda was being effectively mounted. People were motivated to take an active part in discussions during these and other forums. Success of the process was evident from the fact that nearly 100 percent of the villagers attended question-cum-opinion sessions that lasted two to three hours each.

The action learning groups also considered the highly prevalent dental diseases. It was determined that children at the Atiu primary school should be provided with toothbrushes and toothpaste to brush their teeth during the school period. Most of the children had developed the toothbrushing habit by the end of one year. Recognizing the need for school dental services, the action learning partners were able to attain a dental unit and dental chair for the school.

At the village level, we began mass treatment for intestinal worms, head lice, and scabies, and mass hair trimming, especially of the children, followed. Similarly, a program of providing iron, folic acid, calcium, and fluoride supplementation was put in place for most pregnant and lactating women.

Every feasible method of health education was followed to provide the public with information from various angles. Consequently, a regular feature on health needs and disease prevention and remedies was brought out in *Atiu Journal.* All the common health, disease, and nutritional problems were discussed one by one, in a total of about fifty articles. They included information about the local herbs and their beneficial effects, as well as about how and when they could be used.

The action learning programs helped create a sense of urgency in the community regarding the upgrading of toilets and personal hygiene facilities. Also, the research and networking formed the basis for getting a $40 thousand grant from the U.S. government for provision of flush toilets to the school and college, a first for any of the outer Cook Islands. These were installed within one year.

Partners' efforts formed the basis of an eight-day workshop entitled "Girls' Guides: Health Training Week." The girls were given theoretical and practical training in the field of personal and environmental hygiene, food and nutrition, first aid, and basic nursing procedures.

After many sessions with the religious advisory council, parents' committee, and teaching staff at the college, it was concluded that adolescent pregnancy was a critical social problem. Pregnant teenagers had normally not been allowed to continue further studies, for fear that their presence at school would escalate the problem. Atiu was the first island to set aside this rule. There was no adolescent pregnancy reported during the two-year period following this change of rule. This was considered to be an achievement of the project, and the college-bound pregnant adolescents were seen as propagators of healthy sex education.

Collective action on the part of the health department, the public works department, the island council, and the administration resulted in a dramatic improvement in the proper collection and disposal of garbage. The positive results of this approach were visible in the form of near-total freedom from mosquito nuisance within a year.

The philosophy that community involvement is the surest way to long-lasting health development in a society prompted the partners to organize the island's people into the Atiu Health Promotion Committee, which also included employees from various government departments on the island. The committee became an active participant in every health planning and implementation activity on the island of Atiu. The partners felt that now their voice was being heard at the national level.

The long-term results of action learning were seen to offer considerable benefits in planning the overall development of the Atiuan community. Most important, new public health awareness had been created at every level of society. Public health officials had, for the first time, comprehensive statistical reference points for planning overall development needs, whether for the extension and upgrading of public amenities or for the construction of private housing.

Action learning groups also helped increase public health awareness among the young. Four nights a week, some thirty students would meet with health department officials to hear lectures, undertake practical work in designated homes, effect environmental improvement, recommend treatment, build public awareness, and evaluate their own roles in Atiuan public health development.

The Atiu experience clearly demonstrates how action learning can be used to develop an entire island community in terms of public health and building the people's confidence that they can solve problems on their own.

The Power of Action Learning in Problem Solving

While engaged in the process of solving problems via action learning, organizations and individuals gain four additional benefits: organizational learning, team development, leadership development, and individual growth and professional development. We will explore these benefits in the next four chapters.

Creating Learning Organizations

As we approach the twenty-first century, we are entering a new era in the evolution of organizational life and structure. The immense changes in the economic environment caused by globalization and technology have forced organizations from around the world to make significant transformations in order to adapt, survive, and succeed in the new world of the next millennium.

These changes are not only in the external elements of the organization—its products, activities, or structures—but also in its intrinsic way of operating—its values, mind-set, even its primary purpose. Harrison Owen (1991) states this message well in *Riding the Tiger: Doing Business in a Transforming World* when he writes:

> There was a time when the prime business of business was to make a profit and a product. There is now a prior, prime business, which is to become an effective learning organization. Not that profit and product are no longer important, but without continual learning, profits and products will no longer be possible. Hence the strange thought: the business of business is learning—and all else will follow [p. 1].

Organizations must learn faster and adapt to the rapid change in the new environment or they will not survive. As in any transitional period, there currently exist, side by side, the dominant, dying species (i.e., the nonlearning organization) and the emerging, more adaptive species (i.e., the learning organization). Within the next ten years, only learning organizations will survive. Companies that do not become learning organizations will soon go the way of the dinosaurs, unable to adjust to the changing environment around them.

Why Organizational Learning Is Critical

The demands put on organizations now require learning to be delivered faster, cheaper, and more effectively to a fluid workplace and mobile workforce. Some of the critical issues facing today's corporations include:

▲ Reorganization, restructuring, and reengineering for success, if not just survival
▲ Increased skills shortages due to workers who are inadequately prepared for work in the twenty-first century
▲ Doubling of knowledge every two to three years
▲ Global competition from the world's most powerful companies
▲ Overwhelming breakthroughs in new and advanced technologies
▲ Spiraling need for organizations to adapt to change

Dilworth (1998) remarks:

Change now tends to outdistance our ability to learn. Existing knowledge tends to misdirect inquiry rather than facilitate problem resolution. People and organizations need to learn new ways of coping with problems. Only by improving the learning capacity of organizations can we "deal with change dynamics" [p. 34].

Thus, learning inside the organization must be equal to or greater than change outside the organization or the organization will not survive. Revans (1983) aptly notes that

in any epoch of rapid change, those organizations unable to adapt are soon in trouble, and adaptation is achieved only by learning—namely, by being able to do tomorrow that which might have been unnecessary today. The organization that continues to express only the ideas of the past is not learning. Training systems . . . may do little more than to make organizations proficient in yesterday's techniques [p. 11].

Learning that is both corporatewide and systemwide offers organizations the best opportunity of not only surviving but also succeeding. As foreseen by leaders of the Rover Automotive Group in England,

The prospect that organizational learning offers is one of managing change by allowing for quantum leaps. Continuous improvement means that every quantum leap becomes an opportunity to learn and therefore prepare for the next quantum leap. By learning faster than our competitors the time span between leaps reduces and progress accelerates" [Marquardt, 1996b, p. 16].

To obtain and sustain competitive advantage in this new environment, organizations will have to learn better and faster from their successes and failures. They will need to transform themselves into learning organizations, where groups and individuals continuously engage in new learning processes.

Shoshana Zuboff, in her 1988 classic *In the Age of the Smart Machine,* observes that today's organization may indeed have little choice but to become a learning institution:

> One of its principal purposes will have to be the expansion of knowledge— not knowledge for its own sake (as in academic pursuit), but knowledge that comes to reside at the core of what it means to be productive. Learning is no longer a separate activity that occurs either before one enters the workplace or in remote classroom settings. Nor is it an activity preserved for a managerial group. The behaviors that define learning and the behaviors that define being productive are one and the same. Learning is the heart of productive activity. To put it simply, learning is the new form of labor [p. 395].

Characteristics of a Learning Organization

A learning organization is a company that has the powerful capacity to collect, store, and transfer knowledge and thereby continuously transform itself for corporate success. It empowers people within and outside the company to learn as they work and utilizes technology to optimize both learning and productivity. There are a number of important dimensions and characteristics of a learning organization:

▲ Learning is accomplished by the organizational system as a whole, almost as if the organization were a single brain.

▲ Organizational members recognize the official importance of ongoing organizationwide learning for the organization's current and future success.

▲ Learning is a continuous, strategically used process, integrated with and running parallel to work.

▲ There is a focus on creativity and generative learning.

▲ Systems thinking is fundamental.

▲ People have continuous access to information and data resources that are important to the company's success.

▲ A corporate climate exists that encourages, rewards, and accelerates individual and group learning.

▲ Workers network in an innovative, communitylike manner inside and outside the organization.

▲ Change is embraced, and unexpected surprises and even failures are viewed as opportunities to learn.

▲ The organization is agile and flexible.

▲ Everyone is driven by a desire for quality and continuous improvement.

▲ Activities are characterized by aspiration, reflection, and conceptualization.

▲ There are well-developed core competencies that serve as taking-off points for new products and services.

▲ The organization possesses the ability to continuously adapt, renew, and revitalize itself in response to the changing environment.

Paradigm Shifts

There are seven key paradigm shifts that make a learning organization different from the traditional organization, as shown in Table 5.1. As a result of these paradigm shifts, there must be a whole new mind-set and way of seeing organizations and the interplay between work and learning. Learning must take place as an ongoing by-product of people doing their work, in contrast to the traditional approach of acquiring knowledge before performing a particular task or job.

The learning in organizational settings therefore represents a "new form of labor" (Zuboff, 1988) in the following ways:

▲ Learning is performance-based (tied to business objectives).

▲ Importance is placed on learning processes (learning how to learn).

▲ The ability to define learning needs is as important as answers.

▲ Organizationwide opportunities exist to develop knowledge, skills, and attitudes.

▲ Learning is part of work, a part of everybody's job description.

The need for individuals and organizations to acquire more and more knowledge will continue unabated. But what organizations *know* takes second place to what and how quickly they can *learn*. Learning skills will be much more important than data. Penetrating questions will be much more important than good answers.

Table 5.1 *Paradigm Shifts of a Learning Organization*

Traditional Focus	Learning Organization Focus
Productivity	Performance
Workplace	Learning environment
Predictability	Systems and patterns
Training and staff development	Self-directed learning
Worker	Continuous learner
Supervisor/manager	Coach and learner
Engagement/activity	Learning opportunity

How Action Learning Contributes to the Learning Organization

Peter Senge, dubbed "Mr. Learning Organization" by many people around the world, believes that a learning organization must be able to integrate work with learning—that only through continuously reflecting on our activities can we become a learning organization. As Revans (1982a) notes, action learning creates constant learning opportunities for people. It creates a culture and morale for learning.

Perhaps no tool is more effective in building a learning organization than action learning. Dilworth (1995) has called action learning "the DNA of a learning organization" because it directs the learning function of the organization and allows the organization to better adapt to the continuously changing environment.

Keys (1994) sees action learning as a unique organizational process that is growing in acceptance. Although originally designed as a managerial learning process, it offers excellent opportunities for promoting strategic organizational learning. Two significant events are occurring within action learning groups that help to create learning organizations: (1) team members are resolving problems, the solutions to which are passed to clients and are themselves learning processes and relevant information valuable for future problem-solving episodes; and (2) the body of institutional knowledge and the pace of institutional learning is accelerating in user organizations.

There are many elements of action learning that contribute to the building of a learning organization. Action learning has the following characteristics (Marquardt and Reynolds, 1994):

▲ Is outcome-oriented
▲ Is designed to systematically transfer knowledge throughout the organization
▲ Enables people to learn by doing
▲ Helps develop learning-how-to-learn skills
▲ Encourages continual learning
▲ Creates a culture in which learning becomes a way of life
▲ Is an active rather than a passive approach
▲ Is done mainly on the job rather than off the job
▲ Allows for mistakes and experimentation
▲ Develops skills of critical reflection and reframing
▲ Is a mechanism for developing learning skills and behavior
▲ Demonstrates the benefits of organizational learning
▲ Models working and learning simultaneously
▲ Is problem-focused rather than hierarchically bound
▲ Provides a network for sharing, supporting, giving feedback, and challenging assumptions
▲ Develops the ability to generate information
▲ Breaks down barriers between people and across traditional organizational boundaries
▲ Helps an organization move from a culture of training (in which someone else determines and provides the tools for others' development) to a culture of learning (in which everyone is responsible for his or her own continuous learning)
▲ Is systems-based
▲ Applies learnings to other parts of the organization as appropriate

Subsystems of the Learning Organization

In this systems-based model of the learning organization, there are five subsystems that interact and support one another, all of which are strengthened via action learning (see Figure 5.1).

The core subsystem of the learning organization is learning, and this dimension permeates the other four subsystems. Learning takes place at the individual, group, and organizational levels and requires acquiring systems thinking, applying mental models, striving for personal mastery, and maintaining continuous dialogue.

Each of the three other subsystems—organization, people, and knowledge—is necessary to enhance and augment the quality and impact of the learning. These subsystems are the indispensable "partners" essential to building, maintaining, and sustaining learning and

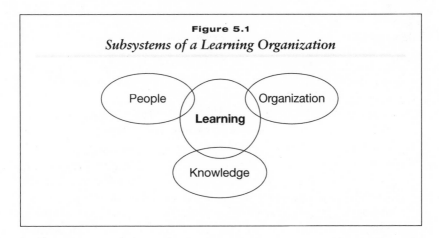

Figure 5.1
Subsystems of a Learning Organization

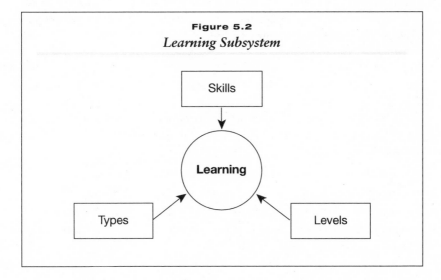

Figure 5.2
Learning Subsystem

productivity in the learning organization. If any subsystem is weak or absent, the effectiveness of the other subsystems is significantly weakened.

Learning

The learning subsystem refers to levels of learning, types of learning, and learning skills (see Figure 5.2).

Levels of Learning

There are three levels of learning present in learning organizations:

Individual learning—the change of skills, insights, knowledge, attitudes, and values acquired by a person through self-study, technology-based instruction, and observation

Group or team learning—the increase in knowledge, skills, and competency accomplished by and within groups

Organizational learning—the enhanced intellectual and productive capability gained through corporatewide commitment to and opportunities for continuous improvement, differing from individual and group/team learning in two basic respects: organizational learning occurs through the shared insights, knowledge, and mental models of members of the organization, and organizational learning builds on past knowledge and experience (that is, on organizational memory that depends on such institutional mechanisms as policies, strategies, and explicit models used to retain knowledge)

Types of Learning

There are several types or ways of learning that are of significance and value to the learning organization. Although each type is distinctive, there is often overlap and complementarity between types. Therefore, a particular learning occurrence may be classified as being of more than one type.

Adaptive learning—learning from experience and reflection

Anticipatory learning—the process of acquiring knowledge from expectations of the future (a vision-action-reflection approach)

Generative learning—learning that is created from reflection, analysis, or creativity

Single-loop and double-loop—types of learning that are differentiated by the degree of reflection brought to bear on action that has occurred in the organization

Learning Skills

Four key skills are needed to initiate and maximize organizational learning:

Systems thinking: This provides the conceptual framework one uses to make full patterns clearer and to see how to change them effectively.

Mental models: These are deeply ingrained assumptions that influence how we understand the world and how we take action. For example, our mental model or image of learning or work or patriotism affects how we relate and act in situations where those concepts are operating.

Personal mastery: This indicates a high level of proficiency in a subject or skill area. It requires a commitment to lifelong learning so as to develop an expertise or special, enjoyed proficiency in whatever one does in the organization.

Dialogue: This denotes a high level of listening and communication between people. It requires the free and creative exploration of subtle issues, deep listening to one another, and suspension of one's own views. The discipline of dialogue involves learning how to recognize patterns of interaction in teams that promote or undermine learning. For example, patterns of defensiveness are often deeply ingrained in how a group of people or an organization operates. If unrecognized or avoided, these patterns undermine learning. If recognized and creatively brought into the open, they can actually accelerate learning. Dialogue is the critical medium for connecting, inventing, and coordinating learning and action in the workplace.

How Action Learning Builds the Learning Subsystem

Action learning programs encourage and enable significant learning to occur at the team and individual levels. Perhaps there is no greater demonstration of true team learning than what occurs during action learning meetings where the entire group is developing common basic assumptions, common understanding of the problem, and common growth in developing new knowledge. Usually, at the end of the action learning meeting, the group seeks to identify ways in which its learning can be applied organizationwide.

All types of learning are sought and developed in action learning programs. In reflecting on past actions, the group attempts to adapt its new actions to a better response to the environment. Anticipatory learning is acquired through the group's analysis of a variety of possible future scenarios or of the possible impact of various actions. Almost continuously, action learning groups are generating innovative, creative knowledge. The time and space provided for deep and frequent reflection during the action learning program provides the avenue for single-loop and double-loop learning.

Action learning provides the opportunity for people in the organization to build each of these learning disciplines. In action learning groups, we can reflect on our actions and the assumptions that underlie them. Action learning promotes "a depth and intensity of dialogue that is uncommon in the normal life experience" (Dilworth, 1998).

Revans (1982a) notes that it is the "social dimension of action learning that provides the challenge to misconceptions and ingrained mental schemata which predispose a person to overlook the ways in which he/she needs to change." In action learning we can explore real problems in a nondefensive way with supportive colleagues who feel free to criticize, question, and advise. Inherent in this approach is the ability to acknowledge that we frequently act in ways that may be incongruent with what we espouse.

Mumford (1995a) has identified ten learning behaviors that organizations need to become learning organizations, all of which can be developed with action learning programs:

▲ Asking questions
▲ Suggesting ideas
▲ Exploring options
▲ Taking risks and experimenting
▲ Being open about the way things are
▲ Converting mistakes into learning
▲ Reflecting and reviewing
▲ Talking about learning
▲ Taking responsibility for one's own learning and development
▲ Admitting to inadequacies and mistakes

Action Learning at Arthur Andersen

Action learning is at the heart of the learning organization being built at Arthur Andersen Worldwide. The firm's new learning model recognizes that learning, as the process of getting the right answer, is the most important issue. A critical task now is to make learning more efficient and effective. The emphasis is on the learning needed by the learner. The former role of instructor/presenter has been shifted to that of coach/mentor/facilitator.

According to Joel Montgomery, an education specialist at Andersen's Center for Professional Education, learners are now "much more active in the learning process, and are jointly responsible for their learning. Learners are asked to use what they have learned rather than repeating or identifying what they have been exposed to."

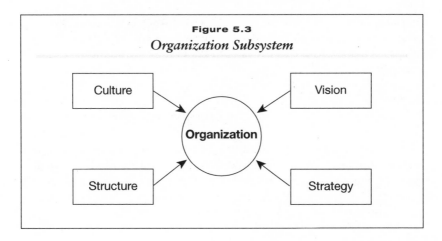

Figure 5.3
Organization Subsystem

Culture

Vision

Organization

Structure

Strategy

Andersen now designs its learning programs in a way that stimulates the learners to engage in activities that allow them to focus their learning on what they know they need. In the process, they are given the tools to reflect on what they are doing, to evaluate it according to some standard, and to give and receive feedback about what they are doing and learning. After they have gone through this process once, Montgomery notes, "we again stimulate them to reengage in learning, bringing with them what they learned the first time, again reflecting on, evaluating, and giving and receiving feedback on what they are doing and learning. This ensures a greater depth of learning." ■

Organization

The second subsystem of a learning organization is the organization itself, the setting and body in which the learning itself occurs. The four key dimensions or components of this subsystem are culture, vision, strategy, and structure (see Figure 5.3).

Culture
The cultural component of the organization subsystem includes the values, beliefs, practices, rituals, and customs of an organization. It helps shape behavior and fashion perceptions. In a learning organization, the corporate culture is one in which learning is recognized as absolutely critical for business success, one where learning has become a habit and an integrated part of all organizational functions. This rich adaptable culture creates integrated relationships and enhances

learning by encouraging values such as teamwork, self-management, empowerment, and sharing. It is the opposite of a closed, rigid, bureaucratic architecture. Risks are encouraged and past methods are to be challenged.

Vision

The vision of an organization captures its hopes, goals, and direction for the future. It is the image of the organization that is transmitted inside and outside the organization. In a learning organization, vision depicts and portrays the desired future picture of the company, in which learning and learners create continuously new and improving products and services. A shared company vision is one that fosters genuine commitment and enrollment rather than compliance.

Strategy

Strategy relates to the action plans, methodologies, tactics, and steps that are employed to reach a company's vision and goals. In a learning organization, these are strategies that optimize the learning acquired, transferred, and utilized in all company actions and operations.

Structure

The structure of an organization includes its departments, levels, and configurations. A learning organization is a streamlined, flat, boundaryless structure that maximizes contact, information flow, local responsibility, and collaboration within and outside the organization.

How Action Learning Builds the Organization Subsystem

The culture created in action learning programs is one where learning is the most important and valuable objective. Throughout the action learning process, there is an emphasis on how the group can continue to expand upon and speed up its knowledge and learning capacities. Members are encouraged and expected to take risks and try new ways. They recognize that many of the greatest leaps in learning have come from learning from mistakes made.

Garratt (1991) remarks that action learning is particularly valuable in helping organizations develop a vision and culture committed to continuous learning. Schein (1993), a pioneer in understanding organizational culture and organizational change, notes that "for change [learning] to occur, the organization must unlearn previous beliefs, be open to new inputs and relearn new assumptions and behaviors." Action learning is a powerful tool in helping to change values and create these new visions.

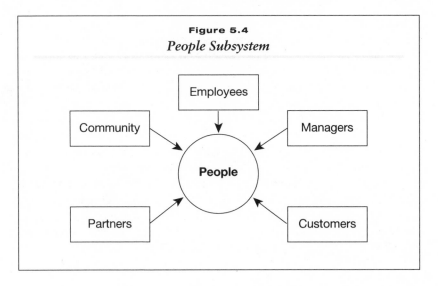

Figure 5.4
People Subsystem

Learning organizations have a bias toward reflection in action. The capacity to quickly take action and generate information is critical to organizations. Senge (1990) observes that "learning cannot exist apart from action. Action provides a basis for the critical dimension of reflection." It is the expressed strategy of an action learning program to build in time, space, and opportunities for learning. And no strategy is more powerful for producing organizationwide learning than getting large numbers of employees involved in action learning programs.

The structure of an action learning group is very fluid and flexible. Keeping the flow of questions and knowledge as clear and complete as possible is critical in processes such as reframing the problem, identifying possible actions, and providing frank feedback. Needless protocol and bureaucracy are discouraged. Leadership flows easily throughout the group.

People

The people subsystem of the learning organization includes employees, managers/leaders, customers, business partners (suppliers, vendors, and subcontractors), and the community itself (see Figure 5.4). Each of these elements is valuable to the learning organization, and all need to be empowered and enabled to learn.

Employees

As learners, employees are empowered and expected to learn, plan for their future competencies, take action and risks, and take the initiative to solve problems. In learning organizations, they should be treated as mature, adult learners and given authority and responsibility according to their learning capacities.

Managers/Leaders

As learners, managers and leaders carry out coaching, mentoring, and modeling roles with a primary responsibility of generating and enhancing learning opportunities for people around them. In addition to managing people, they should become proficient at managing knowledge. Revans (1980) has remarked that "encouraging autonomous learning is not managerial abdication." Finally, leaders should become champions of learning projects, including action learning programs.

Customers

Customers can be a valuable source of information and ideas. They should thus be closely linked into the learning system and strategy of the organization. When possible, they should be offered training so as to become wiser customers and better able to advise relative to their future expectations from the company.

Partners

As learners, business partners, including suppliers and dealers, can receive and contribute to instructional programs. They can also benefit by sharing competencies and knowledge with the organization. Learning from and with suppliers, dealers, and other partners should be a regular strategy of learning organizations.

The Community

The community includes social, educational, and economic agencies that can share in the providing and receiving of learning. Involving the potential diversity of all these groups enhances product and service development.

How Action Learning Builds the People Subsystem

Action learning recognizes the importance of involving people from throughout the business chain in the problem-solving process. Action learning groups are most effective when customers, suppliers, and interested community members come together to ask fresh questions and share fresh perspectives.

Empowering people to take responsibility for themselves rather than waiting for outside expertise is a key value of action learning. Limerick et al. (1994) point out that there is within action learning programs "the explicit recognition that management's role is to provide continuous opportunities for employees' self-development."

Pedler (1991) notes that in learning organizations, a primary task of managers is to facilitate the staff's learning from experience. Through the experience of action learning, managers will recognize the importance of making time for seeking feedback, obtaining data from a variety of perspectives, and encouraging new actions for old and new problems. They will also perceive the value in questioning their own ideas, basic assumptions, attitudes, and actions.

Building learning alliances helps organizations achieve continuous improvement and develop the capacity to cope with discontinuous change. Learning from fresh faces is critical for success in action learning, as it is in organizations. According to Limerick et al. (1994, p. 6), adding new partners and perspectives can accomplish the following:

▲ Enlarge the range of the continuous environmental scanning ability of those in the alliance
▲ Bring a wide analytical range and a wider range of assumptions to the learning process so that discontinuities are more likely to be recognized
▲ Help members recognize and overcome defensive routines so that they can be more transcendent
▲ Improve the learning of members at multiple levels within the alliance
▲ Open up the boundaries of the organization and make possible completely new organizational forms, constantly open to importing chaos and evolving new forms of order

Action Learning at Honda

Honda is an exemplar company in empowering its people. Honda does not just talk empowerment; it permits people to set out and create new cars. Robert Simcox, a plant manager, says that Honda people are learning together because they have been "given the power to use their own creativity and imagination." This is action learning at its best because the people on the line meet to discuss how to fix the problem, and they learn from fixing that problem. ■

Knowledge

The knowledge subsystem of a learning organization refers to management of the acquired and generated knowledge of the organization. It includes the acquisition, creation, storage, and transfer and utilization of knowledge (see Figure 5.5).

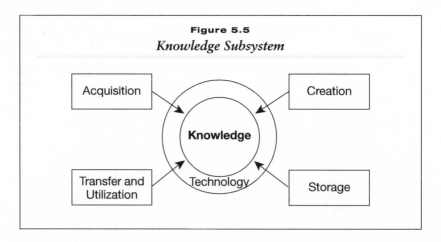

Acquisition
Acquisition refers to the collection of existing data and information from within and outside the organization via benchmarking, conferences, environmental scans, the Internet, use of consultants, publications, and research. Rover, Andersen, Xerox, and Sony regularly benchmark and systematically participate in information exchange programs.

Creation
Creation involves new knowledge that is created within the organization through problem solving and insights, as well as through the conversion of tacit to explicit knowledge. Experimentation, demonstration projects, and reflection on past and current programs increase the innovativeness of the company.

Storage
The coding and preserving of the organization's valued knowledge for easy access by any staff member, at any time, and from anywhere, is what is referred to as storage. The knowledge should be categorized according to learning needs, work objectives, user expertise, and function. It needs to be structured and stored so that it can be found and delivered quickly and accurately.

Transfer and Utilization
The transfer and utilization of knowledge are its mechanical, electronic, and interpersonal movement, both intentionally and uninten-

tionally, throughout the organization, as well as its application and use by members of the organization.

The knowledge elements of organizational learning are ongoing and interactive instead of sequential and independent. The collection and distribution of information occur through multiple channels, each having a different time frame. An example is an online newsletter that systematically gathers, organizes, and disseminates the collective knowledge of the organization's members.

Technology

To quickly and adequately implement all four stages of knowledge, technology is essential. Technology includes the supporting, integrated technological networks and information tools that allow access to and exchange of information and learning. It includes technical processes, systems, and structures for collaboration, coaching, coordination, and other knowledge skills. It encompasses electronic tools and advanced methods for learning, such as computer conferencing, simulation, and computer-supported collaboration. All these tools work to create knowledge freeways. Good knowledge management is not possible without the use of technology.

Knowledge Management at McKinsey & Company

McKinsey & Company uses some of the following knowledge-management strategies:

▲ A director of knowledge management coordinates company efforts in creating and collecting knowledge.

▲ Knowledge transfer is a part of everyone's job and is considered as part of the personnel evaluation process.

▲ Employees must prepare a two-page summary of how and what they have learned from a project before they get a billing code.

▲ Every three months, each project manager receives a printout of what he or she has put into the company's information system.

▲ An online information system called the Practice Development Network is updated weekly and now has over 6,000 documents, including the *Knowledge Resource Directory,* a guide to who knows what in the company.

▲ For any of the thirty-one practice areas of McKinsey, an employee can find the list of its expert members and core documents by tapping in to the database.

▲ A McKinsey Bulletin featuring new ideas appears two to three times per week.

How Action Learning Builds the Knowledge Subsystem

Action learning builds the knowledge subsystem in four ways:

Acquiring knowledge: Learning organizations are information-rich. In action learning groups, members recognize the importance of acquiring information not only from external resources but also from the tacit, internal wisdom and experience of other members. The internal networks developed in action learning groups heighten the awareness of organizational resources, facilitate the exchange and sharing of ideas, and generate knowledge.

Creating knowledge: Participants in action learning programs understand that they should seek new ways of solving old problems, and that the old knowledge may no longer be sufficient. Thus, members are constantly creating new knowledge and encouraging innovation within the set. Nonaka (1991) suggests that information creation is a fundamental requirement for the self-renewing (i.e., learning) organization. An autonomous self-organizing group begins to be realized when members are given the freedom to combine thought and action at their own discretion and are thereby able to guarantee unity of knowledge and action. The actions of action learning clarify and generate meanings.

Storing knowledge: Knowing which knowledge to store and why is based upon the organization's ability to make sense of the data encompassing and surrounding it. The company must then develop sense-making categories for coding and retaining value-added knowledge. Through ongoing reflection on learning and the knowledge acquired, action learning programs lend themselves well to the Kantian school of thinking, which "positions sense-making above mere sensing" (Botham and Vick, 1998). By reflecting on action, the set develops the ability to "make meaning" of the data collected and stored.

Transferring and utilizing knowledge: During reflection periods, learning becomes more explicit and intentional. Group members capture and store for themselves the knowledge and wisdom that will help them become better in both their professional and personal lives. Finally, action learning groups continuously seek ways in which they can transfer the learnings, wisdom, and experience gained in resolving the group's problem(s) to the organizations and communities in which they work.

Actlist: Action Learning Through the Internet

Sankaran Shankar

What Is Actlist?

Actlist is a free, online action learning set (group) for managers who are interested in using action technologies, which include action learning, action research, and action science, to reflect on and learn from their own on-the-job experience as well as from the experience of other managers.

Actlist was set up to be useful to managers doing formal postgraduate studies that use action technologies. Actlist expects to provide a forum for such managers to reflect on the papers, projects, and thoughts that they are developing for these formal studies. It is also expected to help practicing managers who would like to use action technologies in their workplaces, to improve their practice.

Actlist Is Actually a Learning Set

Actlist was formed as a virtual learning set. Members are expected to be able to reflect on their experiences, "warts and all," and to learn from their mistakes, rather than explaining or excusing them. Members are also expected to listen to the experiences of others and to offer careful and constructive support by asking challenging questions.

Actlist has grown since its formation and now has nearly seventy members, with equal proportions of managers and action technologists. It has served as a platform for some useful and pointed discussions.

An Online Conference

In 1998, Actlist decided to venture into running an online conference to expand the discussions among its members. The topic chosen for the conference was "The Reflective Practitioner," based on the writings of the late Donald Schön (author of *The Reflective Practitioner* and *Educating the Reflective Practitioner*) as well as on several books by Chris Argyris.

In March 1998, the conference was held on Actlist and attracted nearly 400 participants. The conference lasted for five weeks, with the last week reserved for reflection. Discussions on the conference were very engaging, and the participants shared several interesting experiences.

If you want to join Actlist, please send e-mail to elogue@mbox2.signet. com.sg and give a brief introduction of yourself and your interest in action technologies.

Action Learning: Cornerstone of a Learning Organization

Marquardt and Carter (1998) observe that "perhaps action learning's most useful role is in creating learning organizations." Revans (1982a) states that "the most precious asset of any organization is the one most readily overlooked—its capacity to build on lived experience, to learn from challenges and to turn in a better performance by inviting all and sundry to work out for themselves what that performance might be" (p. 286).

Learning quickly and systemically is critical for surviving in the twenty-first century. The organization that makes learning its core business can rapidly leverage its new knowledge into new products, new marketing strategies, and new ways of doing business. Learning organizations will become places where global success is possible, where quality is more assured, and where energetic and talented people want to be. More and more organizations are seeing action learning as the vehicle to help them become learning organizations and to move safely and well into the next century.

CHAPTER 6

Building Teams

Teams have become the heart and soul of organizational life and productivity. Teams are being used to manage cross-functional projects, work on the assembly line, reengineer business processes, and develop marketing strategies.

Tom Peters (1992), the noted guru on the future of organizations, has placed teams as the foundation for organizational survival for the twenty-first century. He offers the following predictions about the importance of teams and their composition as we enter the next millennium:

▲ No matter their size—whether 200,000 or 20—organizations will be broken down to work in fast, learning-efficient units of four- to forty-member teams.

▲ Most of tomorrow's work will be done in project teams. The life span of a project team might be indeterminate or just a few hours. Dynamic, short-lived project configurations will be commonplace.

▲ It will not be uncommon to work on four or five project teams in a year—but one might never work twice with the same configuration of colleagues.

▲ The typical project team will include "outsiders" such as vendors, customers, and distributors.

▲ Who reports to whom will change over time, and one will routinely report to a person for one task while that person reports to you for another task. Thus the ability for everyone to lead and guide groups will become an almost universal skill.

▲ Developing world-class teams with world-class members will be more important than any single business victory.

▲ Performance appraisals will be based primarily on team skills and success and will be done by fellow team members.

▲ There will be constant reorganizing, restructuring, and reengineering that will be based on endless reconfiguration of project teams.

In this chapter we will look at the characteristics needed by world-class teams and how action learning helps to develop such teams. In particular, we will explore the key element of team learning as a part of the team's contribution to organizational success. Case examples of teams being built and team successes via action learning will be presented throughout the chapter.

Team Building at General Electric

Action learning has been extensively used at General Electric to build world-class teams. Working in project teams composed of people throughout the organization reflects the boundary-free work environment that GE is striving to create (Noel and Charan, 1992). As they collaborate with different businesses, GE leaders must learn how to manage group processes and sustain group synergy. And they must accomplish those objectives "in the stressful environment of competing teams, highly visible projects, and time constraints. At the conclusion of the action learning projects, participants spend half a day to discuss team output, processes and members' contributions. A remark often heard at the conclusion of the leadership programs at GE is, 'our groups became teams.'" ■

Building World-Class Teams and Team Skills

Organizations must build new, better, and more teams as they enter the twenty-first century. They will need to equip their people with the skills and attributes that will make them better team members and team leaders. An effective team is defined as an energetic group of people who are committed to achieving common objectives, who work well together, and who produce high-quality results. Effective teams continue to learn and improve on both an individual and a team basis. Team members feel responsible for the output of their team and act to clear difficulties standing in their way.

World-class teams exhibit seven common characteristics:

▲ Cohesiveness and caring
▲ Clarity of objectives and purpose
▲ Communication and dialogue
▲ Commitment to task and ownership of results
▲ Creativity
▲ Competence
▲ Cooperation and collaboration

Action learning provides the perfect tool for developing such capabilities, since the values, principles, and skills practiced in action learning sets encourage and develop each of these attributes.

Cohesiveness and Caring

Effective teams have an underlying sense of "tightness," of bonding to achieve a common purpose that is both highly important and immensely personal. Cohesiveness refers to the overall attraction of group members to each other and the way in which they stick together. Members have a sense of belonging and are dedicated to the well-being of the group. It also refers to the morale, teamwork, and spirit of the group.

A strong union is built in action learning programs as people focus on seeking to clarify the real problem and acquire a commitment to action. In addition, when one shares one's feelings about self-awareness, significant learnings, and frank appraisals of oneself and others, one develops powerful links with other members.

Cohesiveness is also built by the egalitarian nature of action learning sets. Dilworth (1998) points out how action learning sets operate "without a designated leader. Any mantle of authority is left at the door." This makes action learning a "good fit with self-directed work teams which are rapidly become a feature in organizations worldwide" (p. 37).

Action learning has a very powerful effect of increasing trust levels in groups (Marquardt and Carter, 1998). As a result of sharing problems, group members share important aspects of their lives with each other. This sharing generates a common understanding of others' situations and creates a bond among group members.

As group members learn effective questioning by the manner in which they challenge and confront each other, they become committed to each other's progress and to the task of the group. As they learn to take action so as to be able to report back to the members what they have tried and where they are in resolving their problem, they continuously redefine the issues as the group continues to meet. This maturation process occurs on multiple levels. The individual becomes increasingly aware of his or her own power for influencing a situation, and the group becomes committed to the success of the other individuals in the group.
—Terry

Clarity of Objectives and Purpose

Many teams fail because there are no clear objectives, or there is confusion about what the group is attempting to accomplish. Answering the following questions will quickly enable the group to discover and/or develop clarity around its objective(s): What are we trying to accomplish? What are the obstacles? How can we overcome these obstacles?

Of course, a common and critical objective of every action learning group is to identify personal and group learnings that can also be applied to other parts of members' lives and to other parts of the organization.

Communication and Dialogue

Humans must learn to talk and think together. The most difficult problems in organizations are those that are complex and ambiguous and involve multiple stakeholders with differing points of view. Technical solutions either do not exist or do not work in these cases—human adaptation and change are required.

High-quality communication is critical to the successful functioning of high-performance work teams. Action learning helps to develop the highest form of communication—*dialogue.* Dialogue is a deep form of communication that requires the free and creative exploration of issues and problems, sincere listening to one another, and the suspension of opinions and criticisms.

Dialogue is important in action learning and in building teams, since it promotes powerful collective thinking and communications. It better allows the group to tap the collective wisdom of its members and to see the situation more as a collective whole than as fragmented parts, and it forces group members to focus on uncovering and inquiring into how and why internal perceptions are influencing how they perceive the problem.

Dialogue can be extremely valuable in problem solving because there is great emphasis on listening, on asking questions rather than posing solutions, and on gaining shared meaning rather than imposing one's own meaning. Dialogue encourages win-win situations as opposed to advocating or convincing others, which often result in win-lose situations.

Group members who use dialogue successfully have the following characteristics:

▲ They recognize more readily when they are jumping from an observation to a generalization.
▲ They balance inquiry and advocacy.
▲ They face up to distinctions between espoused theories (what they say) and theories used (what they tend to do).

Action learning changed how we felt about each other. What I remember most from the action learning experience is not that we solved a bunch of problems, but that there were now fewer barriers between us. The facades had come down, and we were able to engage in open, honest communication.
—Charlie

Commitment to Task and Ownership of Results

Teams will not optimize the processes under which they are working nor produce high-quality results unless participants take responsibility for and ownership of their products. People must be committed to helping one another and to a high level of effort. Action learning develops strong commitment as a result of intense personal sharing and selected actions by group members.

One afternoon one of my co-workers came to me to ask for some help with an organizational intervention that had mushroomed from a straightforward request for supervisory training to much more complex issues of power and control in the organization. The two of us found four others from various parts of our organization, and we began to meet as part of an action learning group. We met three times.

The first meeting started to clarify the underlying issues and helped my co-worker with options for how to proceed in the client organization. After the third meeting, he was ready to ask for the CEO's commitment to a new plan of action to assess the organization's readiness for change. Not only did my co-worker feel supported in his problem, he was also able to get some very valuable feedback about how he handled the situation. The synergy of the action learning experience focused his approach. The group members became genuinely interested in the outcome of the situation. It was group ownership of a problem such that I had never before seen in my organization.
—Bryan

Creativity

Teams are utilized because there is an inherent belief that members will be much more creative than they could be as individuals, since shared ideas and actions encourage innovativeness. Unfortunately, this is too often not the case. Groups become bogged down in tedious, bureaucratic, mind-numbing activities and frustration. Isaacs (1993) notes that even in the face of challenges, teams often act in more and more ineffective ways. They revert to win-lose dynamics, face-saving, and defensive routines while remaining unaware that they are doing so. As a result, group members remain cynical, tolerate mediocrity, and bypass difficulties.

The reflective questioning and accountable action inherent in action learning groups, however, generate the opposite effect. People who have participated in action learning groups enthusiastically report them to be creative and exciting experiences, where difficult, complex problems get solved in wonderful ways. Action learning enables team members to access their collective wisdom and ignorance, work together in meaningful and reflective ways, and produce coordinated action.

Competence

Research and experience have demonstrated that action taken on a problem changes both the problem and the people acting on it. There are several team-related skills and competencies developed through participation in the action learning process:

▲ Ability to focus on process and product issues interchangeably, as necessary

▲ Ability to gain self-understanding and self-awareness from the feedback of others in the groups

▲ Questioning and problem-solving skills

▲ Knowing how to be an effective, supportive, and challenging member of a group, and learning how to work with others

▲ Knowledge about the organization—its products, people, and processes

▲ Facilitation, advising, and leadership skills

▲ Effective communication skills, including giving and receiving feedback

Cooperation and Collaboration

Action learning groups, unlike other groups (for example, task forces, quality circles), cannot work without a high degree of cooperation and collaboration. Members need to seek ways in which they can work together, particularly if they are accountable as a group for the action to be recommended and taken by the group.

The importance of cooperation and collaboration can be seen in the fact that such terms as "comrades in adversity" or "partners in pursuit of opportunity" are often used to describe group members.

Team Learning at Ford Motor Company

The Ford Motor Company was one of the first U.S. companies to use action learning in project development and team building. Recently, the Product Launch Success Team of Ford's Electrical and Fuel Handling Division (EFHD) applied action learning to the process of launching new products in automobiles. As a result of action learning, the team identified several key assumptions —about the purchase and maintenance of equipment, the production process, the work ethic and administrative support—that would never have been discussed in traditional meetings or even during root-cause analysis (Bierema, 1998).

Action learning helped Ford produce an involvement roster that lists which personnel should be involved at various stages in the process and why. The company was also able to produce, via action learning, a listing of equipment specifications that were collectively written by employees in engineering, manufacturing, and purchasing, by hourly employees, and by vendors. Action learning also provided participants with a better understanding about the effectiveness and ineffectiveness of their actions and about how to keep improving.

On the basis of its action learning experiences, Ford Motor Company developed a six-step model for capturing and sharing learning. That model is now used in all learning projects:

1. Provide a process for capturing the learning that is the purpose of the model.
2. Actively reflect about work-related problems and vision through the process of dialogue.
3. Generate and cluster issues by similarity.
4. Generate actions and decisions from the critical clusters.
5. Record and own information.
6. Determine success, and begin the cycle again.

The model emphasizes shared learning by developing and documenting processes, policies, and stories. The objectives of the team learning project include the following:

▲ Creating or reengineering a process critical to maximum performance
▲ Sharing the leaning via documentation and process maps
▲ Practicing Senge's five learning disciplines (systems thinking, personal mastery, team learning, mental models, and shared vision) to encourage empowerment, dialogue, and community in the organization.

Bierema (1998) notes that the Ford process incorporates action learning techniques that help to clarify observations and assumptions as well as providing opportunities to apply process reengineering, focused improvement, and quick-hitting methods for improvement. ■

Team Learning and the Learning Organization

As organizations must deal with increasingly complex problems, they are discovering that they must become skilled in group/team learning. Work teams must be able to think, create, and learn as an entity. They must learn how to better create and capture learning. Team learning can and should occur every time a group of people are brought together, whether to attend a single meeting, conduct a short-term project, or address longer-term organizational problems.

It is important to recognize that team learning differs radically from a team's merely acquiring group skills. In team learning, the emphasis is on self-managed learning and on the free flow of ideas and creativity. A successful team learning system ensures that teams share their experiences, both negative and positive, with other groups in the organization and thereby promote vigorous corporate intellectual growth.

Figure 6.1
Teams as the Connection Between Individual and Organization

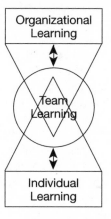

Source: Adapted from Watkins and Marsick, 1993, p. 10.

Teams should be able to generate knowledge through analysis of complex issues, innovative action, and collective problem solving. Team members need to learn better from their own experiences and past histories. They should experiment with new approaches, quickly and efficiently transferring knowledge among themselves and to the rest of the organization.

As teams learn, they can become a microcosm for learning throughout the organization: insights gained by the team are put into action, and skills developed by the team can be transferred to other individuals and to other teams. The team's accomplishments can set the tone and establish a standard for group learning for the larger organization. Team learning, as Senge (1990) proclaims, is at the heart of organizational learning.

Watkins and Marsick's team learning model, represented in Figure 6.1, captures the relationships and learning among individuals, teams, and the organization. The key to this model is the overlap. It is where teams function and bring the benefits of the learning organization. The utilization of the combined resources and energies of individuals, teams, and the organization is what creates the learning organization.

Learning organizations seek to create a full range of teams, including continuous improvement teams, cross-functional teams, quality

Building Classroom Teams at George Washington University

Terry Carter, Fellow, Executive Leadership Program

In the fall of 1996, I was one of eighteen students around a table in George Washington University's Executive Leadership Program who wondered how we could benefit from a course in action learning. Were we really supposed to believe that something as simple as asking questions in a small group could help us solve difficult organizational issues? Surely, the members of this cohort program were already well versed in problem-solving strategies. We understood from our personal experience the political nature of give-and-take that so often accompanies problem solving in organizations.

Yet here we were, grouped in sets of four or five students, trying to become teams and solve problems at the same time. It was the beginning of our second semester in a two-and-a-half-year program of doctoral studies in human resource development. We knew each other by name and by the usual exchanges of casual acquaintance. Little did we realize that this action learning experience would set the tone for the remainder of our educational experience together, forging deep and enduring personal friendships and relationships of mutual support. We had no idea that we were about to begin a lesson in trust.

Our task was to introduce a problem from work to our action learning group members. Each of us in turn served as the owner or "client" for the others. True to Reg Revans' requirement that the client own the problem, these were not puzzles but difficult and intractable issues that affected each one of us in important ways in our organizations. They were problems for which there were no "right" answers. We quickly discovered we needed to learn the fine art of asking better questions instead of jumping to solutions for our cohort members. This was harder to do than we thought.

During the next few months, our fledgling questioning skills began to improve as we explored the nature of each other's problems. The atmosphere among the group members began to change from one of required participation to one of thoughtful introspection and gentle, probing inquiry.

In my set, those who were initially uncomfortable with the questioning process forgot to be uncomfortable as they became committed to helping their fellow students gain insight into their organizational problems. We discovered that questions that probed beneath the surface of our issues required us to suspend taken-for-granted beliefs and ideas, something most of us had never really been challenged to do before. Each of us was faced with examining his or her own underlying assumptions about the problem.

Pedler (1991) has referred to this as the dual public and private nature of all problems, requiring internal changes in people as well as external changes in organizations. Our problem solving was transformed into reconstructive learning by reframing and double-loop learning (Argyris and Schön, 1978).

Since then, I have had time to reflect on this first action learning experience and to recognize the extraordinary benefit it afforded us in developing close personal and professional relationships. I have learned that the simplicity of action learning is deceptive. Its power lies in the discovery that problems are never what they seem to be. It is a power that comes from realizing that collective entities—teams, work groups, and even action learning groups—have ways of knowing and perceiving that are socially constructed.

In every case, we found that the problem was inevitably redefined through the process of questioning. The most insightful questions were those that arose out of curiosity, ignorance, or statements of the obvious. The effect for the owner of the problem was to realize how rigidly he or she had become entrapped in particular ways of thinking and acting. Action learning freed us to think in new and fresh ways about old issues.

As a result of my group members' discussion of problem issues from work, we each shared with the others something important about our lives. By trusting the others with our unsolvable problems, we opened ourselves up to the concern and caring that engenders true teamwork and commitment in a group. We had learned the importance of trusting relationships, shared insights, and mutually supportive behaviors that would carry us through the remainder of our program. We had become a team.

management teams, and even organizational learning teams. These teams take time for reflection and for action learning. They serve as vehicles for causing fundamental organizational change and renewal. Teams are encouraged not only to solve problems but also, according to Redding (1994), to generate a fundamental new understanding of the business through the process of "collective learning."

Team learning will occur more quickly and fully if teams are rewarded for the learning they contribute to the organization. Learning at the team level requires practice and reflection. High-level team learning enables high-level collective thinking and communication and allows team members to work creatively and constructively as a single entity. These are elements of the action learning process.

Building Teams as Well as Cars at General Motors

In 1994, General Motors' Global Task Teams (GTT) were developed. The purpose was to build teams of eight to ten high-potential employees who could work together to address important organizational issues. In these teams, designed by GM, members from sites around the world come together for global action learning. Over the last four years, tasks and sites have included the following:

Site	Task
India	To contribute to the design and implementation of a lean manufacturing system and related support systems
Indonesia	To develop manufacturing systems for new operations
North America	To identify marketing indicators for new products
Australia	To design a materials-flow process for a new body shop
England	To review marketing strategy for improving customer satisfaction

After the initial launch process, according to Dixon (1998b), each team spends four weeks visiting the companies that represent the "best practices" of the task it has been assigned. GM's goal is not limited to transferring a preferred approach from that site to a GM site but rather seeks to examine the many ways that the assigned task could be accomplished in different settings. For example, the team might seek to implement unfamiliar tasks in unfamiliar settings so as to gain maximum potential for expanding members' experience, knowledge, and creativity.

The next eight weeks are spent at the GM site, to develop what the team has learned as a result of its benchmarking efforts. At the end of the three-month program, the team makes recommendations and, in some cases, begins the implementation process. Also, time for extensive reflection is allocated to optimize members' learning from the experience and to anticipate their reentry into their positions at GM.

There are several critical junctures of the three-month program, at which two GM facilitators meet with the Global Task Teams. At these junctures, the two facilitators help the team members think through what they hope to achieve, what they have learned, and how they might apply these learnings to their home units. These interactions, according to Dixon, constitute "lessons in reflective learning, team process, and planning that help the team understand how to learn from its own actions" (p. 109).

To maximize the development of team members, GM looks for tasks that have both a systemic element (i.e., tasks that take the whole system into account) and a strategic element (i.e., tasks that include the development of a strategy for implementing recommendations). Without the systemic element, as Dixon notes, the scope is too narrow for team members to gain the comprehensive picture of GM that they will require as future executives, and without the strategic element, the task is too abstract for developmental learning.

Throughout the program, but especially during the closure week, team members provide each other with in-depth feedback on a wide variety of leadership behaviors. The facilitators also interview key people at the sites to gain insight into the teams and provide this information to the teams. The Global Task Teams have quickly earned a growing reputation within General Motors for the quality of both their work and their teamwork. ■

Powerful Teams and Team Skills via Action Learning

Teams have become the cornerstone of organizational life and corporate success. They form the foundation for accomplishing more and more of the work of the organization. Corporate success increasingly depends on the ability of talented people working together in cohesive, creative, and competent teams. Leaders must be able to inspire and facilitate teams. The problem solving, communication patterns, and action-selection competency of effective teams all need to be transferred to everyone else in the organization.

Action learning, as illustrated in this chapter, provides a unique vehicle not only for building teams throughout the organization but also for developing the leadership and team-building skills that will be needed by workers in tomorrow's organizations.

CHAPTER 7

Leadership Development

New times demand new kinds of leaders. Never before have there been so many demands and expectations put on our leaders—leaders who must continuously change themselves. Leadership styles and skills that may have worked in stable, predictable environments will be inadequate in an era of radical uncertainty, at a time when organizations can't even define the problem, much less engineer a solution.

Many organizations and most of the world have responded to this demand for better leaders by creating more training programs. The number of business schools worldwide has continued to increase. Corporations have opened up management training centers and corporate universities. Management consultants in increasing numbers have been called on to advise managers and training staff.

However, as McNulty and Canty (1995) note,

> there is even more dissatisfaction with management and executive development programs than ever before. The increase in education and training, formal development systems, specialist staff, and overall expenditure has done nothing to halt the loss of competitiveness in certain industries. Mangers and educators alike are calling for change, with both sides putting a new emphasis on learning practical things about the working world [p. 53].

Marsick and Cederholm (1988, p. 7) decry the limitations of most management development programs, which "typically focus on a single dimension of managerial work—the personality of the leader, professional competence at specific tasks, or competence in dealing with the organization's culture and environment." Action learning, on the other hand, "derives it power from the fact that it does not isolate any dimension from the context in which managers work."

It is important to recognize that *what* leaders learn and *how* they learn cannot be disassociated from one another, for how one learns necessarily influences what one learns. Action learning's real-world approach to problem solving and professional development is thus causing more organizations to turn to action learning as the most efficient and effective way of developing their present and future leaders.

In this chapter, we will look at the leadership qualities deemed most critical for the next millennium and at how the values and procedures of action learning fit into helping develop these attributes. Interspersed throughout the chapter will be examples of how such companies as General Electric, Bristol-Myers Squibb, and Ameritech, as well as management centers in Sweden and England, use action learning for leadership development.

Leadership Roles for the Twenty-First Century

A review of a wide array of literature (Kanter, 1997; Rhinesmith, 1996; Senge, 1990; Spears, 1995) and statements of leading executives from around the world leads one to conclude that there will be seven critical roles for a leader in the twenty-first century:

▲ Systems thinker
▲ Change agent
▲ Innovator and risk taker
▲ Servant and steward
▲ Polychronic coordinator
▲ Instructor, coach, and mentor
▲ Visionary and vision builder

Systems Thinker

Effective problem solving requires the ability to be a systems thinker. Senge (1990), Wheatley (1992), and others have illustrated the importance of this attribute for any leader. Systems thinkers have the ability to see connections between issues, events, and data points—the whole rather than its parts. Systems thinking requires the ability to frame structural relationships that result in dynamic networks as opposed to staid, patterned relationships predicated on one's position in the hierarchy.

Isaacs (1993) rightly notes that leaders in today's world must shift their perspective from mechanistic and reductionist ways of thinking and action to one that encourages attention to the whole. Since the seventeenth century, we have operated on the premise that analysis of single parts will give understanding of the whole. This was the basis of Newtonian physics. Hobbesian policies and Adam Smith's free market economics took their lead from this mechanistic approach, and Taylor's scientific management stressed internal competition, control, predictability, and relativity.

Today we are living in an age of intensive global interdependence, one in which this old way of seeing the world no longer fits. Building on the new quantum physics of the twentieth century, a new model emerges where the whole organizes and even partly defines the parts. Within organizations, the new framework requires that we pay attention to the relationships between people, to the validity of each person's unique reality, and to the multiple creative possibilities that exist at any moment in time.

Leaders in organizations must help people see the big picture, with its underlying trends, forces, and potential surprises. They need to think systematically and be able to foresee how internal and external factors might benefit or destroy the organization. The ability to decipher and analyze massive amounts of often contradictory information demands patience and persistence. Some key elements needed to accomplish this way of thinking include the following:

▲ Avoiding symptomatic solutions and focusing on underlying causes
▲ Distinguishing detail complexity (many variables) from dynamic complexity (when cause and effect are distant in time and space, and when the consequences over time are subtle)
▲ Seeing processes, not snapshots
▲ Focusing on areas of high leverage
▲ Seeing interrelationships, not things
▲ Seeing that you and the cause of your problems are part of a single system

How Action Learning Develops Leaders
to Be Systems Thinkers

Action learning is built around a diverse group of people asking new and fresh questions so as to gain a full picture of the problem and its context before attempting to solve it. The core questions asked in action learning focus on examining underlying causes and long-range solutions. They seek to provide the greatest leverage, and they recognize the importance of relationships and one's own role in problems and solutions. Reflecting on how to make connections, how to analyze seemingly contradictory data, and how to seek new possibilities rather than old answers are inherent parts of the action learning process.

Change Agent

Kanter (1985) has long been a prophet with respect to the importance of leaders' being change agents. He insists that all leaders must develop an understanding of and a high degree of competence in creating and managing change for their organizations to survive. Wheatley (1992) talks about how change is the essence of the new global environment, and about how new leaders need to have the ability to bring order to chaos, as opposed to trying to control it.

Since change is a function of leadership, being able to generate highly energized behavior is important for coping with the inevitable barriers to change. Just as direction setting identifies an appropriate path for movement and just as effective alignment gets people moving down that path, successful motivation ensures that they will have the energy to overcome obstacles (Kotter, 1995).

How Action Learning Develops Leaders
to Be Change Agents

McNulty and Canty (1995) remark that how action learning "develops the ability to create change and not be afraid to do so. It enables members to see and understand the concomitant change that is happening inside themselves so that they can do it again with ever greater facility" (p. 57). Revans (1980, p. 277) adds that "the action learning process is founded on the concept that one cannot change the system unless one is changed in the process. The change in the system is 'action.' The change in the individual is 'learning' so that learning to act effectively is also learning how to learn effectively."

Innovator and Risk Taker

Leaders of the twenty-first century must be willing to take risks. Not only should they themselves be creative, they should encourage and reward creativity around them. New leaders must be truly open to the wide range of perspectives and possibilities essential to identifying trends and generating choices.

Many corporate leaders now say that it is "imagination and not resources that is scarce." Thus the twenty-first-century leader should listen to many new voices in the strategy process if he or she wants to increase the odds of helping the organization move into the future.

Often new ideas are not allowed to occur in an organization, since they might conflict with existing, established mental models or ways of doing things. The new leader has the task of confronting existing assumptions without evoking defensiveness or anger. He or she is able to uncover and test the mental models and basic assumptions of colleagues. Specific skills in this area include the following:

▲ Balancing inquiry and advocacy
▲ Distinguishing between what is espoused and what is practiced
▲ Recognizing and defusing defensive routines
▲ Seeing and testing leaps of abstraction

Jack Welch, CEO of General Electric, challenges his managers with the following questions: Are you dealing with new things? Are you coming up with fundamentally new approaches for getting things done? Are you generating new programs? For General Electric and its leaders, the generation of new ideas is the lifeline to continued success. Although everyone is encouraged and expected to be creative, it is the managers who can best create this environment. They can invite risks as well as protect and encourage those whose risks have not been successful. The twenty-first-century leader should be continuously attempting new things and challenging the old ways.

How Action Learning Develops Leaders to Be Innovators and Risk Takers

Action learning enhances the ability to think in new and fresh ways about existing reality and problems by using critical reflection, reframing, and context shifting. The synergy of diverse groups asking fresh questions generates creativity. Risk taking is encouraged in action learning groups to generate numerous solutions and inspire action.

Marsick (1988) remarks that "the capacity to dig below the surface layer of perception and examine taken-for-granted assumptions and

Breakthrough Leadership at Ameritech

Darlene Van Tiem, University of Michigan–Dearborn

At Ameritech Corporation, action learning teams are formed with representatives of various business units. The teams seek to make significant organizational changes, eliminate unnecessary work and waste, and improve service to internal and external customers. Sanctioned by higher management, the action learning team defines the current process flow and searches for improvement, possibilities, and solutions. The teams are expected to explore, decide, and implement changes quickly, frequently within two months or less.

Examples of action learning projects include developing a new billing system, creating a competency-based training approach, and establishing a cross-functional, cross-level approach to marketing and development methodology. One action learning group created a Training and Development Kit, which included an assessment instrument for the HR practitioner and manager and recommended methods of developing each skill through independent learning, job assignment, coaching, and/or training.

Breakthrough leadership is an intense action learning process that has increased productivity, created a greater customer and shareholder awareness, and instilled an urgency for continuous change and organizational improvement at Ameritech.

values" is necessary in order to determine whether or not one is addressing the right problem. Members take risks in being frank and honest in helping others learn about themselves. Adapting and applying the learning to one's organization and to one's own professional life requires flexibility and creativity.

Servant and Steward

The words *servant* and *leader* are usually thought of as opposites. When opposites are brought together in a creative and meaningful way, however, a powerful paradox emerges.

The servant-leader concept was introduced in the 1970s by Robert Greenleaf, an AT&T manager for over thirty years. His book *Servant Leadership* (1977) sparked a radical rethinking of leadership. Influential business theorists such as Senge, Vail, and Block cite the attribute of stewardship as one of the most critical for the twenty-first-century leader.

Greenleaf's insight was inspired by his reading of Hesse's (1932) short novel *Journey to the East,* about a journey by a group of people on a spiritual quest. A character named Leo accompanies the party as the servant who sustains them with his caring spirit. All goes well with the journey until Leo disappears one day. The group quickly falls into disarray, and the journey is abandoned. The group cannot manage without Leo. After many years of searching, the narrator of the story stumbles upon Leo and is taken into the religious order that sponsored the original journey. There he discovers that Leo, whom he had known as a servant, was in fact the head and guiding spirit of the order—a great and noble leader.

Leaders, according to Greenleaf, must first serve others. This simple fact is central to a leader's greatness. True leadership emerges from those whose primary motivation is a desire to help others. Serving others—employees, customers, and the community—must be the number one priority. Servant-leadership emphasizes increased service to others, a holistic approach to work, a sense of community, and shared decision-making power.

The first concern is to make sure that other people's highest-priority needs are being served. The best test is this: Do those served grow as persons? Do they, while being served, become healthier, wiser, freer, more autonomous, more likely themselves to become servants?

Servant-leaders must be willing to suspend their need for control. In order to process multiple levels of experience, they must be able to see their own values, backgrounds, and experiences and to recognize that thinking that their own backgrounds or areas of experience are superior to those of others can be a fatal flaw.

Spears (1995) identifies ten key characteristics of the servant-leader:

Listening: Leaders must have a deep commitment to listening intently to others, in regard to both what is being said and what is not being said. Only then can they truly be able to identify and clarify the will of a group.

Empathy: Employees need to be accepted and recognized for their special and unique spirits. Leaders should assume the good intentions of co-workers and not reject them as people, even when forced to reject their behavior or performance.

Healing: Many people have broken spirits and have suffered from a variety of emotional hurts. Servant-leaders help make whole those with whom they come in contact.

Awareness: A leader should be fully aware of the needs of others as well as of his or her own. Issues of ethics and values are inherent in this characteristic.

Persuasion: The servant-leader seeks to convince rather than coerce. He or she is effective at building consensus within groups and recognizes the need to democratize the strategy-creation process.

Conceptualization: The leader should be able to dream great dreams. Thinking beyond day-to-day realities requires discipline and practice. The servant-leader stretches his or her thinking to encompass broader-based conceptual thinking.

Foresight: The tremendous ability to foresee the likely outcome of a situation, as well as the likely consequence of a decision for the future, requires someone who is deeply rooted within the intuitive mind.

Stewardship: Servant leaders recognize that they are merely holding an organization in trust for a period of time, for the greater good of society.

Commitment to the growth of people: For servant-leaders, people have an intrinsic value beyond their tangible contributions as workers. As a result, servant-leaders are deeply committed to the personal, professional and spiritual growth of every individual.

Building a community: The servant-leader works to build a community of caring people both within and outside the organization.

How Action Learning Develops Leaders to Be Servants and Stewards

The facilitator, in many ways, is a model of the servant-leader. The roles that are employed by the facilitator mirror in a remarkable way the roles just listed for the servant-leader:

▲ Designing opportunities for participants to find their own answers to problems
▲ Designing opportunities for participants to learn from each other's perspectives, successes, and mistakes
▲ Encouraging a climate where participants will both support and challenge each other
▲ Refraining from displaying one's own knowledge and understanding
▲ Challenging individual and group assumptions
▲ Providing difficult feedback to members
▲ Asking questions that assist participants in exploring the reasoning behind their assumptions
▲ Acknowledging mistakes publicly and framing them as learning experiences

Polychronic Coordinator

Twenty-first-century leaders will need to be able to coordinate many things at the same time (that is, be *polychronic*). They must also be able to work collaboratively with many others, often in unfamiliar settings on unfamiliar problems. These leaders require the dexterity to focus on the big picture as well as on the details. When juggling fifty balls at once, the leader can concentrate on the one that is in his or her hand at the time.

In the changing organization, with its increased use of project teams, managers will more likely be leading and coordinating three, five, even up to ten different task-focused teams, each carrying out a variety of activities on a totally different time schedule. The ability to quickly enter into and become a trusted partner of these teams is a taxing challenge. To plan, manage, balance, and juggle these many "balls" requires an agile, caring, and well-organized individual.

Walter Kiechel (1994), managing editor of *Fortune* magazine, predicts that tomorrow's managers will need to be simultaneously and consecutively specialists and generalists, team players and self-reliant, able to think of themselves as a business of one and plan accordingly. The new leader will need to be internetworked rather than a practitioner of the old-style, brilliant-visionary, take-charge approach. He or she will need to possess both analytic and strategic thinking skills.

A twenty-first-century leader must think in terms of whole systems, seeing the business as part of a wider environment. He or she should view business opportunities not simply as a solo player, but as one player among many, each coevolving with the others. This is sharply different from the conventional idea of competition, in which companies work only with their own resources and do not extend themselves by capitalizing on the capabilities of others. In the new global market, leaders need to make use of the other players—for capacity, innovation, and capital.

Within the new technologies, structures, environment, and resources of an organization, the leader must be an architect who can "fit" or "sculpt" these elements into a system that will thrive in the rapidly changing marketplace. The leader helps to redefine the organization, reshape the networks and teams, and reinvent new methods for selecting, training, and rewarding people so that everyone can participate in the new global environment. The leader must also help create and design new and appropriate policies, strategies, and principles.

Like an orchestra conductor who encourages each player to play his or her instrument more magnificently, the twenty-first-century leader empowers individuals to perform at their best while being part of the organization as a whole. The leader utilizes a repertoire of approaches and styles to track information, polish products and services, and energize people from within and outside the organization.

How Action Learning Develops Leaders
to Be Polychronic Coordinators

During action learning programs, group members learn how to handle many problems, often in the same meeting. They learn how the problems interconnect. When serving in facilitator roles, they must note the numerous dynamics occurring simultaneously between and among several members.

Through action learning, leaders recognize the importance of carving new paths, of living in a state of constant inquiry. They recognize the importance of continually asking questions, gathering information, and analyzing the situation. Dealing with all these uncertainties is fraught with risk and requires a willingness to admit the things one does not know, something no one likes to do. Yet it is when we are overwhelmed with possibilities and things go wrong that we achieve our greatest accomplishments. Reg Revans relates that the great successes at the Cavendish Laboratory occurred when the scientists admitted and shared their "bloody ignorance." Handling problems and confusions is what leadership is all about, and leadership is what action learning develops.

Instructor, Coach, and Mentor

Helping others learn is one of the critical responsibilities for a leader in tomorrow's organizations. This requires a variety of approaches, including those of instructor, coach, and mentor. Which of these roles a leader chooses to play depends on several factors (see Table 7.1).

The leader is not there just to tell others what to learn. He or she should encourage, motivate, and help workers to learn and to continuously improve their skills as well as their learning abilities. He or she should assist them in identifying learning resources. The leader should also be a devoted learner, one who takes time to learn and demonstrates a love for learning. Practicing action learning, taking risks, seeking innovative answers, and asking fresh questions all exhibit solid learning practices and skills to employees.

An analogy might involve the coach of a soccer team who transforms individuals into a cohesive unit in which every member is responsible for the success of the team, and in which they can all see how individual plays affect the whole game. The manager motivates,

Table 7.1   *Factors to Consider in Choosing Leadership Roles*

	Instructor Role	Coach Role	Mentor Role
Focus of Help	Task	Results of job throughout life	Development of person
Timespan	A day or two	A month or year	Career or lifetime
Approach to Helping	Show and tell; give supervised practice and set up opportunities to try out new skills	Explore problem with others	Act as a friend; listen and question to increase awareness
Associated Activities	Analyze task, give clear instruction; supervise practice and give immediate feedback on results	Jointly identify the problem; create development opportunities and review	Link work with other parts of life; clarify broad and long-term aims and purpose in life

implores, inspires, and promotes all team members so that they are able to successfully play the game, with minimal input from the sidelines.

Gaining workers' participation in challenging and sometimes unenjoyable activities requires skills in coaching and facilitating. No task is more important for the new leader than encouraging and inspiring learning.

How Action Learning Develops Leaders to Be Instructors, Coaches, and Mentors

All members of the group, not only the facilitator, are encouraged to assist fellow members in the learning process. Thus learning occurs in action groups naturally, as individuals and teams reflect on their thinking, actions, and learnings.

Coaching skills are enhanced and developed in the group. Members help the presenter identify the true problem and assist him or her in developing possible actions to take in resolving it. They seek to empower the presenter to take "appropriate levels of responsibility in discovering how to develop themselves" (McGill and Beaty, 1995, p. 37).

Mentoring is also developed in the action learning process when members enable the presenter to work through his or her issues. Through this process, the presenter gains an understanding of what it is like on the receiving end of mentoring.

Visionary and Vision Builder

Finally, the twenty-first-century leader must be able to help build the company's vision and to inspire workers, customers, and colleagues. The leader must envision, together with his or her fellow employees, the type of "future world" the company desires. This world is, ideally, one that is exciting and challenging enough to attract and retain the best and brightest workers. To the extent that the leader is truly able to build a shared, desired picture for the organization or unit, the people will be willing and committed to carry out the vision. Leaders should attempt to:

▲ Blend extrinsic and intrinsic visions
▲ Communicate their own vision and ask for support
▲ Encourage personal visions from which emerge shared visions
▲ Keep visioning as an ongoing process

Kotter (1998) points out the importance of leaders being visionaries when he says:

> The best leaders know something about challenging the status quo, about developing a vision that makes sense in light of economic realities, and about how to create strategies for achieving the vision. They're compulsive communicators. They know what they need to get people all over the place to understand and believe in those visions. They're compulsive empowerers. They realize that they have to give people enough rope to implement those visions [p. 5].

The twenty-first-century leader looks for *white-space opportunities* —that is, for new areas of growth possibilities that fall between the cracks because they don't naturally match the skills of existing business units. He or she looks for *strategic intent*—that is, a tangible corporate goal or destiny that represents a stretch for the organization and implies a point of view about the competitive position a company hopes to build over the coming decade.

The ability to conceptualize complex issues and processes, simplify them, and inspire people around them is essential for the twenty-first-century leader. Charisma may be helpful, but it is much more important to lead through a caring confidence in the people for whom one plays the steward role. Leaders create stories about the future of their organizations. These stories create a case for change, a vision of where the organization is going, and an understanding of how to get there.

How Action Learning Develops Visionary Leaders

Action learning groups are often challenged with a problem in which initially no one knows toward which direction to steer. Yet, through the process of sharing their ignorance, the group members begin developing a vision of where they need to go to solve the problem. Ann Brooks (1998) notes that action learning builds leaders who "metaphorically speaking, [have] the capacity to find a new and better path through the jungle, rather than be the first one down a path that already exists" (p. 53).

Learning how to conceptualize complex issues is a skill gained through action learning. Creating visions, particularly shared visions, occurs frequently in action learning groups as the members develop system-oriented, holistic resolutions to complex problems.

Trying to get people to comprehend a vision of an alternative future is also a communications challenge of a completely different magnitude than organizing them to fulfill a short-term plan. It is much like the difference between a football quarterback's attempting to describe to his team the next two or three plays and his trying to explain to them a totally new approach to the game to be used in the second half of the season. Action learning gives people the skills of understanding and preparing such a vision of the future.

Why Action Learning Is Effective in Developing Leaders

It was during his lecture-based courses that Reg Revans became aware of the fact that students and managers were relatively passive and lacking in energy in the classroom. They came to life, however, when they discussed their own "back home" problems with one another. The message was loud and clear to Revans: Managers are people of action who learn from action. The other message was that managers will help each other in the right environment and will be prepared to share their experience and insights.

As Revans (1983) notes, "action learning is the Aristotelian manifestation of all managers' jobs: they learn as they manage, and they manage because they have learned—and go on learning" (p. 49). As professor at the Manchester Business School, Revans pushed for a faculty and board composed of business leaders rather than just academics. Also, when working with the coal mines and hospitals, he felt that better management skills and self-awareness could be attained through actual work on problems rather than through a consultant's or teacher's telling people how to gain these skills and awarenesses.

Using Real-Life Conditions Faced by Managers

In the real world of work, learning for most managers generally occurs from the process of doing a job. However, for most managers, learning is rarely identified beforehand as an opportunity, nor do managers know how to tap learning opportunities.

Action learning creates the conditions in which managers learn from their own experience in a real-life problem, helped by and helping others facing similar situations. Developing the two key skills of problem solving and personal development is part of the same learning process. The process in the sense that a manager actually changes the way he or she manages is based on reality.

In action learning groups, managers submit their actions to the constructive scrutiny of persistent but supportive colleagues. Through this process of enforced self-revelation, managers are able to get in touch with why they say the things they say, do the things they do, and value the things they value. The managers also begin to transcend self-images that are falsely built on the assumption that their actions are entirely congruent with their epsoused intentions.

Every person who participated in action learning–based management programs matured five years during the six-month program.
—A senior executive

As a result of my action learning experiences, I have much better relations with my staff. I am able to motivate them and to communicate more effectively with them. I have learned better how to delegate and how to empower. I have a much better understanding of what management is all about and am more organized and prepared for my leadership role.
—Jim

Leadership Development at Britvic Soft Drinks

Britvic Soft Drinks produces approximately 20 percent of the fizzy drinks, mineral waters, and dilutables in the United Kingdom and employs 3,000 people at more than thirty locations.

In 1993, Britvic introduced its Developing to Lead (DTL) program for frontline supervisors and those with leadership potential. The program's success is measured by candidates' ability to develop key competencies and lead work teams to influence change, achieve key performance indicators, and demonstrate value to the business. Candidates work with real problems and are encouraged to challenge the status quo.

DTL participants form action learning groups, each of which works at its own pace with its own ground rules and priorities. The group becomes the arena for peer discussion, assessment, and evaluation, with each group member negotiating his or her own target dates for assignments and project work. These groups meet on eight occasions during the program.

Each candidate is expected to identify four problems or opportunities for change. At first, candidates were reluctant to take the initiative and looked to facilitators for leadership. As their confidence grew they became less inhibited and more willing to take control.

The variety and quality of the work in the action learning groups has exceeded expectations, and tangible benefits are apparent. Savings gained as a result of the first DTL program exceeded five million dollars with just the first group of thirty students. ■

Action learning creates conditions in which managers learn from their own experiences of real-life problems, helped by and helping others in similar or dissimilar situations. A manager actually changes the way he or she manages, on the basis of reality. The focus of action learning is on learning about the process of managing change by actually managing an organizational change. It stresses the importance of learning about oneself and the influence that one's attitudes and assumptions have on how one leads and makes decisions.

Mumford (1995a) believes that action learning is so effective because it incorporates the following elements necessary for training managers:

▲ Learning for managers should mean learning to take effective action; this is the focus of action learning. Acquiring information and becoming better at diagnosing and analyzing have been overvalued in traditional management development programs.

▲ Taking effective action _necessarily_ involves actually _taking action_, not recommending action or undertaking an analysis of someone else's problem.

▲ The best form of action for learning is to work on a specific project or an ongoing problem of actual significance.
▲ Managers learn best with and from each other.
▲ As "comrades in opportunity," managers can share problems on which to take action.
▲ In action learning, the people providing help are crucially different from the inexperienced professors found in many management training programs.
▲ Rather than being taught through case study or simulation, participants in action learning learn from exposure to real problems and to each other's insights.

Flexibility and Universalism

Action learning can be effective in developing leaders in all fields of endeavor, in all cultures, and at all levels because it is so flexible and adaptive. The process respects and builds upon each person's independence and experience.

It is less structured because it responds to the variety of managers and problems on which it draws. It has no syllabus of its own, no textbooks, and few classrooms. It makes its own use of teachers and professional staff. It is a self-guided course of education that is unique to each manager and his or her problem, for "never again will the same problem with the same set of characters meet in history" (McNulty and Canty, 1995).

The questioning insight of action learning becomes a way of life for leaders who have grown and developed through action learning programs. Action learning graduates have a greater aptitude to listen, negotiate, resolve conflict, and stand tall in the face of change.

This habit of seeking insight about themselves is the most basic source of learning for all leaders. Our character cannot be taught but must be learned. Academic programs have difficulty in applying what is learned back at work. In action learning, that lesson is learned as the program progresses.

Leadership Development at General Electric

Executive education at GE is composed of two four-week programs: an executive development course (EDC), conducted once a year, and a business management course (BMC), taught two to three times a year. The participants in these programs are determined via an annual organizational staffing review and succession planning process.

Prior to 1986, GE's leadership programs consisted primarily of lectures, case studies, computer simulations, and outdoor activities. Curriculum included modules on leadership, teamwork, global competition, and business strategy. The program ended with an integrating activity that synthesized these various themes. CEO Jack Welch recognized that leadership learning was not sufficiently intense and impactful in developing the new GE leaders.

GE therefore decided to move from a model that was based on individual cognitive learning to one that is based on problem solving by teams—that is, action learning. The teams faced real problems, real team challenges, and real risks and were to solve some of the most vexing problems facing GE businesses.

New leadership programs would have four key objectives, all of which were deemed to be best achieved through action learning:

1. Enable participants to learn, apply, and receive feedback on business concepts and skills applied to real GE business issues
2. Provide help on issues important to GE businesses
3. Help participants develop leadership and team skills essential to leading and working in high-performing, multifunctional business teams
4. Assist participants in developing personal action plans for applying new business and leadership skills in their work settings

The Problems for Leadership Development

Action learning teams are built around GE problems that are real, are relevant, and require decisions. Formats may vary, but, typically, two teams of five to seven people, who come from diverse businesses and functions within GE, work together on the problem.

Before the course begins, Management Development Institute staff work with the businesses being studied to define the issues and compile a dossier of pertinent market, customer, and financial information on each issue that the participants review as they begin the program.

Action learning projects are identified by the company's top executives or heads of GE's major divisions and include:

▲ Transportation system—evaluation of transportation systems' market strategy to enter the locomotive lease/maintenance business
▲ Plastics—development of a marketing strategy for a new resin and continuous porous process
▲ Lighting—recommendation on whether the lighting business should enter a new market segment in a mature business
▲ Aircraft engines—analysis of aircraft engines' "service shops" competitiveness, and recommendation for their charter with the aircraft engines business

▲ Information services—evaluation of artificial intelligence applications for GE information services

▲ Industry sales and service—development of a national accounting marketing plan

▲ Medical systems—recommendation on how best to leverage the new centralized marketing function

▲ Marketing—determining the market for GE financial services in India

▲ Competition—examining how GE stacks up against foreign competition, such as Electrolux, Toshiba, and Asea Brown Boveri

Initially, some people at GE were concerned that GE's business leaders would want to air their problems in an open forum. Fortunately, the business leaders viewed the projects as excellent opportunities to have a group of bright, experienced managers work on their problems (Noel and Charan, 1988). The leaders felt that having participants come from other businesses provided a fresh perspective.

Schedule

The first week of the leadership program is spent in a variety of team-building exercises, as well as in receiving briefings on the projects with which the leaders will be involved. During weeks two and three, the teams begin developing plans, asking questions of key managers, and carrying out a variety of diagnostic activities. In the final week, participants make their presentations to the business leader (client) who provided the project. At this presentation, the business leader brings along a team of key players who are involved with the critical issues of the project. GE builds into the action learning model opportunities for reflecting upon and receiving feedback on leadership and teamwork.

A GE action learning project that was held in Heidelberg, Germany, focused on potential new GE markets in Europe. The first week was spent gaining an overview of GE operations in Europe. During the second week, the focus shifted to projects from GE's plastic, lighting, and electrical distribution and control businesses. One action learning team looked at the lighting strategy for Europe, reflecting the sharp rise—from 2 to 18 percent in only eighteen months—in GE's share of the western European consumer lighting market, mostly resulting from the acquisition of Tungsram in Hungary and Thorn Lighting in the United Kingdom. The teams were encouraged to be creative and think of serious ways in which GE could change the market and excite retailers and customers by finding new ways to add value. The participants traveled across Europe to conduct interviews; they also experienced firsthand the effects of local culture, language, currency, legislation, tax laws, and consumer preferences for national brands. Between interviews, the participants debriefed each other and prepared their final reports to present to GE leadership, including Jack Welch. ■

Leadership Development at Bristol-Myers Squibb

Rebecca Kraft, Organizational Consultant

A key BMS strategy is to gain and sustain competitive advantage by attracting, developing, and retaining employees of the highest caliber. In order to build on that strategy, the company created the Center for Leadership Development, whose goal is to ensure the development of future leaders by increasing the depth and breadth of management talent.

One of the key activities of the center is the Global Leadership Development (GLD) program, which is designed to develop critical management skills for high-potential managers on a global cross-divisional basis. The primary objectives of the GLD program are for each participant to gain an understanding of and enhanced effectiveness in solving critical BMS problems and develop high-level leadership skills and attributes.

During the three-month program, all the high-potential managers work on the following:

▲ Enhancing their ability to think and act strategically for competitive advantage

▲ Focusing on practical skills and their application to current business issues

▲ Developing business and leadership skills, and understanding the diversity and complexity of the business in today's competitive environment

▲ Developing and leading high-performance teams

▲ Establishing a worldwide network of internal contacts

▲ Benefiting from increased exposure to senior management

The program includes two one-week classroom sessions. Week one focuses on global strategic management concepts, the challenges of change, and breakthrough thinking concepts. In week two, the theme is organizational behavior issues that drive management actions within a constantly changing work and market environment.

The weeklong classroom sessions are separated by a three-month period during which participants return to their jobs. During this hiatus, they work in teams on action learning projects that directly relate to their businesses. Several business challenges currently faced by the organization are worked on during this period. These projects are intended to represent "stretch" opportunities for the individuals and lead to creative and innovative solutions. The teams present their findings and recommendations during the second week of classes.

The GLD program has been in place for four years. Nearly two hundred individuals have participated since 1994. Because this is an exclusive experience, nominations are accepted from business divisions only once each year. Selections are made by the Center for Leadership Development in conjunction with line management and the Human Resources Vice Presidents in each division. Classes are formed with equal representation from divisions and with diversity of the group an important goal.

The GLD program has continued to achieve impressive results, but, most important, it has seen the significant development of a number of valuable leadership capabilities, including:

Openness: Learning to be truly open to the wide range of perspectives and possibilities essential for identifying trends and generating choices is a critical attribute for BMS leaders. Related to this characteristic is the ability to suspend the need for control, be open to listening, and ask questions rather than give answers.

Patience: A better manager, for many, is too often seen as being in constant action. Revans (1983) warns against this compulsive drive to take action:

> Most managers, tormented by the ticking of the office clock and the fall of the days from the factory calendar, will respond sooner to the urgencies of the moment, however inconsequential, than to the suggestion that they ought to clear the decks and heed the long-term warnings. This is Gresham's law of management: "Short-term issues drive out the long."

Creativity: Action learning has increased the personal flexibility and willingness of BMS managers to takes risks; they now have an increased ability to be innovative while encouraging creativity around them.

International Management Centres

The International Management Centres (IMC) of Buckingham, England, conduct MBA and doctoral management programs that are based almost exclusively on action learning. Students are involved in numerous action learning projects throughout their years in the program. These projects are written up for accreditation. Professors, many of whom are practicing managers, occasionally present, but more often serve as group advisors. The IMC program boasts over 1,000 MBA graduates from most of the largest corporations in the world. ■

Swedish Management Institute

The Swedish Management Institute hosts action learning programs of thirty to forty days' duration over nine-month periods, which intersperse seminars with action learning projects. The original flagship program included managers from seven or more companies. There is a special emphasis on fresh questioning; thus, the institute often brings in a visiting manager from another company, a stage actor, or an artist to generate previously unasked questions.

Three groups of participants are involved in the Swedish leadership development programs:

Members—(often referred to as *fellows*), who are assigned to tasks and fields quite alien to their backgrounds (e.g., bankers to telemarketing for an oil company, an importer of cars to product innovation in a steel mill, a telecommunications engineer to poultry-feed marketing)

Clients—organizations/business units that are faced with significant challenges (these units may submit their problems to the group members or have a manager actually be a part of the group; in either case, they must commit themselves and their employees to working out the problem with the fellows assigned to them)

Teaching staff—made up of businesspeople and faculty with business experience ■

Leadership Development and Organizational Performance Intertwined

Leadership development programs, as practiced by most corporations and institutions of higher learning, according to Dilworth (1996, p. 49), "produce individuals who are technologically literate and able to deal with intricate problem-solving models, but are essentially distanced from the human dimensions that must be taken into account." They may be good at downsizing and corporate restructuring but cannot deal with a demoralized workforce and the resulting longer-term challenges. These so-called development programs provide excellent technical skills, but the "social and interpersonal aspects of the organizations that largely create the dynamics of corporate culture are left unattended."

Action learning has the power to provide both the best content and the best methodology for building the vital attributes of leadership for the twenty-first century. Leadership is built on the premise and expectation of getting things done. To take effective action is an essential task. Action learning programs introduce real-life, real-time practice of the necessary skills, focusing on the learner/leader, and not just on the tasks to be undertaken by the learner/leader. As Reg Revans noted over thirty years ago, managers do not change situations without themselves being changed in the process.

Personal Development

Action learning recognizes that you cannot change the problem without changing yourself. Solving an organizational problem and developing the individual group members are intertwined. Dixon (1998) points out that organizational problems cannot be solved unless the people within organizations change themselves. If an organization sacrifices individual learning, it risks the organizational capacity to change.

In action learning, group members learn about themselves. People are able to change themselves when they are working on problems or issues that truly involve them. The kind of development that individuals are able to achieve through action learning, according to Dixon, is unique in organizational settings. Action learning has the power to develop individuals to be "more self-aware, be more cognizant of their impact, and . . . have a more differentiated frame from which to view the organization and its future issues" (p. 58).

The Process of Personal Development

Personal development, according to McGill and Beaty (1995), demands "a complex weave of reflective practice and opportunities for development of knowledge and skill." The reflection on practice that takes place in action learning is the "oil in the wheel" that enables effective personal growth as well as reconstructive and additive learning.

Two Cycles of Learning

Learning begins in a cycle of experience whereby some problem or challenge is identified. The problem is shared with the group to further clarify and reframe it. Upon critical reflection, solutions are planned and a decision is made to experiment or test the proposed action. This action, in turn, is then examined for further learnings, the development of generalizations, and future actions. Action ensures that the learning is tested and based on real outcomes. Reflection is a continuous part of the process. This cycle is described in Chapter 2 and illustrated in Figure 2.2.

In addition, there is another cycle of learning occurring during action learning programs. There is an inner cycle of growth and development, and it is illustrated in Figure 8.1. First, there is unease with the experience or an insight. This results in awareness of a desire to change. With some courage and support, the person takes a risk from which he or she gains an understanding and new insight and, perhaps, a new level of awareness. He or she then begins a transformative learning experience and is ready to put the possible solution into action.

Personal Development Defined

Dixon (1998) defines personal development as "the movement the individual makes in achieving a more *open*, differentiated, and integrated perspective." Being *open* implies a willingness to entertain alternative perspectives. *Differentiated* refers to the ability to draw finer distinctions between concepts. *Integrated* relates to the capacity to weave these differences into an increasingly complex whole.

According to Mezirow (1991), development implies a movement toward a systems view and away from an ethnocentric or fragmented view. As adults become more developed, they are able to deal with increasing complexity, as opposed to being stuck in rigid and highly defended thought patterns that make them less able to adapt to changing conditions and less able to change themselves.

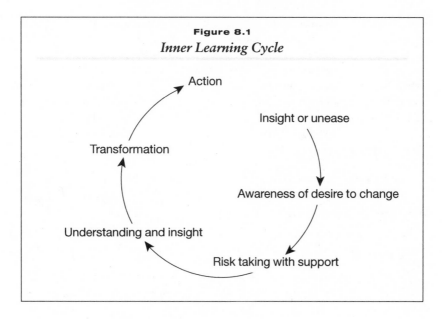

Figure 8.1
Inner Learning Cycle

Action

Insight or unease

Transformation

Awareness of desire to change

Understanding and insight

Risk taking with support

Development requires reflection so that people can reframe their understanding of themselves in the world or in relation to the system of which they are a part. Readiness is a prerequisite for development and is often engendered by some type of internal dissonance or external circumstance. An action learning group may provide the opportunity for internal dissonance, while the problem and/or action may provide the external trigger.

How People Develop Through Action Learning Programs

Action learning programs progress through distinct phases that inherently accentuate self-awareness and personal development. First, individuals are placed in unfamiliar settings and/or unfamiliar problems. In these new settings, fresh questions are automatically and naturally induced. Being out of one's comfort zone forces one to look at things through a different lens.

Once fresh questions are introduced, group members begin to unfreeze and reshape their underlying assumptions, thereby transforming how they see and respond to situations. As these assumptions get questioned, they may be confirmed, modified, or rejected. Those that are changed lead to our creation of new mental models (an important discipline for organizational learning, as we discussed in Chapter 5).

The new mental models cause a reassessment of our programmed knowledge, some of which we accept and some of which we reject and replace with new knowledge. As we keep adding and renewing our knowledge, we increase our learning capacities and performance levels.

Weinstein (1995) identifies and distinguishes three levels in the learning that occurs in action learning groups:

Level 1—Understanding something intellectually

Level 2—Applying some newly acquired skill (i.e., taking action and doing something differently)

Level 3—Experiencing (i.e., undergoing an inner development that touches on beliefs and attitudes and leads to personal development)

Academic and professional training programs introduce opportunities to learn at levels 1 and 2; level 3 is rarely developed in most educational and training activities but is a common and natural occurrence in action learning programs.

Individual development requires time, often more time than we are willing to commit. It requires becoming aware of our blind spots and our weaknesses as well as our strengths. In our day-to-day interactions, we get little real feedback on our limitations and strengths. In action learning groups, however, we spend a significant amount of intense time with each other. Thus we are able to observe each other as we struggle with challenges, limitations, and professional issues. We have the opportunity to understand and see people with their problems. Members are willing to give feedback, support fellow group members, and seek to be frank and truthful with one another. Having developed some investment in each other's well-being over a period of time in the action learning group, members are more likely to give and receive feedback and reflection that lead to personal growth.

Personal Attributes Developed via Action Learning

In addition to the teamwork skills and leadership competencies that can be built through the use of action learning programs (see Chapters 6 and 7), participation in action learning develops a number of personal characteristics and attributes that are highly valued in organizations:

▲ Critical reflection
▲ Inquiry and questioning
▲ Openness and willingness to change
▲ Clear personal vision
▲ Personal mastery
▲ Empathy
▲ Active listening
▲ Courage and frankness
▲ Skills in advising and helping others
▲ Facilitation and presentation skills
▲ Wisdom and common sense
▲ Self-awareness

Critical Reflection

A core activity of action learning programs, and one that is important for their success, is *critical reflection.* Group members are encouraged to continually reflect on what is happening in the process, both implicitly and explicitly, and on the words, actions, and thoughts of all the members. During the action learning process, participants have the opportunity to practice reframing questions and perspectives and to examine taken-for-granted assumptions that may have been preventing them from acting in new and more effective ways.

Critical reflection, or what Brookfield (1988) calls a *healthy skepticism,* is necessary for transformative learning—that is, learning that causes people to see the world in a new light, to be able to evaluate their values, beliefs, actions, and ideas in the context of the new reality, and to transform present knowledge. Bierema (1998) points out that action learning is a process of "exploration and discovery" during which members reflect on "how assumptions and action interact."

Inquiry and Questioning

Bierema (1998) notes that, throughout our lives, we accumulate knowledge, and this knowledge gives us confidence that we have the right answers. Thus there is a natural tendency to advocate our present opinions. *Advocacy,* as generally defined, is a state of pushing one's personal opinion or promoting the commonly held viewpoint. There are many rewards in organizations for having the right answer in a crisis; hence our impulse for developing and using our advocacy skills.

On the other hand, few rewards exist for admitting, "I don't know" or "I might be wrong." When you are in a mode of selling an existing idea, openness to alternatives vanishes. However, advocacy or present knowledge is not necessarily helpful when you are faced with new, complex issues.

In action learning there is an open orientation toward new information and knowledge, which encourages a willingness to ask fresh questions and to counter conventional wisdom. Instead of immediately advocating our position, we see a wider picture, a more common ground. The ability to have good questions is what counts. To develop inquiry skills, individuals need to acknowledge that they may not have the answer and learn to ask good questions in search of it. They need to recognize that the answer may not yet be within the current set of knowledge and assumptions on which action is being based.

As illustrated throughout this book, action learning is built on inquiry rather than just answers, on asking the right questions rather than jumping into boxed solutions. Participants in action learning groups have the opportunity to learn how to pose questions, when to inquire, and when to advise. They see vividly the impact of good questions and are therefore encouraged to use questions as well as directives in their day-to-day lives.

What struck me is how much more you gain by framing issues in a nonthreatening manner, by asking good questions. I've discovered that people are more likely to elaborate when they are not entrenched in supporting their own positions. You learn more when you ask "why" questions. When someone says something that I disagree with, I now try to frame my disagreement as a question instead of immediately excluding what others have to say on the basis of my personal biases.
—Todd

There are, according to Beaty et al. (1993), two types of questions that help improve one's competence in inquiry. *Open questions* cannot be answered in a word or two; they require discussion and explanation. Unlike closed questions, which tend to close down exploration, open questions force the respondent to go deeper. They include questions such as:

▲ What resources do you have to do that?
▲ What other options can you think of?
▲ What questions provided you the best insight?

Questions that ask specifics help to get people in touch with the realities of the problem. They include questions such as:

▲ Can you give us an example of that?

▲ What caused that response?

Openness and Willingness to Change

Persons who appreciate the value and importance of asking questions will be more open to changing their basic assumptions and previous "perfect solutions." They may be more willing to see that the old ways may no longer work in a new world of chaos, uncertainty, and challenges. Kanter (1985) and others have remarked that the willingness to embrace and manage change is one of the most important competencies of today's worker.

Action learning can be a freeing experience. Participants discover that questions that may arise out of curiosity, ignorance, or lack of self-understanding may cause them to become aware of how rigidly they are entrapped in their own ways of thinking and acting (Revans, 1982a).

Butterfield et al. (1998, pp. 493–494), in their research on the key benefits of action learning, discovered that participants experienced "breakthrough learning" when they became aware of the need to "reach beyond [their] conscious belief[s] and to challenge [their] assumptions about [their] present worldviews." Action learning caused a "new awareness relative to the impact of reactions and interactions." Butterfield et al. quote similar reactions of other participants: "I discovered the extent to which my own assumptions, frame of reference, and worldview impact how I approach problems. I find that my level of awareness about this has been increased, and I've become more reflective about what I say and think and why"; "Much of my career has required me to learn models and techniques causing me to look at problems in a linear fashion. Action learning has freed me from this programmed bias to view a problem in a less structured manner."

A Clear Personal Vision

The presenter, particularly in open groups dealing with multiple problems, is bombarded with questions that force him or her to seriously examine and reflect on what is truly important relative to this problem and relative to his or her own life. When asked questions such as "What are you trying to accomplish? Why is this important to you? What will happen if . . . ?" one is obligated to examine values, goals, and personal vision.

Having a personal vision provides a foundation, meaning, and system for determining future directions and efforts. It provides a rudder to guide the person through constant change and conflicting expectations.

Organizations are well served by people who have the skill of articulating a desired outcome while honestly assessing their present reality and understanding the gap between the desired and actual realities. Such a personal understanding is important for career assessment and development.

Personal Mastery

Senge (1990) lists personal mastery as one of the five disciplines necessary to build a learning organization. Personal mastery is also a skill sought after by organizations who seek special levels of proficiency. In order to obtain personal mastery, one must have energy and patience and seek to continually clarify and deepen one's own personal vision.

In open action learning groups, each person is encouraged and expected to be the world expert on his or her problem. There is an expectation of self-responsibility; that is, the owner of the problem, with the assistance and support of the group, will ultimately master this important challenge in his or her own life. As a result, the presenter of the problem will gain greater self-understanding and self-awareness from the feedback and information of others in the group. Thus action learning promotes empowerment and self-reliance as well as confidence.

Empathy

Empathy is one's ability to project oneself into another's situation; it is an understanding of the world from the other's point of view, including that person's feelings, experience, and behavior. A sense of empathy is critical to effectively communicating and connecting with others in the workplace and in the community. A deep level of caring for others builds stronger organizations and better products and services for customers. Empathy enhances one-to-one relationships and adds quality to group interactions. McGill and Beaty (1995) cite empathy as "one of the most valuable, if not the most valuable" of the relationship skills developed in action learning.

Action learning groups depend on members supporting and being concerned about the well-being of others. Beaty et al. (1993) remark that "in order to have the energy and capacity to help solve another's problem, you need to care for the other person." You need to care enough about the other people in the set to "want them to succeed with their project and to learn from so doing" (p. 355).

In action learning, we begin to gain a sense of what it feels like to be that person with that problem. We develop an attitude that is curious and thoughtful about the way the problem owner feels about the problem, and we develop a willingness to share another person's feelings and thoughts.

Empathy provides the best data on how to help another person solve his or her own problem. Empathy is important in action learning groups because when a person believes that others appreciate how it would feel to be in his or her shoes, then the person will be more trusting toward the others. Thus we say in action learning groups, "How do you feel about?" rather than "What would I do if I were in your situation?"

In action learning groups there are times when it is appropriate to offer a shoulder to lean on, to express how much you hope a fellow set member succeeds, or to share another's disappointment with a failed action. Beaty et al. (1993) have found that such support "enables the recipient to move forward through areas where . . . feelings are blocking . . . progress. Empathy conveyed is more powerful then empathy concealed. This is a powerful encouragement that enables the problem owner to allow himself to share" (p. 355).

Active Listening

In action learning groups, members need to listen to what others say as well as attend to the nonverbal cues that indicate unspoken feelings and attitudes. A good listener has the ability to capture and understand the messages communicated, regardless of whether these messages are transmitted verbally or nonverbally, clearly or vaguely (Egan, 1990). To be truly helpful, group members must give full attention to the problem of another member.

Typically, our own agendas dominate our minds while another is speaking, and we are simply waiting for the other person to stop talking so that we have our opportunity to speak. We typically listen just enough to develop our own response, and we seek to relate what we hear to our own experience.

Active listening involves paying close attention to what the other is saying and conveying to the other that you are doing so. In action learning groups, participants seek to recognize the underlying feelings and the thoughts behind the words. Patterns of defensiveness that may be deeply ingrained in a person's thoughts need to be identified and creatively uncovered. In reflecting on the actions of a group, members are asked to identify when and how they were actively listening, and when they were filtering, generalizing, and forcing.

Courage and Frankness

Action learning groups work best when members are frank and honest with each other and with the challenge in front of them. Uncovering assumptions and differences ultimately results in better solutions.

In the action learning process, there will be times when the group needs to confront a member with direct, tough questions, such as:

▲ How would you handle that differently next time?
▲ What did you learn from that experience?
▲ Why didn't you do that?

These types of questions are necessary for people to work through their hidden biases and face their problems directly. Anything less than this kind of courage and honesty does not work.

Advising and Helping Others

Most of us do not know how to advise others in a way that will be accepted by them. Often our "wise" counsel is rejected because it is seen as being offered out of context, or without empathy for the other person. The other person may dismiss the advice as simply our own solution.

A popular management game referred to as "broken squares" places five individuals around a table, each with various pieces of different squares. The goal is to complete a square with the parts in front of them. There are two rules: no talking, and no taking pieces from someone else's pile. When a person sees a possible solution for another, it is extremely difficult not to tell the person, and when one is allowed to show the other person the answer, there is inevitably resentment. People first want to see if they can solve the problem alone; when someone else tells them how to do it, it makes them feel inferior and stupid. Only when people are ready to receive help will they ask for it, and it will be from someone who has demonstrated keen interest in and support for what these people were doing on their own.

Action learning works much more effectively when, instead of giving our solutions to fellow members, we help them to discover solutions to their own problems and to learn from this. When we find solutions for others, we deny them the opportunity to use a problem as a means of learning and developing.

In action learning programs, we learn and practice how to give and receive help and feedback. We allow the problem presenter to decide which queries, comments, and suggestions are truly helpful and which only serve others' own purposes, such as trying to appear more knowledgeable. Being an effective helper requires lots of discipline and practice, and feedback should be given in a way that:

▲ Is clear and concise
▲ Emphasizes the positive
▲ Is specific
▲ Focuses on the priorities
▲ Focuses on behavior rather than on the person
▲ Focuses on behavior that can be changed
▲ Is descriptive rather than evaluative
▲ Is owned by the person providing the feedback (uses "I" rather than "you")

Facilitation and Presentation Skills

As a presenter in an action learning group, an individual can learn to enhance his or her ability to clearly, logically, and concisely present what can be complex and confusing information. The group members all help the presenter determine the key points through focused questions. As a result of participation in action learning programs, presentation skills become more poised and polished.

When serving in the facilitator role, an individual develops one of the most critically important skills in both the workplace and the community: the ability to help individuals and groups solve problems and learn while doing it.

Wisdom and Common Sense

Revans notes that common sense is in fact the exception. True common sense, or wisdom, involves the deliberate effort to explore what cannot be seen in the problem. This differs fundamentally from cleverness, which enlarges upon what is already known to be there. Wisdom is interested in posing fertile questions; cleverness is interested in elaborating brilliant answers.

Putting ideas and suggestions to continuous testing is the essence of every action learning program. The utility of wisdom, rather than the elegance of cleverness, is what organizations and leaders are seeking.

Self-Awareness

The final and perhaps most important attribute developed in action learning programs is self-awareness. The adage "Know thyself" remains absolutely critical for anybody to truly succeed in any endeavor in life. Throughout the action learning process, members have the opportunity to become aware of the *why* behind their words and actions. The facilitator and other group members raise questions and provide reflective feedback on the individual as a worker, a learner, and a person.

Action learning develops a capacity for self-diagnosis and self-development on an ongoing basis, so that people become what Morgan (1988) describes as "competent at being competent."

Self-Awareness and Action Learning

Laura Frey Horn

True understanding comes from true practice.
—Thich Nhat Hanh

Mindfulness is a Buddhist term that means total presence in the moment. It includes total presence in thought, word, and deed. Mindfulness is the practice of knowing what is going on within and all around us. "When we are mindful, touching deeply the present moment, we can see and listen deeply, and the fruits are always understanding, acceptance" (Hanh, 1995). Mindfulness inspires an understanding of why one thinks and acts in a specific way. True mindfulness also inspires change in behavior and touches others' lives when practiced in the community.

Action learning, when practiced as designed, is mindfulness in action. "Action learning is concerned to do something about reality—including helping those involved to see more clearly what they are about" (Revans, 1983). Like mindfulness, action learning requires that individuals apply new knowledge and skills in their daily work. Also, like mindfulness, action learning has a powerful, multiplying effect.

Revans (1983) states that "by talking about things, one may claim to 'know' them, but only by actually doing them can one demonstrate, alike to oneself and others, that one does, in truth, 'know' them. There can be no learning without action, and no action learning." Through the action learning process, the problem owner will "rapidly perceive, using this incontrovertible scheme of classification, enlightenment and advance." Like mindfulness, action learning brings enlightenment.

The goal of action learning is not simply to define the problem. The reflection process must lead to action—a workable solution. Mindfulness also seeks not just knowing, but doing. "Touching deeply is an important practice. We touch with our hands, our eyes, our ears, and also with our mindfulness. . . . When you practice this way, your mind and body come into alignment, your wandering thoughts come to a stop, and you are at your best" (Hanh, 1995).

Action learning group members can address the purposes of a group most effectively when they have "a concern for the well-being of the other set members, a belief that each person is the leading expert in their own problems, and empathy" (Beaty et al., 1993). Group members must display behaviors that support these attitudes, including active listening and having the right purpose in listening, as well as skills conveying empathy and providing support.

The concept of mindfulness is better accepted and understood in non-Western cultures, whereas action learning is more widely used in Western cultures, yet the similarities between the two concepts are quite strong. Although action learning does not use the term *mindfulness*, the attitudes and behaviors demonstrated in action learning groups are similar to the concept of mindfulness in a community. In the Buddhist community, a group of individuals come together in a *sangha* to "practice together to encourage the best qualities in each other" (Hanh, 1995).

Action learning has not achieved the same degree of popularity and success in non-Western cultures because of the vast differences in culture, norms, and behaviors (see Chapter 9). If people and organizations in cultures accustomed to traditional Eastern philosophies identified the concept of mindfulness that embodies action learning, perhaps their understanding, use, and success with action learning would increase.

One way to introduce action learning from the mindfulness approach would be to address the process from an Eastern perspective. Respect for the varying rules of culture would have to be addressed. It's possible to establish groups and describe the process as a way of working with mindfulness to approach and solve problems. A group facilitator should teach or reaffirm the concepts of empathy and active listening and provide feedback, solutions, and challenges as a way to increase the group's and individuals' mindfulness. From this approach, it may be possible to introduce action learning in a gentler manner that would be more conducive to success in cultures comfortable with Eastern philosophy. It may also serve Western culture to learn a bit about mindfulness to improve the way in which group members approach the action learning process and the organization itself.

Marsick et al. (1992) state that participants tend to be highly committed to finding solutions and often begin implementing solutions while action learning groups are still in process. Finding workable solutions is energizing. Individuals who come together to solve problems find a sense of calm and satisfaction in working out viable solutions. Mindfulness is an active state that thoroughly engages one in finding solutions. When one is fully aware, solutions become obvious.

"The concept of action learning teaches participants to *act themselves into a new way of thinking, rather than think themselves into a new way of acting*" (Revans, 1982a, p. 65). Action learning is effective because it creates solutions by changing behaviors. Mindfulness works in much the same way: through an active focus on the present, behaviors change. Lawrie (1989) notes that action learning creates powerful reasons for success because the design is simple and the criteria for successful performance by participants are clear and actionable.

These same precepts of action learning apply to the practice of mindfulness. When Revans designed action learning, more than fifty years ago, success of an action learning group was determined by real-life solutions. Lawrie (1989) reinforces this: "If true action learning were to take place, members of the group would have to go beyond diagnosis to prescription and, ultimately, engage in treatment." Action learning is the way to new solutions.

Using Action Learning for Career Development

Action learning is ideally suited to helping individuals explore and take action regarding career options. In action learning groups that are built around career development, each person has the opportunity to share career hopes and frustrations and to check out possible directions and possibilities.

In the career development group, members receive frank but helpful feedback regarding their values and expectations and the quality of their thinking and actions. The supportive and creative environment generates a wonderful array of meaningful choices.

Weinstein (1998) describes how action learning successfully assisted four unemployed senior managers: a managing director who had massive debts necessitating employment; a finance director who was feeling very hurt and angry; a human resources director who was an older person but wanted some form of work; and a training manager who wanted to become self-employed. The problem or task of each was to become employed. They worked on "their needs, their desires, their dreams, their values, as well as their skills and the reality out there" (p. 155).

By the end of the action learning program, the human resources director had become a steward at a racecourse (always a secret wish of his). The managing director had received three different job offers and was making a decision based on job location and the effect on his quality of life. The training manager had become self-employed, and the finance director had become involved in venture-capital schemes.

Personal and Professional Development via Action Learning

Revans (1980) notes that "one cannot change the system of which one is in command (at least not in any new sense) unless one is also changed in the process, since the logical structure[s] of both changes are in correspondence with each other. The change in the system we call action; that in the self we call learning, so that learning to act effectively is also learning how to learn effectively" (p. 277).

Participating in action learning programs can significantly change a person and generate tremendous intellectual, personal, psychological, and emotional growth. The intense energy and synergy generated by action learning has the potential to result in significant leaps in professional, personal, and social capacities.

Marriott Virtual University: Providing Career Development in the Workplace via Action Learning

Jim O'Hern, Vice President, Training and Organization Development

Welcome to Marriott Virtual University, which seeks to provide a radically different form of educational development for Marriott employees. Internet-based tutoring and mentoring will be supplied directly to the hotel where you are working. In the brave new world of Internet resourcing, it is finally possible to provide the same level of access to colleges and the same education support to learners wherever they work in the world.

Workplace/Action Learning Approach

Workplace or action learning is the learning approach used by individuals and teams to tackle issues, solve problems, and find answers to the challenges and opportunities facing the hotel industry. Marriott will work with the International Management Centres (IMC), a global business school based in Buckingham, England, and dedicated to action learning. IMC resources all of its action learning programs by Internet, with a full range of on-line information services.

Courses are designed for hourly, supervisory, managerial, and executive study so as to enable our people to engage in career-long, just-in-time development. All courses are crafted to fit existing patterns of work. Learning occurs on the job with issue-led courses designed to assist you in solving your day-to-day challenges. The format allows the sharing of resources and mutual support of one another via either in-company sets or open sets (with people from different organizations).

Participants must take responsibility for their own learning so as to identify their own development needs and exploit the well-structured, searchable, rapid-management intelligence resources built into all courses. In this way, they draw what they need when they need it. Our goal is to facilitate learning, to encourage active learning, and to use the global domains of on-line knowledge to help in resourcing three forms of return on investment: personal (enhancing qualifications), developmental (acquiring an active learning habit), and organizational (using real issues and challenges for learning and development).

At best, this approach enables workplace learners to travel from *programmed knowledge* to *questioning* and back again, via the action learning cycle that involves capturing and disseminating real-time practitioner knowledge from the sets.

In summary, the new action learning experience at Marriott is designed to help participants become more effective in their jobs. It is driven by outcomes, not content. All assignments reflect real workplace challenges—there are no formal exams. Our approach is to test the application (not recall). Participants undergo "exams" at the end of the course to draw out what they have achieved, both personally and for the company.

CHAPTER 9

Action Learning Around the World

Action learning, as illustrated throughout this book, has been implemented with growing frequency and success in the Western, Anglo-Saxon cultures of the world (by "Western," cultural anthropologists generally refer to the United States, Great Britain, Australia, Canada, New Zealand, and parts of northern Europe). Action learning is a prime management-development and problem-solving tool for numerous corporations and public agencies in Western countries and the former British colonies (e.g., Singapore, Nigeria, Malaysia, Hong Kong).

Despite its amazing accomplishments in Western cultures and Western-headquartered corporations, action learning appears to have been rarely implemented in the remaining 90 percent of the world for several possible reasons. Maybe people and organizations in the rest of

This chapter is adapted from "Using Action Learning with Multicultural Groups" by M. J. Marquardt, 1998, *Performance Improvement Quarterly*, *11* (1), pp. 113–128. Copyright 1998 by the Learning Systems Institute, Florida State University, Suite 4600 University Center, Bldg. C, Tallahassee, Florida 32306-2540. Reprinted by permission from *Performance Improvement Quarterly*.

the world are not yet familiar with the basic principles of action learning. Although this is a possibility, the fact that other Western trends and fads, such as reengineering, quality management, and 360-degree feedback, were quickly discovered and adopted worldwide would tend to discount it. Another possibility is that the non-Western world is simply unaware of the inherent power of action learning to change organizations and people. Yet another possible reason for the limited use of action learning in non-Western cultures is that action learning is built on primarily Western cultural values and practices. The questions we must answer are these: Are there, in fact, some cultural elements inherent in action learning that would discourage the use of action learning in Latin America, Asia, the Middle East, Africa, and southern Europe (see Wigglesworth, 1987)? And have action learning practitioners been insensitive to the fact that action learning must adjust to the values, basic assumptions, and behaviors of other cultures in order to be successful?

The answers to these questions are important for Western companies as they go global, employ multicultural workforces, and form multicultural alliances. Many of these organizations recognize that solving global problems and developing global leaders will depend on their ability to "translate" the power of action learning programs to their multicultural employees and customers.

The fact that there are a growing number of non-Western organizations and communities successfully using action learning indicates that it can be equally valuable and powerful in all parts of the world. Action learning programs are emerging in Mexico, Colombia, Romania, China, and Egypt. I personally have achieved tremendous results using action learning in academic programs with multicultural groups of students and with African, Asian, and Latin American leaders at the United Nations Staff College. These experiences have led me to conclude that action learning is and can be universally effective and powerful. However, sensitivity to cultural differences, as well as modification and adaptation of the elements of action learning, are necessary for action learning to work in multicultural settings.

In this chapter, we will explore the definitions and dynamics of culture and how and why Western cultures differ from other cultures of the world. We will then see how each of the six components of an action learning program can be affected by culture. The chapter will conclude by identifying possible principles and strategies that one can employ in adapting and implementing action learning programs in non-Western settings.

Figure 9.1
Human Nature, Culture, and Individuality

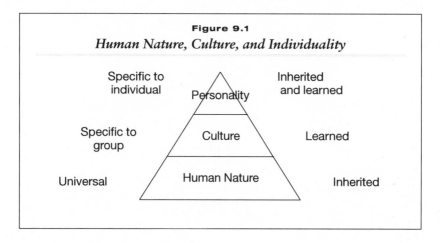

Definitions of Culture

Culture can be described in many ways. Most definitions contain three elements: (a) it is a way of life shared by all or almost all members of a group; (b) older members of the group pass on cultural information to younger members; and (c) it is a method of shaping one's perceptions and behavior. Culture provides systematic as well as implicit and explicit guidelines for how people should conduct their thinking, doing, and living. *Thinking* (ideas) encompasses values, beliefs, myths, and folklore. *Doing* (norms) includes laws, statutes, customs, regulations, ceremonies, fashions, and etiquette. *Living* (materials) refers to the way one interacts with machines, tools, food, natural resources, and clothing.

Hofstede (1991) distinguishes among human nature, culture, and personality. *Human nature* is what all human beings universally have in common and is inherited. The human ability to feel anger, fear, love, joy, sadness, and loneliness is part of this human programming. However, what one does with these feelings, how one expresses oneself or behaves, is modified by the *culture*. *Personality* refers to how a person individually and uniquely acts; it is modified both by the influence of culture and by one's personal experiences (see Figure 9.1).

An example of the distinctions among the three levels would be the following: (a) all *humans* eat, (b) different *cultural* groups eat in different ways, and (c) *individuals* in a cultural group may eat similarly to as well as differently from other members of the cultural group.

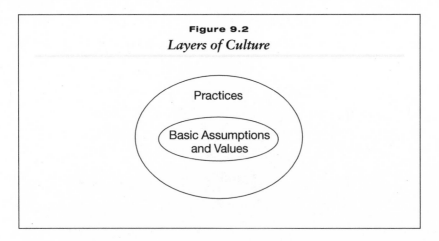

Figure 9.2
Layers of Culture

Culture is multilayered (see Figure 9.2). *Practices,* including behaviors, symbols, rituals, and artifacts, are more visible to someone outside the culture. They are more easily influenced and changed than the core of culture that is formed by *values* and underlying *basic assumptions,* not so easily recognized or understood by outsiders. These values are among the first things children learn—not consciously, but implicitly.

Simply put, culture provides people with a meaningful context in which to meet, think about themselves, and face the outer world (Trompenaars, 1994). It is important to realize that culture is logical and rational to the members of the culture, even though it may appear irrational or illogical to someone outside the culture. This represents the greatest challenge to anyone trying to work or live in another culture.

Factors Creating Culture

There are nine factors that create a culture and, in turn, are influenced by the culture: religion, language, education, economics, politics/laws, family, class structure, history, and geography/natural resources. What distinguishes one culture from another is not the presence or absence of these factors, but rather the patterns and practices found within and between these factors. Each of these factors can and does influence how a cultural group responds and reacts to action learning (see Figure 9.3).

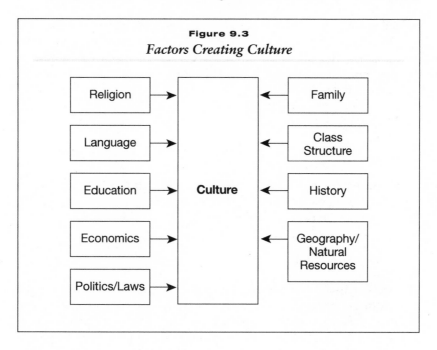

Figure 9.3
Factors Creating Culture

Let us briefly examine how Western and non-Western cultures evolved so that we can begin to see why action learning fits more easily with Western ways of thinking and behaving and why adaptations are needed for it to make "better sense" to non-Western cultures.

Religion

Western
The dominant religious influence is that of Protestantism, with its emphasis on individualism, personal salvation, and the work ethic. Individual morality prevails over social morality. Westerners feel *guilt* when not meeting their *individual* expectations (versus the feeling of *shame* in other cultures, when one does not meet the group's expectations).

Non-Western
Buddhism and Hinduism preach the importance of harmony with nature and one's fellow human beings, of accepting the world as it is, and of seeking collaborative means to resolve problems. Humility is a

valued virtue. The Islamic religion influences every part of the daily life of a Muslim, such that the phrase *insha'Allah* (if God wills) punctuates discussions. The more traditional Catholicism influences southern Europe and Latin America with its historical emphasis on hierarchy, patriarchy, and fatalism.

Language

Language is the carrier and conditioner of all cultures. The words and structures available in a language strongly influence a speaker's values, beliefs, relationships, and concepts.

Western

English has become the global language. In English *I* and *no* are the two most common words. These words are not even found in some languages. Being a low-context culture, Western culture places a high value on written language. English is a very direct and active language. If a person reads a book and enjoys it, in English she might say, "I think it's a good book," clearly defining herself as a person entitled to make such a judgment. In Japanese, a less direct language, one would say the equivalent of "With regard to me, the book is good." The assumption of authority and objectivity is less present in non-English languages.

In English, there is only one form of *you*, which implies equality and informality. Thus it is easy to see how it is natural for an American to be informal and egalitarian.

Non-Western

These are *high-context* societies, that is, the environment or context can influence what is being said as much as or more than words themselves. Some of these languages have many forms of *you*, thus recognizing the importance of hierarchy. In Vietnamese, for example, there are over forty forms of *you* depending on age, gender, relationship, number, status, and so on. The languages are more verbal. Arabic, for example, is a language to be spoken and heard. How one says something becomes almost as important as what one says.

Education

Western

Emphasis is on learning that is practical, utilitarian, experiential, and applicable. The inductive approach of thinking is encouraged. Experiences tend to be evaluated in terms of dichotomies (right/wrong, do/don't, successful/unsuccessful, good/evil, work/play, winner/loser, subjective/objective, etc.).

Non-Western

The influence of Confucius, with his high emphasis on education and respect for the educator, permeates most Asian cultures. Learning tends to be by lecture and rote. The Latin education system tends to emphasize the theoretical/deductive approach and the humanities, with less emphasis on the practical. Islamic traditions involve memorization of the Koran, an imitative rather than a creative approach to learning.

Economics

Western

Economies are primarily market-driven and capitalistic. Competition is seen as healthy and desirable. The Western societies have a relatively large middle class.

Non-Western

There tends to be more government involvement in most non-Western countries. Until recently, there were more centrally planned economies, which left little opportunity for local decision making and management development. Small family businesses are common. Governments are gradually relinquishing control of large-scale enterprises. Confucianism encourages entrepreneurship and hard work. Societies are divided between the rich and the poor, with a small middle class.

Politics/Laws

Western

These countries are democracies with universal suffrage. Government is seen as serving the people and should not be too powerful. Individual rights are all-encompassing and legally protected. Laws are made for each situation.

Non-Western
Governments tend to be paternalistic and more deeply involved in the social and economic lives of the people. The good of the community supersedes individual rights. Decisions are made by church hierarchy, charismatic leaders, military dictators, or benevolent elders. Napoleonic, deductive laws are followed.

Family

Western
Families are nuclear, and children are responsible primarily to themselves for career, marriage, and education choices.

Non-Western
The family structure is strongly extended. One is expected to respect and obey elders, even if that goes against the desires and wishes of the individual. Social relationships are needed to accomplish results. In Islamic countries, men may be separated from women and are accorded higher status in decision making.

Class Structure

Western
In this more open class structure, individuals have the ability to choose and to move up in a system, on the basis of their own merits and efforts.

Non-Western
In a closed society, one's position is determined and limited by who one is rather than by individual achievement. In Islamic countries, social organization is highly stratified. The division of labor is primarily on a class basis, so that social mobility is difficult. However, *who* you are is gradually being replaced by *what* you are, so that one can now more easily move up in class through education and money.

History

Western
Although British history is quite extensive, the United States, Canada, and Australia have short histories. America's brief history includes the

rugged pioneers, rapid industrialization and expansion, and successful warfare resulting in confidence relative to controlling the future.

Non-Western

The Chinese, Japanese, African, Arabic, Indian, Malay, and Korean cultures are thousands of years old, and thus time frames are longer-term and involve a greater appreciation of the past, even though some of these countries have been colonized for many centuries by Western powers.

Natural Resources/Geography

Western

Hofstede (1991) positively correlates a country's *attitude* toward equality with a country's *latitude* and observes that colder climates require small power distances between people. The vast spaces, minerals, forests, and farmlands of the Western countries helped form a culture with rugged individualism, optimism, materialism, and independence.

Non-Western

Huge populations strain the food and mineral resources of these societies. Numerous floods and earthquakes contribute to a sense of the inevitability of nature's power and the acceptance of fate.

Summary of Cultural Differences

The differences between Western and non-Western cultures relative to these nine factors have resulted in a clear distinction between these two kinds of culture in the ways people think and act. These key dimensional differences are listed below:

Western	Non-Western
Individualism	Collectivism
Achievement	Modesty
Equality/egalitarianism	Hierarchy
Winning	Collaboration/harmony
Guilt (internal self-control)	Shame (external control)
Pride	Saving face
Respect for results	Respect for status/ascription
Respect for competence	Respect for elders

Time is money	Time is life
Action/doing	Being/acceptance
Systematic/mechanistic	Humanistic
Tasks	Relationships/loyalty
Informality	Formality
Directness/assertiveness	Indirectness
Future/change	Past/tradition
Control	Fate
Specificity/linearity	Holism
Verbal emphasis	Nonverbal emphasis

These two views of the world explain why people of Western cultures will tend to react differently from people of non-Western cultures to the various elements and processes of action learning. Let us now explore those differences and reactions.

Cultural Dimensions of the Six Components of Action Learning

As we noted in Chapter 2, there are six fundamental components to action learning: a problem, the group, the questioning and reflection process, the commitment to taking action, the commitment to learning, and the facilitator.

Each of these components is, in fact, based upon some basic assumptions and values of Western culture. However, with some minor adjustments and cultural sensitivities, action learning can be equally effective and, in some cases, more easily implemented in non-Western countries. Let's now explore the cultural implications inherent in the six components and how to adapt them for non-Western and multicultural groups.

A Problem

Basic Principles
An action learning program requires having a project or task that gives the group something to focus on. There are several criteria to determine if the project is appropriate for an action learning group:

▲ The project chosen by/for the group must represent a real organizational problem, task, or issue that needs to be addressed and exists in a real time frame.

▲ The project must be feasible—that is, within the competence of the group.

▲ Either it should be within the group's sphere of responsibility or the group must be given the authority to do something about the problem.

▲ The project should provide learning opportunities for members and have possible applications to other parts of the organization.

Basic Western Assumptions

Western culture encourages sharing and the discussion of personal as well as organizational problems in a public setting (frankness). It is okay for a Western manager to admit difficulties in solving a problem and thus be willing to turn it over to outsiders or subordinates. It is less difficult for him to trust subordinates and to delegate power to them (egalitarianism).

Non-Western Cultural Reactions

In many other cultures, it would be more difficult for a leader or individual to turn over his most critical problems to subordinates. Even if he delegated such power, some members of some cultures would still not see real power present in the group without the leader being physically there.

The Group

Basic Principles

The core entity in action learning is the action learning group. Ideally, the makeup of the group is diverse. The dynamics of the group and the diversity of its participants are the keys to its success. To be effective, the group members should possess the following attributes:

▲ Commitment to solving the problem
▲ Ability to listen and to question themselves and others
▲ Willingness to be open and to learn from other group members
▲ Valuing of and respect for others
▲ Commitment to taking action and achieving success
▲ Awareness of their own and others' abilities to learn and develop

Basic Western Assumptions

The mixing of people of differing ages, genders, roles, and so on, fits in with the Western values of egalitarianism, equality, and informality. We like variety, different perspectives, new ideas, and the give-and-take among differing groups. The competence of fellow group members is more important than their rank or status. The cultural factors of *class structure, politics, history, religion, family, language,* and *economics* all contribute to our ease in accepting the makeup of an action learning group.

Non-Western Cultural Reactions

In most non-Western cultures, mixing people of differing status opposes the sense of hierarchy and respect. Mixing may be seen as a means of undermining authority and power in the workplace. It may cause embarrassment, confusion, and loss of face.

In Asian countries, young people in a group will hesitate to speak out if older people are present. A person's status is important in determining the degree to which he or she can state his or her opinion. In many African societies, there is a rigid, hierarchical, bureaucratic structure, with great status differences and extreme deference to authority (Jones, 1990). In conservative Islamic cultures, men and women cannot even be in the same room, much less exchange ideas on an equal level. Age almost always comes before competence in decisions about who is to be the most important member in the group.

Cultures that appreciate hierarchy and clear roles find it difficult to bring together different interacting groups. Seating arrangements are determined by status. The language used requires one to be addressed in a superior or inferior fashion (for example, use of many different forms of the word *you*). Formality, especially among those of differing status, is absolutely essential.

In addition, who the members are determines the importance of an activity; therefore, it will be difficult to "volunteer" someone who does not wish to (or cannot appropriately) be seen with a particular group.

Conversely, the collectivism of most non-Western cultures encourages working in action learning teams. Thus these cultures place much more value on teamwork and solving problems as a group. The collectivism of many non-Western cultures is better suited to action learning than is the individualism of Western cultures.

A manager may experience loss of face by admitting the inability to handle a problem himself or herself. In many non-Western cultures, it is the role of managers to solve problems and make decisions, whereas the role of workers is to implement those decisions. Most cultures in Africa and India, for example, would see it as inappropriate for a manager to have others solve his or her problem.

If a problem cannot be solved, some cultures would encourage a manager to accept this as fate and be religious enough to embrace it. In most of these cultures, the sharing of personal difficulties might be seen as crass. Finally, many non-Western companies could never conceive of the idea of involving people from outside the company in working on an internal problem.

The Questioning and Reflection Process

Basic Principles

By focusing on the right questions rather than the right answers, action learning emphasizes what one does not know as well as what one does know. Action learning tackles problems through a process of first asking questions to clarify their exact nature, reflecting and identifying possible solutions, and only then taking action.

Action learning programs attempt to provide the time and space necessary for standing back and reflecting in order to unfreeze thoughts, rise above everyday problems, bring things into perspective, and draw out the experience and practical judgment of the group members. This questioning and reflection process also encourages members to view each other as learning resources.

In action learning, group members should be open to trying out new ways of doing things, experimenting, reflecting on experiences, and considering the results or effects of experiences. They then repeat the cycle by trying out newly gained knowledge in different situations. At the heart of action learning is the process of reflection, which is designed to develop questioning insight, or, as Revans writes, "the capacity to ask fresh questions in conditions of ignorance, risk, and confusion, when nobody knows what to do next."

Basic Western Assumptions

The questioning and reflection process is more comfortable in cultures that value informality and egalitarianism and where people can be more directive and challenging of each other. The Western approach to inductive thinking and problem solving encourages careful examination of the particular event and development of new ways of responding.

The approach of asking questions is built on the Socratic way of learning; it naturally leads to more openness and creativity in handling problems. Discussion tends to be logical and rational, with a moderate show of emotion.

Non-Western Cultural Reactions

Taking time to question, reflect, and discuss would work well in Latin and Arabic cultures where time is flexible and there is less need to rush to results. However, in some cultures, such as the Chinese, there is a high degree of impatience with spending too much time in discussion and reflection; quick results and speed are highly valued.

Arabic and African cultures, because of their educational systems, tend to be imitative rather than creative, and African managers regard their authority, professional competence, and information as personal possessions rather than as part of their organization role. They are therefore reluctant to delegate authority, share information, or involve subordinates in the decision-making process.

Questioning others, and especially questioning people of superior status, is very difficult. With Asians, for example, this can result in ritualized behavior, withdrawal, or even resentment.

The Commitment to Taking Action

Basic Principles

For action learning advocates, there is no real learning unless action is taken, and, conversely, no action should occur without learning from it. Therefore, members of the action learning group must have the power to take action themselves or be assured that their recommendations will be implemented. Action enhances learning because it provides a basis and anchor for the critical dimension of reflection.

Basic Western Assumptions

Western culture is much more action-oriented than most other cultures. It encourages making decisions and taking action. People tend to prefer tasks to relationships, and achievement to discussion. They also like to do things that have immediate utilitarian value. Time is money and should not be wasted on things that do not achieve results.

Non-Western Cultural Reactions

Other cultures may give people much less authority to act. In Arabic cultures, the leader may consult others but will then make the decision on his own. Those strongly influenced by the Islamic religion would also be much more aware and respectful of the role of Allah in making decisions.

In many Asian cultures, people are much more circuitous in selecting a course of action. Social and political sensitivity drive the solution, and the action taken must not cause someone to lose face: even if the group thinks a decision is proper, the members may disavow the decision later on.

In most non-Western cultures, there is also a fear of asking stupid questions, since that, too, may cause one to lose face. One avoids exposing one's weakness and faults. Setting a supportive climate may not be sufficient in these cultural environments.

The Commitment to Learning

Basic Principles
Solving the organizational or individual problem provides immediate, short-term benefits to an organization or individual. However, the learning gained by the group members and the application of these learnings throughout the organization will provide an even greater and more lasting benefit.

During the action learning process, individuals should take responsibility for their own, the team's, and the organization's learning and development. Time is set aside to talk about personal learnings and about how the team's learning can be utilized in other parts of the organization.

Basic Western Assumptions
The basic principles of learning just cited are more congruent with Western cultural values and traditions than with non-Western ones. Questioning assumptions, questioning authority or the past, welcoming the urgency and immediate practicality of learning, accepting change and uncertainty, working in a nonhierarchical fashion so as to acquire fresh perspectives, and learning from the feedback of others about ourselves are all actions that fit in more with the Western way of thinking and acting.

Non-Western Cultural Reactions
Asking for feedback and encouraging self-analysis, although fine for Westerners who value frankness and openness, could be disastrous in Asia, where a much higher value is placed on hiding one's feelings and thoughts and not prying into the feelings and thoughts of others. One does not offer constructive advice in public settings. Pointing out a weakness is difficult in Hispanic cultures, since people are not expected to speak negatively of others. For Arabs, "Allah loveth not the speak-

ing ill of anyone." This kind of focus is not one of self-awareness, learning from useful feedback, or admitting errors.

Although many non-Western cultures would appreciate the emphasis on learning, they may have several concerns about the status and quality of learning in action learning programs. Often people equate learning with lectures and rote memorization and feel that it implies obtaining a certificate or diploma.

The Facilitator

Basic Principles
Group members are necessarily involved in reframing the problem, actively listening to one another, and intensely seeking to find alternatives and solutions. It is difficult to also be aware of the group processes that are occurring or the dynamics of interaction around them. Members may also lack the skill, as well as the time, to understand and focus on the learning opportunities that are available. The facilitator is the person appointed to serve this important role so as to optimize the problem solving and the learning efforts of the group.

Basic Western Assumptions
A facilitator is often used to guide the learning in training programs in Western societies. In group discussions, someone is usually designated to facilitate the dynamics, timing, and so forth, of the meeting. To learn from and be questioned by peers or external consultants is a common Western practice.

Non-Western Cultural Reactions
Being observed and questioned in a setting of one's peers can be very threatening in many non-Western cultures. Being asked by the facilitator such questions as "What did not go so well? Why did you do this? What have you learned? Why did the group fail to . . . ? Why did you not say that then?" may be uncomfortable, especially if there is an implicit criticism of another or a diminishing of oneself. Some questions may be seen as too personal to be discussed in the presence of the group.

Adapting and Implementing Action Learning in Non-Western Cultures

Learning, like eating, is universal. However, how people learn varies from culture to culture. Action learning, developed and practiced primarily in Western countries, needs to be *acculturated,* that is, conveyed and transferred across cultural boundaries to ensure that the action learning program is "user friendly." This does not mean that the essential elements of action learning are dropped or radically altered; rather, they are adjusted to the cultural milieu so as to ensure that the maximum benefits of action learning can be tapped. Without this acculturation and adaptation, the power and benefits of action learning will not be realized.

Adapting action learning programs to multicultural or non-Western cultural settings requires a keen sensitivity to the basic assumptions inherent in those settings and to the ways in which their people think and act. The following are just a few suggestions for acculturating action learning programs to multicultural settings.

Selection of Problem or Task

▲ Select problems that are comfortable and appropriate to the values and practices of the organization.

▲ Identify problems for which the manager can delegate power and the group members will accept responsibility.

▲ Appreciate the concern of the culture for fate and for saving face in the selection of a problem.

▲ Begin with smaller issues, yet ones that are important and valuable to the group members and to the organization.

▲ Allow group members, when serving in the role of client, to introduce problems that may be somewhat "external" to their locus of accountability and responsibility.

Composition of Group

▲ Recognize the relative status of the members.

▲ Seek balance between authority and nonauthority figures
Build on the cultural value of working in groups (collectivism).

▲ Gradually include diversity in action learning groups.

▲ Obtain diversity in other ways—different units, technical areas, industries, and so forth.

▲ Begin with some team-building activities to assist members in becoming comfortable and supportive of one another.

Use of Questioning and Reflection Process
▲ Create an environment that encourages asking questions.
▲ Demonstrate with initial questions that the focus is on solving the problem rather than on fixing blame.
▲ Recognize the need to save face and to not cause others to lose face.
▲ Allocate set times for reflection.
▲ Be comfortable with periods of silence or outbursts of expression.
▲ Appreciate indirectness and formality.
▲ Understand nonverbal communication patterns and situational contexts.

Commitment to Taking Action
▲ Ensure that the group has the authority and capacity to take action. If a client is external to the group, ask that he or she meet with the group to clearly state that the group is to determine the final action steps.
▲ Distinguish the action learning mentality from a think-tank or recommendations-only mentality in the group.
▲ Respect the status of those who are responsible for taking action, whether they are internal or external to the set.
▲ Recognize social and cultural limitations on the actions considered.
▲ Respect the acceptance of fate and the belief in an inability to control the future.
▲ Understand the importance of maintaining harmony.

Focus on the Learning
▲ Identify and recognize learnings gained through action learning programs.
▲ Respect the need for modesty and humility in identifying how one has contributed to the group's learning.
▲ Use facilitators, at least initially, to help the group identify and apply learnings.
▲ Acknowledge action learning as a new form of acquiring knowledge.
▲ Connect learning to cultural values that support continuous learning.

Facilitation
▲ Be sure to introduce yourself and your role in a clear and supportive way so that you will be not seen as a threat or as a possible source of loss of face.
▲ Identify positive and constructive areas in the earlier stages of the action learning program.
▲ Pose questions to the group as a whole rather than to individuals.

▲ Demonstrate the value and effectiveness of uncovering and sharing learnings.
▲ Encourage members to begin asking questions of the group.
▲ Emphasize that individual and group disclosure and feedback are confidential to the group.

It is important to recognize that cultural differences need not cancel or postpone the use of action learning programs. Instead of seeing cultural differences as barriers, one should see them as a source of synergy, which contributes to a variety of perspectives that can actually augment the power and success of action learning programs. The non-Westerner's ability to listen carefully, value and respect others, and seek group consensus are important characteristics of action learning groups.

Recent research by Hampden-Turner and Trompenaars (1997) has found that East Asian cultures may, in fact, have several characteristics that make them better suited to action learning. Westerners prefer playing what these researchers call a *finite game,* in which individuals win or lose by specific criteria in universal contests; Easterners play an *infinite game,* in which all players learn cooperatively. Westerners prefer such values as winning, compromise, individualism, competition, universalism (rule by laws), inner-directedness, achievement of status, and a sequential view of time (time seen as a race). Easterners prefer values such as communitarianism, cooperation, outer-directedness, ascribed status (the good should succeed), and particularism (uniqueness and being exceptional). In the finite game, improvement comes from the fiercer competitor rising to the top in a battle, which favors the "survival of the fittest." In the infinite game, improvement comes from the game itself, from players developing "survival of the fittingest" and self-organizing more effectively—and this is what action learning is all about.

Just as there are non-Western cultural factors that hinder action learning programs, so there are cultural factors that encourage them. Several years ago, Zhou Jianhua, after meeting with Reg Revans in England, returned to Wuxi, in a remote part of China, to introduce the concept of action learning. She was surprised that managers there felt so familiar with the process. The managers gave three reasons for their inherent enthusiasm for action learning:

▲ It fit in with Maoist philosophy. In *The Strategy of China's Revolutionary War,* Mao Zedong discusses military training in the following way: "Not only reading is learning, but also doing is learning. Learning to swim through swimming is our major method."

▲ Sharing experiences and perspectives is the traditional and popular method of learning in China.

▲ The managers had found that the principles of Western management did not provide solutions for their problems. They realized that they had to solve their problems by themselves, according to their own cultural ways.

A Global Perspective on Action Learning

As we enter the twenty-first century, multinational companies are recognizing the value of action learning for developing global executives, identifying strategic competitive advantages, reducing operating costs, creating performance management systems, and establishing a foundation for learning organizations. Multicultural workforces and multicultural teams are becoming more common. The acculturation of action learning programs will thus become increasingly critical as more global companies introduce action learning programs to their multicultural managers and workforces.

Establishing and Implementing an Action Learning Program

Action learning is based on a simple and natural process of systematically solving crucial problems in the organization with a diverse group of people who seek to learn as they act. As long as there are problems (i.e., issues, challenges, tasks, or projects), then there is both a need for and a high value in having action learning programs. Once the appropriate conditions are established within the organization, the programs will become valuable, self-sustaining, and ongoing (unless, of course, the organization runs out of problems or challenges—an unlikely scenario).

In Part 3 we will look at the *how to* of action learning—how to establish an action learning program (Chapter 10), how to tailor the form and format of action learning for your organization (Chapter 11), how to facilitate action learning groups (Chapter 12), how to avoid the pitfalls of unsuccessful action learning programs (Chapter 13), and how to comprehensively assess the action learning meetings and programs (Chapter 14).

To be successful, action learning needs to follow a number of clearly defined steps and procedures. Action learning can, however, be adapted to take on a variety of forms and formats in order to provide optimum benefit for its users. Getting an action learning program started is a challenge, but the payoff is well worth the effort. Let's now examine the steps to begin an action learning program in your company.

Setting Up an
Action Learning Program

Establishing an action learning program involves a number of important, sequential steps to ensure its success and sustainability. In this chapter we will discuss five steps for establishing a successful program (see Figure 10.1).

Step 1: Gain Top Management Support

Gaining support requires commitment not only from corporate leadership but also from the people who will be forming the action learning sets. In order for this commitment to be gained, top leadership needs to be convinced that action learning will result in improved problem solving and improved learning and development on the part of the people who participate in the action learning program. Management must become persuaded that action learning will ultimately lead to a higher level of leadership competencies and organizational capacities that will result in better products, services, profits, and reputations.

This belief and commitment must then be conveyed down through the ranks. At some point, leaders should be demonstrating their commitment by participating in action learning groups themselves; it

171

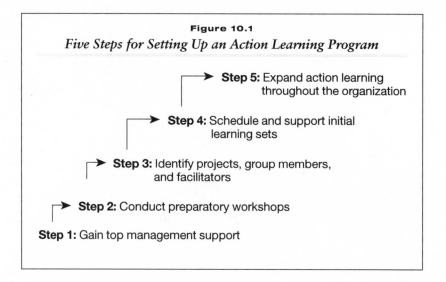

Figure 10.1
Five Steps for Setting Up an Action Learning Program

Step 5: Expand action learning throughout the organization

Step 4: Schedule and support initial learning sets

Step 3: Identify projects, group members, and facilitators

Step 2: Conduct preparatory workshops

Step 1: Gain top management support

should become the way they choose to solve the day-to-day problems they encounter. Reward systems, time availability, and new roles may need to be created so as to demonstrate this commitment.

It generally works best to utilize both internal and external sources in building company support:

External sources: Many organizations find it very valuable to invite an experienced action learning proponent from outside the organization to meet with key leaders and/or conduct an introductory training program.

Internal sources: Action learning advocates continue to meet with leaders and other staff to push for the introduction of action learning into the organization. It provides a great boost for action learning if a few managers become willing to serve as champions for it and are willing to submit some problems to a set or to participate in a set themselves.

Table 10.1 is a checklist of key questions that can be used for determining top management support for action learning programs.

Step 2: Conduct Preparatory Workshops

A workshop is conducted as an introduction to action learning in order to begin the process of overall organizational understanding and sup-

Table 10.1 *Checklist for Top Management Support*

- Is top management committed to the program?
- Does the organization understand the nature and purpose of the action learning programs?
- Is there agreement on overall benefits and objectives for the program?
- Are there champions for the action learning groups?

port of action learning. The preparatory workshop may be conducted by an external action learning consultant and/or staff trained in action learning whose task it is to explain and demonstrate the basic principles and dynamics of action learning.

Experienced action learning leaders have learned that companies that jump right into action learning activities end up getting much slower and lower-quality results and create much frustration among group participants.

Benefits of a Preparatory Workshop

There are several potential benefits to having a workshop prior to initiating action learning in the organization (McGill & Beaty, 1995):

▲ Enables the organization and potential action learners to gain a perspective on what action learning is and how it works
▲ Provides an overview of the why and how of action learning
▲ Helps to develop enthusiasm for action learning
▲ Demonstrates numerous benefits and applications of action learning
▲ Begins the self-screening process in terms of identifying those who would like to be participants in the action learning groups
▲ Reaches a wide number of potential users and clients
▲ Allows organizational and individual experimentation before commitment
▲ Gives future facilitators the opportunity of seeing action learning demonstrated

Preparation Before the Workshop

Prior to the workshop, the instructor(s) and/or facilitator(s) should discuss with organizational people the following:

▲ What are the backgrounds, levels of understanding of action learning, expectations, experiences with experiential learning, and biases toward action learning of those who will be attending?

▲ Is the location convenient, quiet, and sufficient in space?

▲ What will be the length of workshop (three hours is recommended as a minimum)?

▲ What are possible problems (real to the organization) that could be identified and used to demonstrate the action learning process and its power?

Organizing the Workshop

The preparatory workshop is ideally divided into three phases, each of which builds understanding as well as support and commitment to action learning in the organization: overview of action learning, practice, and reflection and questions.

Overview of Action Learning

The first phase includes a description of what action learning is, how it can be used, the types of action learning programs, in what contexts it can be used most effectively, and how it differs from other problem-solving and training/development approaches in the organization. The overview should take no more than thirty to forty-five minutes so that the participants can quickly get into experiencing action learning. Specific activities and content areas include the following:

Warm-up activity: As part of the introductions, it is wise to include a warm-up activity that helps to create an environment that is similar to the environment of an action learning group—namely, one that is trustful, supportive, and open. A useful activity for a group in which members know each other is for each person to tell something about himself or herself that no one in the group yet knows (for example, a favorite travel destination, a childhood experience, a unique achievement). People new to each other can also provide first names, roles, places in the organization, and so on.

Outline of purpose and structure of the workshop: The facilitator then provides an overview of the day, including schedule, objectives, and procedures. The importance of a learning, trusting, supportive atmosphere should also be emphasized. Participants may be asked what they would like to achieve by the end of the workshop, and these points can be put on a flip chart.

Listing of benefits: The various benefits and applications of action learning are highlighted, including problem solving, team building, leadership development, organizationwide learning, and personal growth.

Presentation of the six elements: The six essential elements of action learning (problem, group, questioning and reflection process, commitment to taking action, commitment to learning, and the facilitator) are presented.

Description of roles of presenter, participant, and facilitator: The different roles that occur in action learning groups (i.e., presenter, participant, and facilitator) are described and differentiated. The role of facilitator is presented differently, depending on whether the organization will be designating people who will serve as facilitators only, or whether the groups will be self-facilitated.

Description of types of action learning: The two types of action learning programs (single-project and open-group) will be presented. Of course, if only one type is planned for use in the organization, that one will be emphasized.

Discussion of unique qualities: It is very important to discuss how action learning differs from quality circles, task forces, outdoor adventures, and so on, as well as the pitfalls that the organization and individuals should avoid (see Chapter 13).

Practice

The practice phase conveys the concept and power of action learning by allowing participants to observe and actually experience it.

Select a problem of importance to the organization: If the organization is planning on employing a single-project action learning program, it is wise to identify beforehand a sample problem that the group will tackle. The sample problem should be genuine, common, and important to the organization, and it should be one that is actually being encountered by many of the participants. It is very important that the problem be clearly articulated and understood so that most of the practice time can be devoted to the problem. Also, the clearer the problem, the better the questions and the greater the likelihood of a successful action learning experience.

If the organization will be using an open-group program, it is again advisable that one or two of the volunteers have their problem evaluated with the facilitator.

Recruit five to six volunteers to tackle the problem: These volunteers will attempt to solve the problem by using the action learning process described earlier. They are reminded that this is a practice session and that a facilitator will be guiding them.

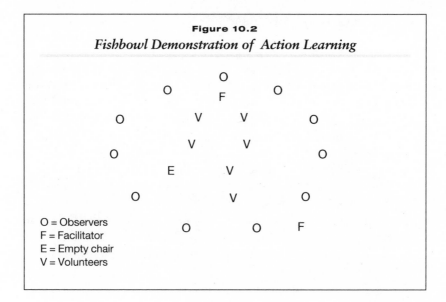

Figure 10.2
Fishbowl Demonstration of Action Learning

O = Observers
F = Facilitator
E = Empty chair
V = Volunteers

Arrange for volunteers to sit in an inner circle: Those who volunteer are placed in an inner circle (fishbowl), with the remaining workshop participants gathered in a larger, concentric circle for observing and commenting on the workings of the action learning set (the *how* of action learning). A vacant chair is set up in the inner circle to allow an outsider to join the action learning group when and if this person deems that he or she can be helpful (see Figure 10.2).

Begin the action learning process with instructors serving as facilitators: The inner circle then proceeds as a normal action learning set. McGill and Beaty (1995) recommend two facilitators, one of whom will take the role of a facilitator in the inner circle (relaxing the group members, ensuring that action learning procedures and principles are being practiced, raising questions, checking understandings of the process, and so forth) while the other facilitator joins the outer circle as a process observer.

Telescope different stages of an action learning meeting: In the workshop, there probably will not be sufficient time for a problem to be fully explored, since there may be only two to three hours for describing and practicing action learning. Of course, additional time may be required to demonstrate both types of action learning programs. Therefore, the facilitator may need to cut the questioning/ reflection phase after fifteen to twenty-five minutes and move into actions and learnings. The facilitator, obviously, will be more directive in this demonstration situation, a fact that should be emphasized to the workshop participants. Thus the facilitator will perhaps interrupt more frequently as he or she observes group members doing such things as jumping immediately into solutions, asking directive questions, being too quick in searching for systems questions, and so on.

Reflection and Questions

After the abbreviated action learning meeting has been ended, the facilitator asks group members questions about what they have experienced, how it worked, what made it more effective, what was difficult to do, what they were unsure of, and so on.

Then the outside observers will be asked to describe their impressions, learnings, and questions. There is a tendency for the outsiders to get engaged in the content; this should be avoided, and the focus should be on the *process*—that is, on how action learning works.

Finally, the facilitator will ask the participants if they have any questions about action learning. Participants can also be asked a variety of questions that will enable them to determine the value and future uses of action learning for themselves and the organization. This allows participants to clarify their understanding of action learning, ascertain their commitment, and begin determining how they will utilize action learning in the organization. Table 10.2 lists some questions that can be addressed in assessing the workshop.

Step 3: Identify Projects, Group Members, and Facilitators

Once the employees have been introduced to the concept of action learning, the organization needs to determine what projects will be chosen and who will be in the action learning group(s). The projects chosen should be those that are meaningful to participants and their jobs as well as important to the organization as a whole. They should also be ones for which employees could offer several viable solutions, rather than problems that could be better solved by an outside expert. Ensuring that the group has the power to act or work toward action is essential.

Table 10.2 *Assessing the Preparatory Workshop*

- Prior to the workshop, were attendees assessed carefully, was the location suitably chosen, and was top management's participation ensured?
- Were all three phases of the workshop well designed?
- Were possible problems preselected for best demonstration purposes?
- Were participants aware of types of action learning, purposes, and key principles?
- Did participants have a solid understanding of the basic concepts and mechanics of action learning and an appreciation of the value of reflective questioning and continuous learning?
- Did the fishbowl exemplify the power and possibilities of action learning?
- Is there now an enthusiasm for action learning?

These and a variety of other choices need to made. For example, what problems will be chosen? Who will choose the problems? Will the "owner" of the problem (i.e., the presenter) be a member of the group, or will someone be designated to represent him or her? How will the composition of the groups be determined? Will members be selected by management or be allowed to volunteer? Will people from outside the company be participants?

Ideally, the composition of an action learning group should be four to eight people from diverse backgrounds and areas of functional expertise. This diversity enables the group to examine problems from fresh and different perspectives. A facilitator also may be assigned to be part of the team, although this is not absolutely necessary. Preferably, the facilitator is someone whom the group members do not already know, so that he or she can act somewhat independently of the group's culture.

Tables 10.3 and 10.4 list some questions that can be asked in assessing the quality of planning for projects, participation, and facilitation.

Step 4: Schedule and Support Initial Learning Sets

Before beginning one or many action learning groups that will initiate action learning for the organization, a number of administrative and programmatic issues need to be considered.

How often will the groups be allowed or encouraged to meet? When and where can the meetings take place? How frequently should meetings occur—daily, weekly, biweekly, or monthly? Should an ending

Table 10.3 *Determining Quality of Planning for Projects*

- Who chooses the projects?
- Do the projects meet the organization's needs and provide learning opportunities?
- Are they problems rather than puzzles?
- Are the projects feasible and manageable?
- Will programs be single-problem, open-group, or both?
- Will group members have the authority to implement their recommendations? Or will the recommendations first need to be presented to higher management for implementation?
- Who will be the presenter for the group if it is dealing with a single-problem program?

Table 10.4 *Determining Quality of Planning for Participation and Facilitation*

- Has group membership been by choice or by appointment?
- Is there diversity within the group so as to provide fresh perspectives?
- How many people are there per group?
- Will groups include outside people?
- Are members committed to the problem and to the process?
- Have members agreed to processes and norms with respect to "airtime," asking questions, and reflection?
- Is there agreement on ground rules relative to confidentiality, starting and stopping on time, being supportive, and taking action between meetings?
- Have members agreed on future dates for meetings and committed to attending them regularly?
- Have convenient locations been identified for participants?
- Will there be a facilitator? If so, will the facilitator be external to the group or one of the group members?
- How have facilitators been chosen?
- Are they trained and prepared?

date be set? Everyone should be clear about the time needed for individual meetings as well as for the overall program. Establishing some organizationwide norms by which the group will proceed is very important.

Introducing Action Learning to the InterAmerican Development Bank

Eleanor Howard, Director, Office of Learning

The InterAmerican Development Bank (IDB) is a regional lending institution that is owned by forty-six countries and has a capital base of $100 billion and an annual lending program of around $7 billion. The lending program and other services are concentrated in Latin American and the Caribbean countries. The bank's financing is for highly diverse, complex projects intended to foster economic growth in these countries while improving the access of less-advantaged groups to the benefits of growth. Bank-funded projects range from investments in basic infrastructure (such as electricity, roads, and water) to health and education reform.

IDB has recently introduced action learning programs in an effort to improve the performance of teams working on loan projects. About twenty teams are participating in the pilot program. An important first step was to identify who should be on the project team, with an emphasis on the importance of incorporating bank borrowers into the team. This was critical for the successful design, and especially the implementation, of the loan project.

The launching of integrated action learning groups is through a two-day workshop. The purpose of the workshop is to create the conditions for effective group interaction so that performance is enhanced by the maximum contribution each member can make to the project. A facilitator is assigned to work with each group. The advisor applies action learning techniques to facilitate dialogue and reflection on key aspects of the project.

The results of the first three workshops have been very favorable in advancing both the project and the quality of interaction within groups. The full impact of the workshops will become evident over time and will depend in part on the continued involvement and effectiveness of group facilitators.

Top management may decide to establish expectations and objectives for the action learning groups. Tapping in to all the applications of action learning (i.e., problem solving, organization development and learning, team development, leadership development, and professional growth and learning) should be encouraged. Organizational leaders and action learning presenters should indicate to the action learning

---

Table 10.5 *Determining Well-Planned/Managed Programs*

- Have the program and its objectives been discussed with potential participants and their managers?
- Do managers and participants understand the time involved?
- How will the groups' recommendations and actions be handled?
- Have members and clients agreed on the problem/tasks to be chosen (if this is to be a single-problem program)?
- Have outside resources and links that may be needed been identified?
- Has a time frame been established for concluding the action learning groups (optional, but important for participants to have a sense of the time being committed)?
- Will the group operate full-time or part-time?
- How often will the group meet?
- Is sufficient time allocated for learning?
- Who will set the group norms?

---

participants how they will be handling their recommendations. Ideally, they will behave as General Electric and other leading action learning companies do and will almost automatically and universally apply the actions recommended by the groups. If they do not, they will quickly destroy the initiative, energy, and creativity of the action learning groups.

As necessary, the group may seek outside expertise between and/or during meetings. Links with other groups may also be necessary. Planning action and exchanging full and frank expectations of actions are required at each meeting. Sufficient time for the individual meetings and for the program as a whole is necessary so as to enable the action learning group to go through the various stages of growth and productivity. Table 10.5 provides a checklist for determining whether action learning programs are well planned and managed.

Step 5: Expand Action Learning Throughout the Organization

If the initial action learning groups have been successful, the action learning program should be expanded to other parts of the organiza-

---

Table 10.6   *Determining the Program's Quality*

- How active are the action learning sets?
- Are participants excited about actions taken and learning acquired?
- Are organizational problems being better resolved?
- Are actions being taken? How effective are they?
- Has there been a review of what has been learned?
- Has systematic analysis occurred of how the learning can be applied to other parts of the organization?
- What were the major benefits for individuals, groups, and the organization from the action learning program?
- Have verbal or written reports been prepared for clients, managers, and interested others?
- How can future action learning programs in the company be improved?

---

tion. Before moving to this step, it is important to assess the quality of the existing groups and the impact of the action learning experience on the individuals and groups involved. Table 10.6 is a checklist of questions for assessing the quality of an action learning program. Also, there should be an examination of how the organization is beginning to change: Are problems being solved better and faster? Are operations more efficient? Are people working better together? Is the company becoming a learning organization?

Action learning programs need not be continuous in all parts of the organization. They can begin in one part of an organization and later be filtered throughout the organization, thus becoming a catalyst for organizationwide change and learning. Action learning programs should be established wherever significant learning is possible and needed.

Cigna International Property & Casualty Corporation

Cigna creates action learning groups that represent as diverse a spectrum as possible, including clients. The Philadelphia-headquartered insurance company puts people in action learning groups that work forty hours a week for four to five weeks. Each group is assigned a single problem that faces one of Cigna's divisions. One or two people in the action learning group will be from that division; every other division will also send one or two people.

A recent group was charged with evaluating the entire business strategy of a segment of the company that was losing money, and with determining whether the business's current strategy was viable. During the first week, the group was immersed in absorbing data about the business problem and strategy and applying theory to strategy. After that, group members went out into the field and interviewed customers, competitors, and employees to determine the soundness of the current strategy. The third and fourth weeks were spent in assimilating the data and presenting an action plan.

Cigna's management was so pleased with the results of this learning group that it immediately began implementing the group's plan of action. ■

Leaders' Circles Program

Carter McNamara, Program Director

The Leaders' Circles program, based in St. Paul, Minnesota, was initiated in 1994 to foster collaboration among nonprofit chief executives and help them increase organizational results, learning, and networking. The program revolves around the action learning process, in which five to seven members meet once a month for approximately three hours.

Interested leaders and funders who do not have an action learning project are allowed to join and serve as reflective questioners for those who do have projects. Each presenter uses twenty to thirty minutes—or more, if negotiated with the remaining members—to work on resolving problems in the organization. A goal for all group members is to network with and learn from each other.

Members help each other by providing highly focused feedback, questioning, support, and even documents and materials—whatever they deem will help. Members are encouraged to take actions, however small, between sessions that will address the problem or issue brought up at the previous meeting.

Examples of Challenges Addressed by Circle Members

Members select issues that are based on major challenges in their lives or workplaces. The following are some examples of goals:

▲ I need emergency budget help.
▲ How do I get my board to be more energized?

▲ Our board meetings are not effective.

▲ How can I evaluate my program?

▲ How can I delegate better?

▲ How do we go from being a volunteer-driven to a staff-driven agency?

▲ How can I incorporate a learning organization into our board structure?

▲ How can I develop an integrating vision for our agency?

Since its beginning, in July 1995, the group has worked on issues ranging from the personal to the organizational and from the strategic to the operational. It is up to each member to select his or her goal on which to work. At the end of each session, members reflect on the quality of the session's process to ensure that it remains highly practical and meaningful to them.

What Happens at Leaders' Circles Meetings

Each new Leaders' Circles program begins with an introductory workshop in which members are introduced to each other and hear an overview of the action learning process. Participants are offered suggestions about maximizing their experience in the circle, review circle ground rules, begin sharing information about each of their individual goals, and set the dates and locations of the next sessions.

During the action learning meetings, members are able to share focused real-world advice and resource materials and thus are able to solve real-world problems in each other's organizations. They are also able to network with others. Members have found encouragement from each other because of the climate of support that is present during the meetings.

In addition, members learn from each other's different values and perspectives. They are able to challenge individual and group assumptions both about the back-home environment and about actions undertaken to achieve their goals.

Members exchange useful materials and other resources. The members themselves control the dates, times, and agendas of each meeting. The members may use a designated facilitator to help the circle's process along, or they may choose to self-facilitate.

The final session of the circle typically includes a process designed by the circle members and geared to accomplish a sense of closure for each member. The duration of a circle depends on the extent of the time for which the members are committed to helping each other achieve their goals and to networking with each other.

Why Leaders' Circles Action Learning Has Been Successful

There are a number of reasons why the Leaders' Circles have been successful:

Ease of organizing, facilitating, and evaluating circles: Five to seven people can organize their own development program without having to defer to an outside "expert" who decides what they should learn, how they should learn it, and how they must prove they have learned it.

Ease of adaptability to busy schedules: The date and the location of each action learning session are determined by the members. Sessions can be scheduled when all members are available, and they can be held at locations that are within practical reach of each member's organization.

Applicability: Information and resources shared among members are focused on meeting each member's needs. At the end of each session, members reflect on the action learning dynamics involved in the meeting. If members believe their meeting is not effective, they can change how it operates.

Affordability: The action learning program is careful not to cultivate dependency on experts, which not only is expensive but also restricts members' ability to value and learn from their own wisdom and experience. Likewise, there is little need for expensive materials, since the learning is based on feedback and inquiry from the members.

Efficiency: Well-managed meetings afford busy leaders the time to reflect, analyze, and plan.

Support: Members support each other through the stresses of building and running their grassroots agencies. Each person gets twenty to thirty minutes of individualized and focused attention at each meeting.

Building resources: Members quickly build a foundation of materials as they exchange valuable and practical resources.

Building networks: The groups build networks of peers who share strong trust and confidentiality.

Tailoring Action Learning to Your Organization

Action learning has the power to transform any organization and catapult the company into excellence and success. However, it is important that the introduction of action learning into an organization be well planned and implemented because skeptical managers may not offer it a second chance.

The success of a company's action learning plan depends on tailoring it to the context and needs of the individual organization. In Chapter 11, we will explore the various options and choices that enable an organization to tailor action learning and thus gain optimum benefits from it.

Tailoring Action Learning Programs to Your Organization

Action learning can take a variety of forms and formats so as to attain the highest level of problem solving and provide the maximum quality of learning and development. Action learning can also be modified and adapted to meet the goals, constraints, and resources of the organizations and/or individuals participating in action learning groups.

In this chapter, we will explore aspects of action learning about which organizations and individuals can make selections and thereby create the type of action learning program that works best for them. It should be noted, however, that none of these choices or options involves elimination or watering down of the six essential components of action learning discussed in Chapter 2.

Decisions About the Program

Type of Program

Action learning programs can be formed to solve company problems (single-project programs) or to solve the problems brought in by each individual group member (open-group programs).

Single-Project Programs

Organizations using the single-project program may chose to have several groups working on the same organizational problem or each group working on a different company problem. When several groups focus on a single problem, many more alternative solutions may be proposed, which can be highly valuable for the organization. This also enables many people in the organization to become aware of one key, complex issue and thus helps to improve morale and commitment to the organization. The disadvantage to having several different groups focusing on the same problem is that the recommendation chosen to be acted on may represent only one group's efforts, and thus the learning from reflecting on action may be limited to that group. When each action learning group works on a different organizational problem, obviously, more problems will get resolved, and each set will be able to learn from the action based on its solution, thus acquiring a deeper level of learning.

Open-Group Programs

In open-group programs, each individual member brings his or her own problem to the table. Each person acts as a presenter in the group. The group members support and assist each other for an agreed-upon period of time. The group may consist of people from different organizations or from different units of the same organization.

Structure of Program

Part-Time Versus Full-Time

Full-time action learning programs require the group members to be released from their normal jobs so that they may be wholly engaged in the program. Part-time programs allow the participants to continue working on their own jobs. Many executive development programs are full-time (e.g., General Electric, InterUniversity Program in Belgium), allowing groups to resolve major corporate challenges during a one-month to twelve-month time frame. Part-time programs (e.g., Bristol-Myers Squibb, George Washington University) may be two to three hours per day, week, or month for one or several months.

Taking people from their jobs for a period of months and placing them in an unfamiliar setting or in another organization has proven to be an extremely powerful executive development strategy (see Chapter 7). It, however, is an approach used in a very small percentage of action learning programs and primarily for high-potential managers.

The advantages of part-time action learning programs include lower cost, allowing the person to continue in his or her regular job, and a learn-as-you-work approach.

Companies are discovering that they must make time to resolve critical problems. Action learning allows the company to fight the day-to-day alligators and at the same time develop the organizational capabilities to drain the swamp. Work, problem solving, and professional development all can and must become part of one ongoing process.

Learning must occur while one is at the post, since there is little time to get away, and action learning provides the best kind of learning. Unlike conventional training, in which only 10 to 15 percent of the learning ever gets applied to the job (Broad and Newstrom, 1991), nearly all of the learning in action learning gets applied.

Length of Program
It is generally a wise policy for the organization and/or the group members to establish some sort of time frame for the action learning program. Should it be for a weekend or for several months? Should members meet a few hours at a time or for the entire day? A definite date for ending the program can assist the members in planning how much time is available for determining possible actions, whether to seek outside knowledge, and so on.

The danger many companies and individuals face is allowing too short a time frame for the action learning groups to carry out their work. Today's organizations tend to be overly concerned about "not wasting time" and "getting back to work." We often focus on the urgent at the expense of the important. If action learning groups are not given sufficient time, they may be unable to fully explore and reframe the problem or to examine the context of the problem from a systems perspective. With limited time, they may not be able to consider solutions that provide the greatest impact and leverage or to thoroughly glean the personal, team, and organizational learnings available.

Length of Meetings
In open groups, it is important that each person have at least twenty to thirty minutes to talk about his or her problem or issue at each meeting, particularly if there are weeks in between each meeting. Thus a group of five to six members would minimally need three to four hours. Less time than that generally leads to frustration and lessening of enthusiasm for the action learning group or the action learning process. Table 11.1 shows a sample schedule for an open group.

Table 11.1 *Sample Schedule for an Open Group*

8:30–9:00	Arrival and coffee; updates and establishing schedule
9:00–9:25	Presenter 1
9:25–9:50	Presenter 2
9:50–10:00	Break
10:00–10:25	Presenter 3
10:25–10:50	Presenter 4
10:50–11:00	Break
11:00–11:25	Presenter 5
11:25–11:50	Presenter 6
11:50–12:15	Review

If the group determines that one member has a particular need for more time, the schedule for that meeting can be altered to accommodate this. Also, time may be given away by a member; however, this may sometimes be a sign that the person is seeking to avoid having the focus on himself or herself, or that he or she has not taken responsibility for action promised at the previous meeting. McGill and Beaty (1995) remark that a member may "feel that she has little to say at precisely the point when the set could be most useful—for example, when confusion makes the presenter unsure about her progress with her project or confused about the issues facing her. At these times, challenge and probing from the other members can be very helpful" (p. 42).

For single-project groups, the range of time set aside for each meeting can vary from one to ten hours, although the three- to four-hour period seems to lead to the most productivity, energy, and satisfaction. Action learning can be both highly energizing and exhausting, so precautions for both should be made. Again, it is wise to establish the time frame at the beginning of the action learning meeting.

Frequency of Meetings
Action learning meetings may occur on a daily, weekly, or monthly basis, throughout the life of the action learning group. Experienced action learning professionals suggest that meetings be held no longer than a month apart to keep the continuity and momentum of problem reframing, testing solutions, and reporting on actions taken. Also, if too much time occurs between meetings, the participants get involved

with "fighting the alligators" (day-to-day symptoms and urgent crises) and forget about draining the swamp (handling the important, system-wide problems).

The priority and importance the company places on action learning are often determined by how much time the company allocates for action learning groups to meet. Some companies, unfortunately, require action learning to occur outside work hours. Obviously, such arrangements lead many employees to conclude that action learning is not important.

Although it is possible to begin and end an action learning program in one session, there are a number of advantages to having time between meetings, including the opportunity to take action and show progress (especially in open-group programs), to reflect, and to obtain outside knowledge.

Finally, it is very important to have periodic reviews relative to the frequency of the meetings to be sure members are comfortable with what was agreed to initially, to evaluate progress and successes, and to determine if more frequent action learning meetings are necessary.

Procedural Norms

Procedural norms for the group may be set by the organization and/or by the members. The norming process is especially important in action learning groups because there is no designated leader. These norms should be clearly developed and stated at the initial meeting, although they may be modified as the groups go forward.

Dilworth (1998) cites the following norms for a group in which he participated:

▲ Meetings will occur only when all members are able to be present.
▲ Debates will be earnest, but members will never attack one another.
▲ All members will carry their share of the responsibility.
▲ Members will listen to one another.
▲ Members will respect the confidentiality of the group.

Decisions About the Group

Inside or Outside the Company

Inside-company action learning programs tend to focus mainly on organizational problem solving and development. They provide a powerful medium for bringing about organizational change and creating a learning culture and a learning organization (see Chapter 5). The length of the action learning program becomes less an issue in inside-company programs, since learning can become an ongoing process.

There are also advantages to employees going outside the organization to participate in action learning groups. Such external programs are more effective in injecting fresh ideas into organizational thinking by bringing together people from very different backgrounds. The participants also get help in launching their own internal programs or handling internal problems.

Volunteer or "Volunteered" Members

Action learning groups may be formed by individuals who have chosen on their own initiative to work on this issue for any of the following reasons:

▲ They care about the problem and/or the people in the group.
▲ They have some knowledge of and interest in the topic area.
▲ The issue has some relevance to their work or life.

Or the organization may appoint members on the basis of the following factors:

▲ Organizational needs—for example, a desire to mix people from certain units or companies, a need to make sure that someone present possesses familiarity with the setting, or a decision to select on the basis of future leadership positions
▲ Meeting the criteria of good action learning principles—for example, fresh perspectives or diversity
▲ Convenience—for example, the availability of people

Group membership in single-project action learning programs is often established by the organization, whereas membership in open-group action learning programs is generally determined by the interested individuals. These groups are composed of people who have voluntarily chosen to be in them.

Internal, External, or Self-Facilitation

Facilitation is an essential element of action learning in that it optimizes the quality of action taken and learning acquired. The role of facilitator may be assigned to someone within the organization (internal facilitation) or from outside the organization (external facilitation), or the role may be rotated among the group participants (self-facilitation). There are a number of key questions that the company needs to ask relative to determining how facilitation will occur within the group:

▲ Can we train in-company staff to become facilitators?
▲ Will having in-company staff serving as facilitators inhibit the group members?
▲ Can we afford the services of outside facilitators? Or can we find volunteers?
▲ Do we believe facilitators will be needed only at the early stages?
▲ Do we want one or two facilitators to serve our many action learning groups? Or should we have many facilitators, thus developing many people with these valuable competencies?
▲ Should we simply ask group members to rotate the role of facilitator?

Real or Appointed Presenter

The presenter of the problem may be either the person who is the true owner of the problem or someone who has been designated by the organization to bring the problem to the group and be responsible for ensuring that the group's solution will be implemented. The true owner is often a senior manager who simply cannot be available to work on the problem or whose presence may lessen the spontaneity of the group in seeking fresh answers and actions.

The advantage of having the real or true owner of the problem in the group is that there may be a stronger sense of caring about the problem and a stronger desire to find a solution. The owner may also be better able to answer fellow group members' questions about the problem in order to implement the group's recommendations.

On the other hand, the appointed presenter may be bringing a problem of much greater importance to the organization, and one that will have considerable impact if solutions are implemented. The energy of the group may derive from an opportunity for members to better their reputations in the organization (or industry or professional field) or from their expected accountability for producing a high-quality solution (e.g., at General Electric). Ensuring members that they have the power to act or work toward action is essential. Lacking this assurance, they are less likely to enthusiastically commit valuable time to something that may never happen.

Size of Group

There are two factors that determine the optimum size of an action learning group:

▲ The number of people necessary for engaging in effective social interaction, acquiring differing perspectives, and attaining necessary support
▲ The time required to deal with the problems requiring attention

Having too many members can interfere with the free, easy exchange of information, ideas, and challenges. Having too few results in less synergy, fewer creative tensions and dynamics, and limited feedback on actions and learnings.

Research and experience relative to the dynamics of groups and the quality and speed of solving problems suggest that the optimal action learning group would be between four and eight members to be both efficient and effective. There are few examples of successful learning groups exceeding ten people.

Decisions About the Problem

Familiar Versus Unfamiliar Problem

When the members of a group work on problems with which they are familiar (e.g., their jobs), there is an opportunity for them to improve their current performance and gain a greater understanding of the systems and contingencies encompassing that job. When dealing with familiar problems, it is important for the presenter to avoid the tendency of playing the "yes, but" game, which is a natural response for someone who is much more aware of his current situation.

Working on unfamiliar problems can be more difficult, but it allows for greater creativity and develops and broadens the perspectives of members in the group. Occasionally, unfamiliar problems may require some outside expertise. One of the dangers of working on someone else's problem is that it may not elicit the same sense of urgency. Reg Revans' description of group members as "comrades in adversity" points out, however, that the action learning process inherently builds an excitement and commitment to getting the problem solved.

Action Learning Students: Working on Unfamiliar Problems in Unfamiliar Settings

Robert Dilworth, Associate Professor, Virginia Commonwealth University

Virginia Commonwealth University is one of several universities offering courses in action learning for senior managers. At VCU students are assigned as a set to work with clients on problems and settings that are unfamiliar to them (a deliberate intent of the action learning design, to maximize fresh perspectives and to demonstrate the power of action learning). The following are two examples of recent action learning projects.

PARI Respiratory Equipment, Inc., a German firm with its U.S. operations in Richmond, Virginia, is a premier manufacturer of nebulizers for those with breathing disorders. The VCU students had no knowledge of this health care–related field and were anxious about dealing with an industry and environment unfamiliar to them. Yet, over a three-month period, the set developed a comprehensive proposal for the company's president, the CEO of the U.S. subsidiary, and his corporate board. Asked to rate the quality of the assistance provided by the action learning set, the CEO said: "On a scale of 1 to 10, I would give this group an 11. Their help was superb!"

The U.S. Army Distance Learning Program at Fort Lee, Virginia, contained a high degree of technological sophistication, yet only one of the VCU students assigned to the set had an in-depth understanding of advanced technology, and none of the students had any experience with the military. By the end of the project, the action learning set was able to offer assistance that enabled the program to be vastly improved and reframed to better fit adult learning principles.

Familiar Versus Unfamiliar Setting

A familiar setting is one in which everyone in the group is from the same organization or community. One of the benefits of everyone being familiar with the setting is that there is less need to explain or describe the context or environment in which the problem is occurring. The key disadvantage is that there may be, initially at least, a common mind-set and a lack of fresh perspectives.

Revans' work with the London hospital is an excellent example of people with problem familiarity working in a different yet familiar setting. Doctors, nurses, and other administrative staff of one hospital worked on the problems of another hospital while the other hospital's staff worked on the first hospital's problems. Not only were the problems of each hospital better clarified and solved, the participants gained confidence in themselves to solve their own problems upon returning to their own hospitals.

The unfamiliar setting is one in which the group is composed of either people from different organizations, backgrounds, or experiences, or people from the same background but working in a setting with which they are totally unfamiliar—for example, marketing people working on personnel problems, or business people working on academic problems.

Who Chooses the Problem

The way problems are chosen and who does the choosing is obviously very important. Of course, the problem chosen must be genuine, in need of attention, and important to the organization. (See Chapter 2 for a discussion of problem selection and examples of types of problems chosen for action learning programs). Given these factors, the following methods are possible in choosing the problem:

▲ A company sponsor chooses the problem.
▲ The problem is jointly determined by the sponsor and members before the action learning program begins.
▲ The problem is determined by members at the initial action learning meeting.

The final two options support the key principle of group involvement in and ownership of the problem. The first option works well when the sponsor assures the group that this is an important company issue and that their recommendations will be implemented (either by the group itself, by the group in collaboration with others, or by some other group).

What Types of Problems to Choose

The more important and complex the problem, and the more leverage gained as a result of its resolution, the better the problem is for the action learning group to tackle. As mentioned previously, the issue undertaken should be a problem (one for which no single solution is

Developing Learning Assessment Criteria
via Action Learning

T. B. Carlson, T. Gorely, D. Macdonald, R. Burgess-Limerick, and S. Hanrahan
University of Queensland, Australia

In 1996 the University of Queensland made a number of recommendations regarding the way courses were to be designed, assessed, and graded by the university. These recommendations had an obvious impact on the way teachers would teach and the way individuals would learn. One of the recommendations that had the greatest impact on teaching and learning was the introduction of criterion-based assessment (CBA).

CBA involves students being rewarded on the basis of their own work, independently of the work of other students. The assessment of student performance is based on a comparison with prespecified performance standards. The establishment of standards requires examiners to describe the type of performance that would result in any given standard.

Establishing the Action Learning Program

The action learning team consisted of five lecturers. Other academic staff were included in the project through an interactive departmental staff retreat designed to develop shared understandings of CBA and how these related to honors theses. An outside facilitator was appointed to assist the process. Students enrolled in the courses experimenting with the CBA procedure went through a series of focus interviews with a research assistant. The research assistant also collected data from team meetings and from individual interviews with team members. In addition, an independent consultant with expertise in CBA was appointed to provide feedback on the criteria and standards developed for a range of subjects.

Individual action learning team members, in conjunction with other members, clarified what CBA meant to them and attempted to reach a common understanding. Members then developed a subject outline and drafted criteria and standards for a first-semester undergraduate subject. Drafts were reviewed by at least one other team member and reworked after feedback was received.

At each team meeting, members discussed the process they were undergoing, their progress, and issues and problems they faced. The assessment tasks were completed by students and evaluated according to the criteria and standards. During and after the implementation, each team member reflected on the criteria and standards. Feedback was sought from students (through focus interviews) on the clarity and fairness of the procedure and on the quality of their learning. Additional feedback was sought, as appropriate, from tutors, markers, critical friends, and the independent consultant. Questions and feedback from other staff members encouraged team members to reflect further on their CBA models and associated teaching and learning practices. The results of these reflections were used to develop subsequent assessment practices.

Benefits of Action Learning

For Students

▲ With the CBA imperative to articulate criteria and standards, assessment tasks became more student-centered, relevant, and authentic.

▲ Students perceived greater inherent fairness in the CBA procedure. One student's statement reflected a typical feeling among the students: "We've had courses that didn't have any criteria—that was just a joke; they couldn't justify why we got our results."

▲ Finally, there was improved understanding of the expectations for the assessment tasks. Students expressed the belief that the criteria and standards gave their efforts a sense of focus and direction.

For Staff

▲ The staff gained exposure to a variety of CBA models and realized that many different CBA models could be equally effective.

▲ Staff gained greater insight into the student learning process. One team member, for example, commented that now, whenever students say that they don't understand what is expected or are confused, it makes him think about how he can be more clear.

▲ The staff has created new procedures (e.g., modeling) to clarify the intended assessment responses.

possible, and which different groups could resolve in different ways) and not a puzzle (one for which there is a single, although yet unknown, answer).

When you are introducing action learning to an organization, select problems that touch different parts of the entire organization, that are not amenable to expert solutions, and that are organizational rather than technical in nature.

Finally, the problem should exist in a time frame (there is a real date by which action needs to be taken), be feasible (it is within the competence of the organization or group), and be deemed important and worthy of solving.

Variations and Options for Tailoring Action Learning Programs

Each organization operates in different ways in response to the unique challenges facing it. Thus, to be most beneficial to an organization, action learning must be tailored to meet the objectives of the company and suit all the parties that will be involved. As long as the essential elements of action learning are in place, a wide array of variations is possible. The cases described in this book demonstrate the multitude of rich possibilities for making action learning work for you.

Facilitating Action Learning Groups

Action learning sets, in order to be able to function in the most effective manner and with the greatest power, need the energizing oil of facilitation. Without facilitation, action learning sets quickly lose their ability to create group solutions and to capture group learnings.

Although each set member should be responsible for contributing to the process of questioning, encouraging reflection, and identifying learnings, the complex and intensive elements of group dynamics necessitate a person's being designated as having facilitation as his or her primary, if not only, role; otherwise, the quality of facilitation becomes neglected and rusty.

In this chapter we will explore the key questions that an organization needs to ask relative to set advisors:

▲ Why is facilitation so important in action learning?
▲ What are the roles of the set facilitator?
▲ What are the ways in which a person can facilitate a group?
▲ How can one facilitate both work and process?
▲ How does facilitation help the learning and development process?
▲ What are the characteristics of an effective set advisor?

▲ When should an external person facilitate a set?

▲ Can we train in-company staff to become set advisors? Is facilitation a good role for developing leaders?

▲ Will having in-company staff serving as set advisors inhibit the set members?

▲ Are set advisors needed only at the early stages of action learning programs?

▲ How can we prepare and train set advisors?

Roles of the Facilitator

Facilitation of the process of action learning is essential for maximizing learning and action. The facilitator's key role is to assist the group in working on the problem(s) and to help the members maintain their commitment to the learning process. Facilitators act as "mirrors" that reflect the learning opportunities back to the action learning group members through questioning, confronting, encouraging, and supporting. They have great influence on the ultimate success of the action learning groups. Chapter 2 provides a list of desired characteristics and attributes of the facilitator.

The facilitator focuses primarily on group processes and learnings. He or she tries to ensure that all group members receive adequate talking time and encourages supportiveness among the members. The facilitator guides the participants to reflect on how they solve problems, on their personal learnings, and on how their learnings might apply to other organizational challenges and situations. Facilitators should help the group members examine their group behavior, especially how they listen, give each other feedback, plan actions and solutions, and challenge one another.

In action learning programs, the facilitator may be called upon to serve in a variety of managerial roles (e.g., planning, briefing, coordinating group meetings, etc.) in addition to the facilitative role described above.

The facilitator plays a final key role, according to Dilworth (1998), in "jump starting" the group activity and orienting the group members to the fundamentals of action learning (e.g., all group members are equal; listening to the views of others is essential, etc.). After that, he or she should fade back to what can be called *mentor status*. The facilitator remains available, as needed, and should provide perspectives relative to the process and the learning.

The facilitator should never tell the group how to deal with the problem; that should be left to the learners. To the extent that the facilitator is involved in the problem or seen as having an agenda, there is the danger of losing credibility and neutrality (since there will probably be differing perspectives on the problem.) This is one of the reasons why many action learning advocates recommend using an external person as facilitator.

Questions That Facilitate Work and Reflection

Facilitators are most effective when they raise questions rather than offer advice or answers. Bader (1998) has identified questions that are most helpful for facilitating work and reflection in the group. The questions for facilitating work include two types—problem-analysis questions and group-process questions. Examples of problem-analysis questions are the following:

▲ What is the group trying to accomplish?
▲ What is preventing you from accomplishing your goal?
▲ What can you do about those barriers?
▲ What have you tried thus far?
▲ What were the consequences of your actions?
▲ Are there any alternatives?
▲ Who knows what you/we are trying to accomplish?
▲ Who can help us?
▲ Who cares about what we are trying to accomplish?

Examples of group-process questions include the following:

▲ How helpful was that comment/question?
▲ Could we turn that statement into a question?
▲ Why did members ignore that point?
▲ What does that really mean?
▲ Does that fit with our ground rules?

Questions that can be asked to facilitate reflection are the following:

▲ What questions were the most helpful?
▲ How can we make this group more effective?
▲ How are we doing thus far?
▲ What ideas from this meeting appear to be most important?
▲ What made it easy or difficult for you to learn?
▲ What actions do you plan to take?

Of course, any member of the action learning group can and should ask these types of questions as well. In fact, questions coming from other group members may be even more effective. However, experience has shown that participants are often so involved in the problem solving that they easily lose track of the process and learning aspects of the group and thus may not be able to recognize the important questions that need to be asked.

Modes of Facilitation

The facilitator should help the group members assume increasing responsibility for their learning and actions, thus encouraging their autonomy. In the early stages, the facilitator inevitably plays a more significant role in guiding and directing how the group operates. Heron (1989) has identified three modes of facilitation to show how the facilitator can move from a more directive to a much less directive role:

Hierarchical: In this mode, the facilitator directs the learning process by clarifying and interpreting questions about procedures, aims of the action learning group, and appropriate and inappropriate behaviors and interventions. However, already at this stage, the facilitator will encourage members to support, clarify, question, and challenge other group members.

Cooperative: As the group becomes more confident with the action learning processes, the facilitator shares power over the learning and dynamics with the group. Group members no longer require the facilitator to help them carry out action learning procedures and processes. The facilitator, however, will still act on something that hinders or helps the learning and may not have been noticed by the members.

Autonomous: At this stage, the members are now on their own way, using other group members to meet the needs they have defined for themselves. The facilitator's main responsibility is to subtly create and support the conditions within which the group members can determine their own learning. The group may or may not, at this point, be ready to self-facilitate—that is, to rotate facilitation among the members.

How Facilitation Accelerates the Learning and Development Process

Research conducted by Heiman and Slomianko (1990) has identified four key activities/skills that significantly increased ability and speed in learning:

▲ Asking questions (forces the brain to neurologically open to better receive data)
▲ Breaking up complex ideas and tasks into smaller parts
▲ Being "tested" to see how much or what one has learned
▲ Focusing the learning on a specific goal or action

The facilitator helps the group members carry out each of these activities and thus increase the quality and rapidity of their learning.

McGill and Beaty (1995) point out that facilitation also helps members learn by both making the process explicit—which helps learners empower themselves and each other—and by facilitating the review of process so that members can become more conscious of process, the range of processes, and the potential application elsewhere.

The facilitator can also help in the reflection process. Mezirow (1991) notes the following:

Learning is the activity of making an interpretation that subsequently guides decision and action. Learning is grounded in the very nature of communication. Becoming reflective is central to cognition for survival in modern societies. It is the way we control our experiences rather than be controlled by them, and it is an indispensable prerequisite to individual, group, and collective transformations.

Boud et al. (1985) note that for the reflection process to occur, there are some key elements:

▲ Learners can only learn for themselves.
▲ Reflection must be an intentional event and complex activity in which feelings and cognition are closely interrelated and interactive.
▲ Reflection is part of a cyclical process.

Facilitators can enhance this reflection process by:

▲ Returning to the experience in the group and replaying it
▲ Attending to the feelings associated with the experience
▲ Reevaluating the experience after attention to description and feelings

Internal, External, and Self-Facilitation

As discussed in the previous chapter, there are a variety of ways in which facilitation can be handled in an action learning group. The role of facilitator may be assigned to someone within the organization (internal facilitation), assigned to someone from outside the organization (external facilitation), or rotated among the group participants (self-facilitation).

Whether the facilitator is a working group member (possessing familiarity with the problem being discussed) or is an "outside" person (not necessarily understanding the problem content or organizational context, but possessing action learning facilitation skills), it is wise that the facilitator not be involved in the questioning, reflecting, and decision-making process. To the extent that the facilitator is active, he or she may lose the needed sense of objectivity, as well as the time for focusing on process that is essential for the team to learn. One of the values of external facilitators is that they do not take their own issues to the group and thus are able to give undivided attention to the effective operation of the group.

Groups tend to be more effective if the facilitator can help the members focus on learning and on questioning the assumptions that may be present. Dixon (1998b) notes that facilitation may be particularly necessary when participants have had past experiences, such as being on task groups or project teams, that focused primarily on the task to the exclusion of process, and that may have established patterns of thinking or behaving that may be hard to break without the help of an outside facilitator or coach.

Many action learning groups may not need the presence of an external facilitator once they have understood the principles of action learning and have broken their old ways of operating in a group. Good facilitators work with the group in a manner that allows and encourages the team members to take over this function on their own, at which time the facilitator can exit from the group.

After groups have become experienced in action learning, some organizations find it wise to make the presence of a facilitator at a group meeting "by invitation only." Other companies believe that a facilitator's presence is necessary for optimal team learning and growth. If one believes, however, that ultimately people must learn how to learn on their own and create their own meaning, then they should not be dependent on the guidance of others.

Reg Revans believes that for group members to ultimately become responsible for their own learning and development, they should not rely on external advisors—each member should take responsibility for these functions. Unfortunately, especially in the heat of the situation, these moments for learning are neglected or even forgotten unless learning is the sole responsibility of a designated person.

In self-facilitated groups, each member takes and shares responsibility for facilitation as part of group membership. Only when acting as presenter will a member relinquish this responsibility. Some organizations find it valuable to use staff as facilitators and/or rotate the role of facilitator as a way of developing many people with these valuable competencies.

Managers as Facilitators at Whirlpool

At Whirlpool, line managers serve as group facilitators for action learning programs. Tom Helton, former director of corporate learning, proudly notes, "We have close to 100 percent of our line managers actually conducting the action training. The role of training and HR people has become largely one of training line managers to be action learning facilitators."

Action learning group successes at Whirlpool include:

▲ A cross-functional team that developed Whirlpool's award-winning super-efficient refrigerator

▲ An action learning group that devised a just-in-time system to supply product kits and components

▲ A team that leveraged knowledge from North America into a new dryer designed for European customers

▲ Several cross-functional groups in Europe that refined complex manufacturing processes ■

When to Use an Outside Facilitator

While a group member can effectively perform the role of the facilitator in many situations, there are occasions when it is preferable to use a facilitator who is not a group member. Schuman (1996) identifies eight factors that might cause a set to consider utilizing an outside facilitator:

Distrust or bias: The person who guides a process has an enormous influence on the process and consequently on the outcome. This may cause the participants to view the facilitator as someone who is promoting his or her agenda and, thereby, whether this is true or not, hinder the process. (This is why bosses or teachers are not advised to serve in this role.)

Intimidation: The presence of an outside facilitator can encourage the participation of group members who otherwise might feel intimidated. This can be especially true when participants are of disparate educational, social, or economic status, different hierarchical levels ator in control relationships (client-provider, purchaser-provider).

Rivalry: Rivalries among individuals can be mitigated by the presence of an outside facilitator; participants may be less likely to reveal personal rivalries or attack one another in the presence of an outsider. And if rivalries do arise, a facilitator can raise the question of their legitimacy and refocus the group on its stated purpose.

Problem identification: If the problem is poorly defined or defined differently by different individuals, the unbiased facilitator can assist in helping the group construct an integrated, shared understanding of the problem.

Human limits: In a difficult situation (which action learning often is), working with the breadth of issues and volumes of important information is challenging enough. As Schuman (1996) notes, it is "too much to expect anyone to also manage the processes that come into play" in an action learning set. Human cognitive capabilities are not great enough.

Complexity or novelty: In a complex or novel problem-solving situation, most groups have developed a set way for addressing problems and thus making repetitive decisions. When trying to get away from this, the outside facilitator, who will not be familiar with the old way, can suggest new approaches.

Timeliness: A facilitator can often speed up the group's work by helping members see their procedural problems.

Cost: By making meetings more efficient and productive, a facilitator can reduce the overall cost in terms of participants' time. Because more is accomplished at each meeting, the total number of meetings might be reduced.

Preparing and Training Facilitators

A key to having a successful action learning program is to identify and prepare facilitators. Harries (1991) recommends that potential set advisors undergo four stages of preparation.

The first stage of preparation involves a brief training and introduction to action learning. This ensures that, at least at the cognitive level, the person has an appreciation of the basic concepts underlying action learning. Input from experienced facilitators is very useful. Although reading and training will not develop the facilitative and managerial skills needed by the facilitator, they will provide the aspiring advisor with an understanding of the need for the acquisition of such skills.

Observation of a group in action is the second stage. This can be done either by observing a group meeting or by viewing one on videotape. One danger to be avoided is to model oneself too closely on someone who is perceived as a good advisor. This can be disastrous, since an action learning facilitator must be true to his or her natural self or the unnaturalness will quickly become apparent.

The third stage involves membership as a participant in an action learning group. Here, the facilitator directly experiences the power of a group, in terms of both its supportiveness and its challenging tensions. This experience is particularly helpful in checking out the development of the group in terms of moving through the reporting, clarifying, and resolution stages (see Chapter 3) and in developing awareness of group processes, interpersonal skills, and the manner in which the group gradually takes over the facilitator's functions.

The final stage involves co-advising. The trainee facilitator *shadows* the experienced facilitator and facilitates whenever the latter feels it to be appropriate. Following the session, the trainee can discuss his or her performance with the experienced facilitator.

Serving as a Set Advisor/Learning Coach

Isabel Rimanoczy, LIM Latin America

In 1996, this Europe-headquartered multinational pharmaceutical company divided its operations into regions, including a Latin American region. The regional manager, facing the challenge of developing synergy among the managers in his region, gathered key people for the purposes of launching a new product and creating a cross-functional regional team. The task was not easy: although Latin America is, with the exception of Brazil, a Spanish-speaking region, there are still significant cultural differences that are not always obvious.

The regional team included executives from Argentina, Brazil, Chile, Colombia, Ecuador, Mexico, Uruguay, and Venezuela. They were scheduled to hold five one-day meetings, spread over six months, hosted in different countries of the region. Establishing a successful project and team were deemed important for several reasons:

▲ From the business side, the launching of the new product was a key factor in facing competitors.

▲ From an organizational point of view, the success of this mission would send a message to the whole region, and to the rest of the regions in the world, that synergy makes sense.

▲ From a team perspective, a cross-functional and cross-cultural team that could perform with success would be seen as a role model for other potential projects.

▲ From personal points of view, the CEO and the group members were exposing themselves to an audacious project.

After the group's second meeting, the CEO, aware of the importance of this pilot test of regional synergy, decided to call in a set advisor/learning coach (i.e., me) to help the team in subsequent meetings. This gave the team a chance to further transform its project into a learning experience. As learning coach, I began by making personal contact with every member before the next meeting, in order to explain the approach that we would be employing for the remainder of the group's meetings.

Action-reflection-learning is an action learning methodology that places extra emphasis on the facilitator as a learning coach. The learning coach pays special attention to the way the group is acting. He or she intervenes when the *process* has become an obstacle to the group's making progress on the *content.* A key objective of the learning coach is to create moments of reflection so that the members of the group have a chance to review their acts, draw conclusions from them, and make the required changes to ensure better progress on the given task. The learning coach acts as a *connector* in this process—designing, observing, questioning, teaching, and coaching—with a just-in-time approach to intervention.

The action-reflection-learning cycle is as follows:

Phase 1: Action
Phase 2: Reflection
Phase 3: Awareness
Phase 4: Assessment of need for change
Phase 5: Planning
Phase 6: New action
Throughout: Planning by learning coach

As the learning coach, my roles during the sessions were to:

▲ Provide tools or concepts if they could help the group work more efficiently
▲ Stop the team to ask a question which would help them reflect on their current performance
▲ Help create awareness of the learnings occurring during the session
▲ Help create the link between that situation and other, similar situations that members would face daily when working on other teams
▲ Help members stay focused on the task
▲ Provide feedback upon request

Key Moments During the Sessions

Two key moments of truth when there were significant changes and learnings occurred during the sessions:

Intervention 1

At one point, I invited the group to suggest one or two norms that members considered important in ensuring a good performance during the meeting (phases 1 and 2: action and reflection). One of the norms that arose was "to use English," which was the official language of the meetings, although English is not the native language of any of the countries of the region. This provoked the sudden awareness (phase 3) of the following:

▲ In this company, if one wants a good career, one must speak English well.
▲ These meetings were being conducted in English because they were meetings of people wanting good careers in the organization.
▲ Some hierarchically superior attendees would be assessing the participants according to their English skills.
▲ English was a second language and nobody felt fully comfortable speaking English.
▲ Some people might rather not express an idea than reveal their imperfect English.

Immediately after this, I asked the group if speaking only in English was an obstacle to communication and if the group accepted that norm (phase 4: assessment of need for change). The group members agreed that it was an obstacle, and, with obvious relief, decided that everyone was free to speak in the language he or she preferred (phase 5: planning). The meeting continued in Spanish (phase 6: new action).

This event shows how an "undiscussable" matter in the organization (namely, the importance of using English) was acting as an obstacle to the group's communication, one of the difficulties they had diagnosed. As the learning coach, I highlighted how setting norms had helped the team members in their performance, fostering their awareness of a learning to be repeated in other situations.

Intervention 2

The meeting had a tight agenda, with a presentation every thirty minutes, each run by a different member who shared his or her progress in the launching of the product. Members used overheads and charts to explain the data. They inspired some questions, but the tight time schedule didn't allow for many questions or much discussion. Even so, after the third presenter, the meeting was already fifty minutes behind schedule. Everyone began to worry, since the group needed to finalize everything by the end of the session.

At that point (phase 1: action) I suggested "stop-reflect-write-report," which is a tool used to include a moment of reflection (phase 2) immediately after an action. I suggested two questions: What are we doing well? What should we do differently from what we are now doing in this meeting?

The group members had two minutes to think and then write down their thoughts individually. Then each one would read aloud his or her two answers. As a result of this intervention, we collected a number of "awareness" thoughts (phase 3) including the following:

▲ The time schedule is not being respected.
▲ There is no time to ask questions.
▲ There is no space for major exchanges.
▲ The data presented in overheads are merely informational, one-way communication.
▲ The time of the meeting should be used better.

The group members then moved to phase 4 (assessment of the need for change) to determine how they might improve their teamwork. They concluded that a meeting of so many people from different countries was such a special and unique opportunity for face-to-face exchange that it should be better used. Everything that could be handled by e-mail, fax, mail, or phone should be avoided at these sessions, thus saving the meeting for questions, generation of ideas, and exchange of experiences.

However, since getting information was still important, the members decided to review the priorities to be discussed during the remainder of that day. The remaining presentations were rescheduled for the next meeting, as was the distribution of additional needed information to each member (phase 5: planning). The learning went one step farther (phase 6: new action) as members planned the information they would mail, fax, phone, or send via e-mail prior to their next meeting so as to keep the same thing from happening again.

Lessons I Have Learned as a Learning Coach Working with Action Learning Groups

I have realized the critical importance of beginning with the question "What are we here for?" As simple as it may seem, once a group takes a moment to reflect on this question, the whole of the work is easily focused. If the Latin American group had begun with that question (answers might have been "to exchange ideas," "to create synergy," "to accelerate the launching process"), the members would have been more aware right from the beginning of the obstacles to their communication (such as language and one-way presentations).

Another valuable insight is awareness about the time required for learning to be assimilated so as to change behavior. The "magic"of learning and changing group behaviors requires more than one day. The cycle needs to be repeated several times.

The Set Advisor: Key to Action Learning Success

Facilitation that enables the group to function at its optimum potential in terms of solving problems and developing the skills and attributes of its members is what separates action learning from all other problem-solving and development programs. Thus it is important to provide the time and the resources for a facilitator. Like the servant leader described in Hesse's *Journey to the East* (see Chapter 7), the facilitator serves the group in so unobtrusive a manner that the group does not even recognize the power and tremendous benefits of his or her service.

Avoiding the Pitfalls

Although action learning is built on some relatively simple and clear principles and can be adapted in a variety of ways, there are a number of ways in which it can be watered down and weakened. If the key elements of action learning are neglected or never introduced, its impact will be lessened and even lost. Therefore, it is important to be aware of the possible pitfalls that can derail the successful operations of action learning programs. In this chapter, we will identify ten of the most common pitfalls and make suggestions for avoiding them.

The Inappropriate Problem

Probably the single most critical cause for the failure of an action learning program is the selection of an inappropriate problem or issue for the group. For action learning, the problem is what creates the purpose, the urgency, the excitement, and the intensity of effort for action and learning. There are several ways in which a problem may be unsuitable for action learning:

Unimportant, too simple, or too small: The problem should be crucial to the organization, one that is deserving of the time and funds being expended by the organization. If it is unimportant and unchallenging, the energy and capacity of the group will not be tested. Members will not commit themselves to coming up with their best ideas.

Not real to the organization: Problems should be genuine for the organization, and not just hypothetical. Otherwise, action learning programs will degenerate into case studies, which Reg Revans describes as "edited descriptions by unknown authors of inaccessible conditions for which participants cannot be responsible and upon which they cannot deploy their most effective managerial talent, namely, the power of observation" (1980, pp. 308–309). In case studies, participants cannot test the validity of their solutions by taking any real-time actions to apply them.

Beyond the authority or scope of responsibility of the group: Problems that are beyond the scope of interest or capability of the group members may cause a sense of impossibility or a feeling of guaranteed failure. Frustration rather than energized commitment will be the response of the members.

Too large and complex: Problems that are overcomplicated result in confusion and unguided chaos. When a situation involves many variables and the variables are hard to identify and measure, the problem overwhelms rather than invigorates the group.

Offering little opportunity for learning or applying learning: Almost any problem offers an opportunity for some learning. However, it is wise for a company to select problems that provide the greatest amount of learning, since this is where the long-range benefits of the action learning occur.

Some questions that can be asked regarding the appropriateness of the problem for the action learning group are listed in Table 13.1.

Lack of Organizational Support

For action learning to be successful, there must be top-level support for the program as well as for those participating in the action learning groups. Top managers should be champions of the program. They demonstrate their support by allowing and encouraging participation during work hours as well as providing appropriate space and facilities.

Table 13.1 *Questions to Determine Appropriateness*

- Is the problem significant and important to the organization?
- Is it within the scope and authority of the set members?
- Is it a problem and not a puzzle?
- Does it provide learning opportunities?

Table 13.2 *Questions to Determine Company Support*

- Is top management supporting the action learning program and its participants?
- Are there champions to sponsor the sets?
- Are time and space set aside for the action learning program?
- Is the organization aware and supportive of the cultural changes that are created by action learning?

The company should also demonstrate keen and immediate support for the actions developed by the groups (see the General Electric story, below). If the solutions generated by the sets are rejected or ignored, the energy and enthusiasm of the participants will be quickly dissipated.

In some companies, managers may reject action learning because it threatens those who are authoritarian, who are conditioned to determining answers by themselves, or who fear losing authority and status. These managers do not trust the action learning program, and they fear people poking around in areas that are "reserved" for experts (Froiland, 1994).

Some questions that can be asked to determine whether action learning programs have company support are listed in Table 13.2.

GE's Commitment to Action Learning

General Electric has declared action learning to be a vital strategy in transforming GE into a global-thinking, fast-changing organization. GE leaders are expected to and must be able to operate in global businesses, to develop the ability to work in nonhierarchical settings, and to solve problems across business and cultural boundaries while also solving difficult strategic business problems.

Since 1986, GE's training programs have used action learning for addressing and solving actual business problems. The aim is to provide managers with high-impact, multifunctional global business team experience. James Noel, manager of executive education at GE, acknowledges that action learning is pivotal in GE's recent successes. He states that action learning has made "participants active partners in the learning process. Because the team projects provide value to GE's businesses, [action learning] has an immediate return on investment. Action learning also provides a viable vehicle for dealing with issues of leadership and teamwork."

The action learning model complements other changes going on at GE—cutting bureaucracy, eliminating layers of management, and keeping only businesses that can succeed globally. The new culture and new leadership at GE need to be based not just on bureaucracy and control but also on empowerment of employees. GE wants to create leaders who can lead the organization with speed, simplicity, and self-confidence. ■

Lack of Time

There are several ways in which the issue of time is implicated in the quality of an action learning program:

Not enough time for the group to complete its efforts: Organizations often blunder by not allocating the amount of time needed for action learning projects to go successfully from the incubation period to final implementation. It takes time for the questioning, reflecting, and interim actions to bear fruit. Time constraints also occur when group members have difficulty in integrating their calendars and schedules. It is naturally quite difficult for a group of six to eight people to find mutually convenient times for meetings of three to four hours for up to six months. Group meetings cannot be squeezed into an hour here and there, and so long-range planning is required. Once the group sets its schedule, everyone must be expected to make that commitment as a group member.

Not enough time between group meetings: At the end of the agreed-upon time for each presenter (in open-group programs) or at the end of each meeting (for single-project programs), specific action steps should be developed and agreed to. There should be sufficient time allotted between meetings for the members and/or those group as a whole to apply these actions. Members will thereby have those actions to reflect on at the next group meeting. Having actions to reflect on is crucial for action learning.

Table 13.3 *Questions to Determine Adequacy of Time Allocated*

- Has adequate time for the action learning programs been set aside to qualitatively resolve the problems assigned to the group?
- Is there sufficient time between group meetings to allow for appropriate information collection, reflection, and action?
- For an open-group program, is sufficient time allowed for each person to present and for the group to reflect and recommend action steps?

Not enough time during action learning meetings: In open groups, it is important to negotiate time at the beginning of each meeting (see Chapter 11). If time is not planned or negotiated, timing is not adhered to, and the group can easily become sloppy and less effective. In order to ensure sufficient time for reflection and learning for each member at each meeting, careful attention must be paid to the clock. Each presenter should observe preestablished time limits. Overrunning by one person cuts into the time of others. Thus it may be useful for the facilitator or an assigned timekeeper to inform the presenter when he or she has five minutes left. Time should also be allocated for assessing the overall meeting.

Some questions that can be asked regarding appropriate time allocation are listed in Table 13.3.

Poor Mix of Members

The composition of an action learning group is very important to the overall success of any action learning program. The action learning group should be composed of four to eight individuals who are committed to examining problems that have no easily identifiable solutions. Ideally, the makeup of the group is diverse, so as to maximize various perspectives and obtain fresh viewpoints. The mix of participants should thus be determined with great care and interest rather than randomly. If possible, members should be from various parts of the organization, or even from other organizations, the community, customers, or suppliers. There should be a balance of gender, age, ethnicity, and learning styles, not only to add diversity and richness, but, more important, to elicit "dumb" questions and challenge assumptions and past ways of doing things.

Table 13.4   *Questions to Determine Choice of Participants*

- Have participants been chosen with strategic care?
- Are participants all from the same part of organization or from several parts of the organization or even from other organizations and the community?
- Do group members have a variety of views and mind-sets?
- Do participants have different learning styles and behavioral patterns?
- Is there a balance of gender, age, and ethnicity to add diversity and richness?

Some questions that can be asked relative to choosing members are listed in Table 13.4.

Lack of Commitment by Members

For action learning to work, there must be strong commitment from all the members to helping each other in resolving the problem(s). People must want to be there for the good of the organization and for their own personal growth and development.

Attention needs to be paid to the words and nonverbal questions of the presenter and other members. In ordinary meetings and discussion groups, people often focus only on issues of importance to them and relax their attention when they are less concerned with the issue under discussion. In action learning, however, members must give their complete attention to the problem, even though it may have nothing whatsoever to do with them or may not be to their advantage. The rewards for this effort are very appealing. Having other people focus all their attention on one's problem can be a powerful and heartwarming event. Group members are more likely to give attention and respect to fellow members who carefully listen to and respect them.

Some questions that can be asked relative to members' commitment are listed in Table 13.5.

Poor Problem Framing and Problem Solving

There are a number of reasons why action learning groups do not and/or cannot frame and solve the problem(s) they face:

Table 13.5 *Questions to Determine Commitment of Members*

- Do the members feel any sense of ownership of the problem or project?
- Are members comfortable taking risks and seeking new solutions?
- Are members interested in the problem, and do they have a strong commitment to solving it?
- Do members listen to, respect, and learn from other members?
- Do members attend all meetings?

The problem has been defined by someone else: The group is forced to or agrees to work within the constraints of the problem statement. The more authority or power accorded to the person who gives the group the problem, the more likely the group is to feel constrained to accept, without question, the definition of the problem.

The presenter is not motivated to solve the problem: The presenter needs to have some motivation to solve the problem and implement the proposed solution. He or she must have a desire to do something about the issue or problem and must come prepared to act. If the set member has no intention to further the project, then the action learning process will not work and set members will become frustrated (McGill and Beaty, 1995).

A too-quick solution is desired: If members are overanxious to solve the problem and move on, the problem will not receive the reflection, energy, and attention necessary for a high-quality solution. The group will not have sufficient time to correctly ascertain the true problem.

A low-quality solution is acceptable: If members attach a lower priority to the problem, they are likely to spend less time formulating and solving the problem.

The problem seems familiar: A seemingly familiar problem is likely to get a ready-made solution rather than a tailor-made solution. Familiarity often leads to a quick solution or fix.

Emotions are too high: Stressful or emotional situations often lead to an abbreviated search for a satisfactory statement of the problem.

There is little prior experience in framing and handling challenging problems: For most people, questioning a problem requires training and practice, as well as a culture that supports questioning. The habit of questioning is hard to get into (and easy to fall out of).

Table 13.6 *Questions to Determine Capacity to Frame and Solve Problems*

- Are the presenter and the group enthusiastic about solving the problem?
- Are members willing to accept a low-quality solution?
- Are emotions too high, such that there is an abbreviated search for framing and solving the problem?
- Do group members have experience and skills in systematically solving problems?
- Are ready-made rather than tailor-made solutions being applied to the problem?
- Is the group more concerned about a quick solution than about a high-quality solution?

Some questions that can be asked regarding framing and solving problems are listed in Table 13.6.

Lack of Commitment to Learning

Most of us, particularly in our work lives, are action-oriented. We do not recognize the need for or value taking time to reflect and learn. When there is a problem, we want to get it solved, take action, and then proceed to the next problem.

Although solving organizational problems provides immediate, short-term benefits to the company, it is the learning gained by the group that has the greater, longer-term benefit. Action learning has greater value for the organization, in terms of strategy, than immediate correction of a problem.

In action learning, the learning is as important as the action. Action learning places equal emphasis on the accomplishment of the task and on the learning and development of individuals and the organization. For the learning to be powerful in action learning, it needs to employ all four stages of the learning cycle: (1) the experience phase, where there is learning from reflection; (2) the exploratory, diagnostic phase, where there is learning through identifying patterns in experience; (3) the planning phase, where there is learning through formulating plans for improvement, and (4) the action phase, where the learning/plan is tested in new experience (McGill and Beaty, 1995)

Some questions that can be asked to determine commitment to learning are listed in Table 13.7.

Table 13.7	*Questions to Determine Commitment to Learning*

- Are the organization and/or participants only action-oriented?
- Is facilitation encouraged, and is a facilitator provided?
- Do group members recognize the greater and longer-term benefits of learning over problem solution?
- Are participants interested in and able to tap in to individual, team, and organizationwide learnings?
- Do time restrictions cause participants to race toward solutions because the organization is expecting quick results?
- Are participants clear about how the action learning program differs from task forces and typical problem-solving teams because of the high priority placed on learning?
- Do the group members know how to reflect on the learnings and apply them to other parts of their lives and the organization?

Insufficient Commitment to Action and/or Inadequate Development of Action Steps

There is no real learning unless action is taken, since one is never sure an idea or plan will be effective until it has been implemented. The action plan is a vital component of the action learning meeting. It represents a clear, tangible solution for the problem. The action plan should contain action steps that are specific—that is, that describe what will be done and by what date. They should also be feasible— that is, it should be possible to carry them out between group meetings. Thus progress on the project can be kept up through a constant cycle of taking action and reflecting. Group members should continually check not only for the best action to take next but also for what can be done in the time between meetings, remembering that it is easy to become enthusiastic about taking action during a set meeting and to forget the restrictions of time and energy.

Some questions that can be asked to determine the group's commitment to action and the quality of action steps are listed in Table 13.8.

Poor Facilitation

Facilitation is essential to helping the group slow down the problem-solving process and thus have sufficient time to reflect on activities and

Table 13.8   *Questions to Determine the Commitment to Action and the Quality of Action Steps*

- Are action plans a part of each group meeting?
- Is there a commitment on the part of the presenter and the group members to take action on the problem?
- Are the action steps specific?
- What will be done by what date?
- Are the action steps feasible?
- Are the action steps recorded so as to ensure that they are specific and understood?
- Are they reviewed at the beginning of the next meeting?

maximize learnings. Without a person being designated as the facilitator, the necessary facilitation simply will not occur. It is impossible to be fully involved in the dynamics of solving the problem while keeping track of the intricacies of group process and assisting in capturing group and individual learnings.

The facilitator helps group members reflect on how they listen, how they may have reframed the problem, how they give each other feedback, how they are planning and working, and what assumptions may be shaping their beliefs and actions. The facilitator also helps participants focus on what they are achieving, what they are finding difficult, what processes they are employing, and the implications of these processes.

The facilitator, as noted in Chapter 12, may be a working group member (possessing familiarity with the problem being discussed) or an external participant (not necessarily understanding the problem content or organizational context, but possessing action learning facilitation skills).

Some questions that can be asked to determine the quality of facilitation are listed in Table 13.9.

Too Much or Too Little Structure

Since most of us are unfamiliar with action learning, we have a natural tendency to conduct action learning meetings as we do other activities, such as task groups, business meetings, quality circles, and so on.

Table 13.9 *Questions to Determine the Quality of Facilitation*

- Is there emphasis placed on facilitation during the group meetings?
- Is the element of facilitating process and learning given priority?
- Has an internal or external facilitator been designated?
- Has the facilitator been trained, or does he or she have experience with the action learning process?
- Is there an appreciation of the critical, challenging, and not so common attributes and skills of a facilitator?
- Is the facilitator participating in a way so as not to neglect facilitation and learning responsibilities?

Table 13.10 *Questions to Determine the Quality of the Structure*

- Are the action learning meetings carefully planned with respect to time allocations for problem reframing or for each presenter in the open group?
- Is there avoidance of unnecessary protocol, of deference to hierarchical position, and of other formalities?
- Are there established locations and schedules for meetings?

Action learning requires a specific structure and format so as to ensure the quality of the problem solving and the development of the participants. Action learning programs do not require formal meetings with chairpersons, agendas, and unnecessary rules. On the other hand, they should not be free-flowing discussions or debates that involve everyone in decision making.

The flow of the group discussion is based on the organization's or presenter's issue and the need for support and challenge. The group may mirror formal meetings, for example, by producing minutes, but the minutes are simply the action steps agreed to; they do not contain a record of the discussion.

In evaluations the structure of a group, the questions listed in Table 13.10 can be helpful.

Keeping Action Learning at Full Strength

In this chapter we have examined ten pitfalls that can weaken action learning and make it less effective and less powerful. Unless these pitfalls are avoided, the action learning program may become merely a task force or a case study. The enthusiasm for action learning will quickly be lost, and beginning anew may be very difficult if not impossible.

It is important that the organization and the action learning advocates stand guard to prevent any of the essential elements of action learning from being eliminated or downplayed. The quality of the problem, the group, the questioning and reflection, the action, the learning, and the facilitation are all too valuable to be watered down.

Assessing the Action Learning Program

To ensure that an organization is fully capturing the power and benefits of action learning, it is important that action learning programs be regularly and systematically evaluated. Only through ongoing assessment can we determine the true impact of action learning and identify how it can be modified and adapted to yield even greater results for the organization.

Action learning programs should be continually assessed to ensure that the optimum benefit is gained from them. Feedback can come (1) from members, who are without question "best qualified to remove the bandages from each other's eyes and to shatter illusions about problems" (Lawlor, 1991, p. 258); (2) from facilitators, who help the members give each other feedback, encouraging them to experiment with various approaches to their problems and to honestly assess the impact of their actions; and (3) from presenters, who can provide feedback on how beneficial the suggested actions have been. The organization as well as its clients can identify changes in its people, products, services, and operations.

In this chapter we will examine group assessment of the action learning meetings as well as organizational evaluation of the overall action learning program. We will also suggest some beneficial times for assessment of and reflection on the action program.

Throughout the chapter we will provide questions that will enable the reader to evaluate and measure how well action learning is progressing within his or her organization and what changes may need to be made to create a better fit and greater benefits. Both the action learning meetings in particular and the action learning programs in general should be assessed on a regular basis. Let's first explore how we might evaluate each action learning meeting.

Group Assessment

A brief period of time should be reserved at each group meeting for members to reflect on how well they are working together to solve the problem and to learn from these efforts. For many members, this assessment time provides the most valuable and deeply meaningful opportunities for learning. The seven areas that the group should examine during these action learning meetings are described below.

Quality of Questions

The key to the power of action learning is the quality and flow of questions. Action learning places a high priority on asking good, challenging questions. Asking the right question is not an easy task, especially when the group is struggling with an overwhelming problem.

One of the primary ways in which action learning differs from other problem-solving approaches is its initial focusing on questions rather than on solutions. And, simply put, the best questions are those that, when asked at the right time and in the right way, provide the action learning group with the information and support it needs. The better the questions, the better the solution, the learning, and the team development that can be achieved.

A deeper understanding of the problem, as well as a better process within the group, can be achieved by questions that are

Open—give the person a high degree of freedom in deciding how to respond (e.g., "How do you make such decisions?")

Affective—invite the member to share feelings about an issue (e.g., "How do you feel about . . . ?")

Reflective—encourage more elaboration (e.g., "You said there are difficulties with your manager; what kind of difficulties? How can we be more reflective as a group? What questions have been most helpful to you? To us?")

Probing—cause the person to go into more depth or breadth on a topic (e.g., "Why is this happening?")

Fresh—challenge basic assumptions; often considered "dumb" questions (e.g., "Why must it be that way? What do you mean by . . . ? Has this ever been tried?")

Create connections—help to create a systems perspective (e.g., "What are the consequences of these actions?")

Clarify—further describe and explain (e.g., "Are you saying that . . . ? Could you explain more . . . ?")

Explorative—open up new avenues and insights; lead to new explorations (e.g., "Have you explored/thought of . . . ? Would such a source help . . . ?")

Analytical—examine causes and not just symptoms (e.g., "Why has this happened?")

Closed questions are those that are usually answered by yes or no or by a quantitative response that may be useful in clarifying or seeking further understanding. These types of questions can also be helpful in action learning, if not overused. *Leading questions,* which force or encourage the person to respond in the way intended by the questioner, are less successful (e.g., "You wanted to do it by yourself, didn't you?"). *Multiple questions,* that is, a string of questions that meet the needs of the questioner but are confusing to the responder, also tend to be less successful.

Who asks the questions in the action learning group is also an important consideration. Questioning should not be reserved for those with the most expertise or prestige. These "experts" often ask questions to elicit information from which they then draw conclusions and answers for the problem presenter. Questions should be for the purpose of enabling presenters to broaden and deepen their own views of the situations or issues they are addressing. Thus it is important that the group members adjust their style from one of eliciting or interrogating to one of enabling (McGill & Beaty, 1995).

The questions presented in Table 14.1 are designed to help assess the quality of questions that are asked by the group.

Table 14.1   *Assessing the Quality of Questions*

- Did we jump to solutions before framing the problem via questions?
- Are we questioning to solve the problem or to impress?
- Are we using open, reflective, and probing questions?
- Are questions fresh, clarifying, timely, and supportive?
- Do we avoid closed, multiple, and leading questions?
- Is everyone involved in the questioning?
- Do we provide sufficient time between questions?
- Do group members jump in before the presenter is finished?

Quality of Listening and Reflection

In a truly capable action learning group, each member is carefully listening and reflecting. Effective listening enables people to fully capture and understand the messages being communicated, whether these messages are transmitted verbally or nonverbally, clearly or vaguely. When others listen to the speaker, the speaker knows that they are interested, care, and are open to receiving the message that he or she is trying to communicate.

Unless the members of the group are actively listening to one another, the group is unable to reflect. It takes time and energy to reflect on the actions and learnings of the group. Members need to allow for quiet time between comments and questions. Action learning programs, to be effective, must therefore provide the essential time and space for people to stand back and reflect, unfreeze thoughts, rise above everyday problems, and bring ideas into a common perspective.

Reflection generates mutual support as members listen intently and draw out each other's experiences and practical judgments. This questioning and reflection process also encourages members to view each other as learning resources.

Group members should be open to trying out new ways of doing things, to experimenting, to reflecting on experiences, to considering the results or effects of the experience, and to repeating the cycle by trying out newly gained knowledge in different situations.

Table 14.2 lists some questions that may be valuable for assessing the quality of listening and reflection in the group.

> **Table 14.2** *Assessing the Quality of Listening and Reflection*
>
> - Is there reflective time between questions and comments?
> - Is listening attentive and open?
> - Are we filtering out what the person is saying?
> - Do we listen without interruption?
> - Are we viewing each other as learning resources?
> - Do we give an interpretation of what is said rather than an accurate response?
> - Do we make and convey assumptions beyond what is said?
> - What is the level of interest in listening to each other and to ourselves?
> - Are we open to new ways of doing things?
> - Are new insights arising, and are people making connections with the diversity of questions and opinions being offered?

TK

Quality of Problem Framing and Problem Solving

There are several criteria to determine if the project is appropriate for an action learning group. First, the project chosen by or for the group must be a real organizational problem, task, or issue that needs to be addressed and exists in a real time frame. It should be of genuine significance rather than merely hypothetical to the company or the person.

The project must also be feasible—that is, the group must be able to understand the problem and identify possible solutions—and it should be within the group's sphere of responsibility. If the project is not already in the group's sphere of responsibility, the group must be given the needed authority.

Further considerations for the project are that it should involve a problem or task that participants care about and that, if solved, will make a difference in their lives and that of the organization. The project should also provide learning opportunities for members and have possible applications to other parts of the organization. If the problem is viewed as just an exercise, or if participants doubt that the solution they construct will be implemented, there will be less learning involved.

Table 14.3 lists some questions that will help in assessing the framing and solving of the problem.

Table 14.3 *Assessing the Quality of Problem Framing/Solving*

- Is the problem real, genuine, and important to the person and the organization?
- Is it feasible?
- Does the problem fall within the individual and/or group's sphere of responsibility?
- Is it a truly a problem, and not a puzzle?
- Does the problem provide learning opportunities for the group? for the organization?
- Are we looking at causes and systems and not only at symptoms?
- Have we generated multiple solutions?
- Are we allowing the presenter to tackle the problem himself or herself?
- Have we considered the impact of the solution?

Quality of Action Steps

Advocates of action learning note that the most valuable type of learning in action learning occurs when participants reflect on their action, not just on their planning. Merely producing reports or making recommendations for someone else to implement leads to a diminished commitment on the part of the group. Being required to take action prevents a group from resembling a think tank, which may be intellectually stimulating but may have no real-world impact. Action learning groups must have the expectation and responsibility of carrying out their plans and recommendations.

It is important that action steps be developed at the end of each problem presentation (in open-group programs) or at the end of the meeting (in single-problem programs). These action steps should be specific (Who? What? When?), measurable, feasible (within the capability of the intended parties), and worthwhile. McGill and Beaty (1995) highlight the importance of each presenter making notes of his or her action steps and checking these out with the group during the meeting to ensure that they are understood and agreed to.

Table 14.4 lists questions that can be asked in assessing action steps.

Quality of Learning and the Learning Culture

A critical value for the action learning group is the emphasis on the learning acquired by each individual and the group as a whole. Toward

Table 14.4 *Assessing the Quality of Action Steps*

- Are they specific?
- Are they measurable?
- Are they feasible?
- Are they of benefit to the individual and the organization?
- Are they clear?
- Have they been recorded?
- Have we considered the impact of these actions?
- Were other options considered?

this end, a learning culture must be created such that the focus on learning is never neglected. Individuals are expected to take responsibility for their own, the team's, and the organization's learning and development. Time should be set aside at each meeting to talk about personal learnings and how the team's learnings can be utilized in other parts of the organization.

According to McGill and Beaty (1995), a learning culture has the following attributes:

▲ Members recognize the potential for many different situations to provide learning opportunities.
▲ Problems and crises are seen as especially important occasions for learning and development.
▲ In the group, it is safe to take risks; failure is seen as an event to be learned from rather than to be depowered by.
▲ Individuals take time to reflect on their effectiveness and helpfulness to the group.
▲ Learning and development are seen as active concerns that result in better action and further learning.

In action learning we augment the speed and quality of learning when the following elements are present:

▲ We reflect on what we did in the experience.
▲ We allow adequate time for the process of learning.
▲ A sense of urgency exists.
▲ We can see results.
▲ We are allowed to take risks.
▲ We are encouraged and supported in our deliberations.

Table 14.5	*Assessing the Quality of Learning and the Learning Culture*

- How can the learnings be applied to our organization? our group? ourselves?
- Do we have an environment where it is safe to take risks?
- Are we learning from our mistakes?
- Is our environment one that is collaborative, supportive, and concerned about learning?
- Are we taking time to focus on our learning?
- Are we questioning our basic assumptions?
- Are we taking responsibility as a group for our learning?
- Are we learning from reflecting on our experience in the group, as well as from actions taken outside the group?

▲ We are able to question the assumptions on which actions are based.

▲ We receive accurate feedback from others and from the results of our problem-solving actions.

▲ We do not rely solely on experts, which prevents us from becoming immobilized and from seeking and trusting our own solutions.

▲ We work in nonhierarchical groups from across organizational departments and functions, which allows us to gain new perspectives and augment our learning.

▲ The learners are examining the organizational system as a whole.

▲ We work on unfamiliar problems in unfamiliar settings—this is where the greatest learning may occur. As we work in unfamiliar areas, we unfreeze some of our previous ways of doing things and develop new ways of thinking.

▲ Learning is built upon the entire learning cycle: experience, reflecting, generalizing, and testing.

Table 14.5 lists questions for assessing the learning and learning culture of the group.

Quality of Facilitation

Facilitation is the oil that enables the questioning, learning, and actions to move forward in an efficient and effective manner. The facilitator should be very conscious of how his or her actions assist or hinder the

Table 14.6 *Assessing the Quality of Facilitation*
• Has the facilitator been able to guide us in reflecting?
• Has a learning-and-action climate been established?
• Are interventions timely and appropriate?
• Does the facilitator model good questioning and listening skills?
• How accurate and timely is the feedback?
• Is the facilitator committed to helping us learn and develop?
• How could the facilitator be more effective?

action learning process. He or she should make sure that members are given the time and encouragement to express their thoughts and feelings. The facilitator should also direct the group to focus on the projects in hand and encourage a questioning and reflective approach to the group process.

In assessing the competence of a set advisor, we should look at some of the following skills and attributes:

▲ Listening skills
▲ Speaking and feedback skills
▲ Empathy and openness
▲ Tolerance and patience
▲ Frankness, courage, and honesty
▲ Questioning skills
▲ Good timing for interventions
▲ Commitment to learning
▲ A nonjudgmental approach

Table 14.6 lists questions that can be used to assess facilitation.

Organizational Value

Action learning groups are usually created to benefit the organization as a whole. Organizations expect that the participants they are sponsoring will become not only more competent but also better able to contribute to the organization's success, through improved products, better services, and organizationwide improvements in operations and communications.

Table 14.7 *Assessing the Organizational Value*

- Are learning activities as realistic as possible?
- Are there immediate opportunities for application?
- Is the total person (human and employee) involved in the process?
- Is action learning well accepted by the individuals participating in it?
- Are there clear, tangible benefits to the organization?
- Is the action learning relevant to the organization's needs, recognizing the real world in which the company functions?
- Is there cost-effectiveness, showing that the expenditure is a profitable investment?
- Is it providing true professional development that is of long-term benefit, and not simply a skill that may be used for a few weeks and then fade away?

An action learning program should be undertaken so that it meets the needs of the group members as well as the needs of the organization as a whole. Most organizations would like to see immediate and significant returns from the action learning groups. They would like to see new leadership skills developed that will lift the organization into the twenty-first century. Clear, tangible benefits that are relevant to the real world outside the group are expected.

Providing people, time, and resources for action learning programs are costly to a company, and it naturally wants to be sure that there will be short-term and long-term returns.

Table 14.7 lists questions for assessing the organizational value of the action learning meetings.

Organizational Assessment

In addition to reflecting on and assessing the action learning meetings of the various learning groups, an organization should also evaluate the overall action learning program to determine its long-term impact on the organization and the people within the organization. Action learning, as we have seen in Chapters 4 through 8, has five significant, synchronous areas of application—namely, problem solving, building a learning organization, team development, leadership development, and personal and professional development. For most action learning programs, all five of these applications are desired and valued and therefore need to be measured for impact and future improvements.

Table 14.8 *Assessing the Problems Solved and the Problem-Solving Capacity*

- Were problems better solved through action learning than through other mechanisms used by the organization?
- Did the problems solved involve systems rather than symptoms?
- Were adaptive as well as technical problems handled?
- What was the impact of the solutions generated?
- Are employees better at framing and solving problems?
- Were biases avoided in solving problems?
- Did the problems stay solved?
- Are teams now more effective at problem solving?

Problems Solved and Problem Solving Capacity

As described in Chapter 4, today's world of rapid change and complexity has presented us with problems that are more confusing and more difficult to identify and solve. The days in which one person possessed the information, imagination, and capacity to solve problems are gone, and using the talents, perspectives, and brains of a diverse group has become an organizational requisite.

The most important yet most difficult problems to solve are not the technical ones. The necessary knowledge to solve these problems may already exist; it must simply be obtained and applied in an efficient and rational way. The more challenging problems are adaptive problems. For these problems, no satisfactory response has yet been developed and no technical expertise is fully adequate. In order to solve the adaptive problem, people must make adjustments in their attitudes, work habits, and other aspects of their lives.

If action learning is having an impact on problem-solving results and capacity, the organization should start seeing much better solutions to its most complex problems. It should observe a greater ability to resolve problems on a systems basis, one that works on causes and not only symptoms; it should notice problems staying solved rather than popping up elsewhere. It should see more team-solved rather than individual-solved problems. And, finally, it should notice greater problem-solving abilities from those who have participated in the action learning program.

Table 14.8 lists some questions for assessing the problems solved and the problem-solving capacity of the action learning participants.

Table 14.9 *Assessing the Impact for a Learning Organization*

- Is the learning culture, as practiced in action learning groups, permeating the way the organization learns?
- Is the organization placing a high priority on learning in all of its operations and planning, as in the action learning groups?
- Is the organization expanding its learning via ongoing questioning and reflection?
- Is the learning acquired in one situation applied, as possible, throughout the organization?
- Have new resources and networks for improving learning been created in the organization?
- Are more organizationwide opportunities for learning being created?
- Is learning rewarded and measured?
- How is knowledge being acquired, stored, transferred, and tested?
- Are we becoming a learning organization?

Building a Learning Organization

One of the greatest benefits of action learning is its potential to create a learning organization. Action learning groups develop values and skills for organizational learning and create a model of a learning organization for the organization to follow. As discussed in chapter 5, the learning created by action learning represents a new form of learning for the organization insofar as it is performance based; importance is placed on learning processes; the ability to define learning needs is as important as the answers; organization-wide opportunities exist to develop knowledge, skills, and attitudes; and learning is a part of everybody's job description.

The increasing need for individuals and organizations to acquire knowledge will continue, and learning skills will be much more important than data. These attributes and characteristics are inherent in action learning.

Thus the organization that is using action learning groups on a regular basis should be experiencing a situation and environment in which everyone is committed to continuous learning, learning is valued and rewarded, knowledge is quickly and systematically managed, and technology is exploited for optimum learning.

Table 14.9 lists some questions that can be asked in assessing the impact of action learning on building a learning organization.

Table 14.10 *Assessing Teams and Team Skills*
• Are action learning participants more effective as team leaders?
• Are they better team members?
• Are teams more effective in the organization? How?
• Do participants recognize the value and appropriateness of teams?
• Are participants better able to facilitate the workings and learnings of teams?

Quality of Teams and Team Skills

Action learning, as we have seen throughout this book, and particularly in Chapter 6, is extremely successful in building teams and team membership capabilities. Teams are being used to manage cross-functional projects, work on the assembly line, reengineer business processes, and develop marketing strategies. Individuals who have participated in action learning groups have been shown to be much more effective team members and be much better at developing and leading teams, since action learning innately develops seven characteristics essential to team success: cohesiveness and caring, clarity of objectives and purpose, communication and dialogue, commitment to task and ownership of results, creativity, competence, and cooperation and collaboration.

Table 14.10 lists some questions that can be asked in assessing teams and team skills.

Leadership Development

Numerous organizations have jumped on the action learning bandwagon for the primary purpose of using it to develop present and upcoming leaders. They have seen action learning as the best tool for developing the perspectives and capabilities that will be required of leaders in the twenty-first century. These include:

▲ Viewing people as a key resource and valuing their knowledge, information, creativity, interpersonal skills, and entrepreneurship
▲ Being able to work in organizational hierarchies with flatter, decentralized, self-organizing structures in which facilitation, networking, and remote management are crucial
▲ Developing contextual competencies that help people from different organizations work on shared problems

Table 14.11   *Assessing the Impact for Leadership Development*

- Do the key roles of leaders include the roles of coach, facilitator, and mentor?
- Are leaders better able to work in teams? to manage group processes?
- Are leaders more effective in managing projects?
- Are they better at systems thinking? Do they take more and better risks?
- Are they more innovative?
- Are they more stewardlike?
- Can they create optimism and energy?
- Do they manage uncertainty and ambiguity more effectively?

When serving as a facilitator, a person practices and improves the following skills that Morgan (1998) has identified as critical for all managers:

The skill of managing group process: This includes understanding the dynamics within the group, sustaining a task-related focus, managing time, balancing speculation and discipline, and maintaining optimism and energy.

The skill of adopting a reflective, synthesizing approach to group discussion: This approach summarizes and mirrors issues back to the group.

The skill of making interventions that frame and reframe the issues: This approach avoids myopic or group-think discussions.

According to McGill and Beaty (1995), action learning also develops several other attributes needed by leaders:

▲ Enhanced effectiveness in working with the range of relationships at work, including teamwork, mentoring, and encouraging cultural and transpersonal change
▲ Capacity to learn, reframe, and empower oneself and others
▲ Ability to live with uncertainty and ambiguity
▲ Enhanced capacity to undertake project management
▲ Management of group processes

Table 14.11 provides some questions for assessing the impact of action learning on leadership development.

> **Table 14.12** *Assessing the Impact for Professional Development*
>
> - Are participants more aware of their own strengths and limitations?
> - How they are perceived by others?
> - Are they better able to balance reflection with inquiry?
> - Are they open to change? to questioning their basic assumptions and rigidity?
> - Is there greater commitment to personal mastery?
> - Are participants evidencing active listening and empathy?
> - Are they more forthright, frank, and courageous in dealing with themselves and others?
> - Is wisdom replacing cleverness?

Personal and Professional Development

As discussed in Chapter 8, self-growth requires us to become aware of our blind spots and our weaknesses as well as our strengths. Action learning groups provide real feedback on our limitations and strengths.

They allow members to help each other struggle with challenges, limitations, and professional issues and build strong caring about one another. Having developed some investment in each other's well-being over a period of time, the members are more likely to give feedback and reflection leading to personal growth.

Table 14.12 provides some questions that can be used for assessing the impact of action learning on personal and professional development.

Assessment and Reflection Times for Action Learning

There are four points during the life of an action learning set at which it is appropriate to undertake an assessment:

At the end of presenter's time in an open-group program or at appropriate points during a single-project program: After each presenter has completed his or her time period, there should be a brief time allotted for the presenter to reflect with the group on areas such as the following: Which questions, facilitations, and interventions did he or she find helpful and less helpful? Which questions were most beneficial, and why? What and how did he or she learn during the allotted time? These types of questions also help to create the climate for learning in the group.

At the end of the group meeting: To maximize the effectiveness of actions and the quality of the learning at each meeting, it is important to spend a short time at the end of the meeting to reflect on and assess the results and the process itself. McGill and Beaty (1995) emphasize the value of checking to be sure that

action points have been adequately recorded and that each person feels that they have gained something from the meeting. Ideas on how to improve the process and ideas for other meetings are exchanged at this time and the allocation of roles for the next meeting is made—who will arrange the venue, who will send out the action points typed up, who will time-keep, etc. [p. 56].

At the end of the meeting, the group should spend ten to fifteen minutes reviewing and assessing the quality of the meeting. Asking questions such as the following can be helpful:

▲ What is one thing that I gained from the meeting today?
▲ What is one thing that I learned about the workings of a group?
▲ Is there something I would like the group to consider?
▲ How could we improve our next meeting?

To optimize learning, members need to become aware of how to raise questions to themselves about how they learn, why they may not feel involved, which questions triggered the most response, how they can apply what's happening to their work, and what was the most important thing they learned at the meeting, and why.

At the midway point (if the group operates for an extended number of meetings): McGill and Beaty (1995) suggest that groups review their activities on a periodic basis with some greater depth (perhaps one or two hours after the group meeting), using the following questions:

▲ What have we gained and learned from being in this group for ourselves and for our work (including skills such as listening, giving and receiving feedback, reflecting, managing time, etc.)?
▲ What have we gained and learned about working as a team?
▲ How can we improve the operation of the group to make it more effective?
▲ How do we wish to utilize the group for our meetings?
▲ How can we link up, and for what purpose, with other parts of the organization?

In an organizational setting where group members are sponsored by the organization, it may be appropriate to invite appropriate organizational managers to this meeting.

At the final meeting of the group: After the project is completed, the facilitator helps group members conduct a final reflection on their work so they can learn more about how they identified, assessed, and solved problems; about what increased their learning; about how they communicated; and about what assumptions shaped their actions.

By regularly performing assessment and gaining feedback, the action learning programs in the company can continue to improve, gain greater participation and commitment, and create tremendous growth in learning and success for the organization.

Ready for Launch?

Action learning, as we have hopefully demonstrated in this book, is undoubtedly the most powerful tool available for organizations to simultaneously accomplish five critically important functions—solving complex and key problems, developing leaders, creating the foundations for a learning organization, building self-directed and high-performing teams, and enhancing personal development and learning.

Action learning is built on solid theoretical foundations and evolves around six complementary components—the problem, the group, the questioning and reflective process, the commitment to taking action, the commitment to learning, and the facilitator. Although firm in values and principles, action learning programs are amazingly flexible and fairly simple to establish within a company.

Companies should seek to develop action learning programs to find what works best for them. This will involve risks (as does all significant change and learning), but the rewards will be tremendous. Action learning has indeed become one of the most valuable vehicles now used by world-class companies as they leap into the twenty-first century. Hopefully, you and your company will now be ready to launch your action learning programs and be among the leaders of the next millennium.

Glossary

action learning A group effort that involves solving real problems, focusing on the learning acquired, and implementing systemwide actions. Action learning involves six components: the problem, the group (also known as the *set*), questioning and reflection, the commitment to learning, the commitment to taking action, and the facilitator.

advisor *See* facilitator.

client The person who owns the problem. This person may or may not be the person who actually puts the problem forward for solution in the group—someone else may be presenting the problem.

external resources People or materials that the group may choose to acquire; information needed to help solve the problem, develop the project, handle the challenge, or resolve the issue.

facilitator The person who assists the group in focusing on learning and on group process. Also known as the **advisor** or **set advisor**.

feedback Reflective questions and suggestions to help the presenter/client.

group Four to eight members, including a facilitator, who use the action learning process to solve a problem or problems. Also known as a **set** or **team**.

in-company action learning program *See* single-problem program.

multiple-problem program *See* open-group program.

open-group program Project in which each person in the action learning group brings his or her problem to the group. Also known as **multiple-problem program**.

presenter The group member currently presenting and working on a problem with other members.

problem The challenge, issue, opportunity, or task for which there are a number of possible solutions.

puzzle Problem for which there is a single right but still undiscovered answer.

set *See* group.

setting The environment or context in which a problem or project is located; may be a **familiar** or an **unfamiliar** setting.

single-problem program Project in which all members of the group seek to solve the same problem. Also known as an **in-company action learning program.**

sponsor Person who has nominated a participant to serve as a client, with a view to helping his or her development and producing a more effective manager; person who puts forward a participant for the program and who feels responsible for his or her progress.

References

Adler, N. 1996. *International dimensions of organizational behavior*. Cincinnati: South-Western.

Argyris, C., and D. Schön. 1978. *Organizational learning: A theory of action perspective*. Reading, MA: Addison-Wesley.

Bader, G. 1998. *Action learning*. Unpublished.

Barker, A. E. 1998. "Profile of action learning's principal pioneer—Reginald W. Revans." *Performance Improvement Quarterly* 11, no. 1: 9–22.

Bates, A. W. 1995. *Technology, open learning and distance education*. London: Routledge.

Beaty, L., T. Bourner, and P. Frost. 1993. Action learning: Reflections on becoming a set member. *Management Education & Development* 24, no. 4: 350–367.

Bennett, R. 1990. Effective set advising in action learning. *Journal of European Industrial Training* 14, no. 7: 28–30.

Bierema, L. 1998. Fitting action learning to corporate programs. *Performance Improvement Quarterly* 11, no. 1: 86–107.

Block, P. 1981. *Flawless consulting*. San Francisco: Pfeiffer.

Boddy, D. 1981. Putting action learning into practice. *Journal of European Industrial Training* 5, no. 5: 2–20.

Botham, D., and D. Vick. 1998. Action learning and the program at the Revans Center. *Performance Improvement Quarterly* 11, no. 2: 5–16.

Boud, D., R. Keogh, and D. Walker. 1985. *Reflection: Turning experience into learning*. London: Kogan Page.

Broad, M., and J. Newstrom. 1991. *Transfer of training*. Reading, MA: Addison-Wesley.

Brookfield, S. 1988. *Understanding and facilitating adult learning*. San Francisco: Jossey-Bass.

Brooks, A. 1998. Educating human resource development leaders at the University of Texas, Austin: The use of action learning to facilitate university/workplace collaboration. *Performance Improvement Quarterly* 11, no. 2: 48–58.

Bunning, R. L. 1993. Action learning: Developing managers with a bottom-line payback. *Executive Development* 7, no. 4: 3–6.

Butterfield, S., K. Gold, and V. Willis. 1998. Creating a systematic framework for the transfer of learning from an action learning experience. *Academy of HRD Proceedings* 490–496.

Casey, D. 1991. The role of the set advisor. In M. Pedler (Ed.), *Action learning in practice* (2nd ed.). Aldershot, England: Gower.

Cunningham, B. 1998. Improving training through action learning. *The 1998 Annual: Vol. 1. Training.* San Francisco: Jossey-Bass.

Cusins, P. 1995. Action learning revisited. *Industrial and Commercial Training* 27, no. 4: 3–10.

Dilworth, R. L. 1995. The DNA of the learning organization. In S. Chawla and J. Renesch (Eds.), *Learning organizations.* Portland, OR: Productivity Press.

Dilworth, R. L. 1996. Action learning: Bridging academic and workplace domains. *Employee Counselling Today* 8, no. 6: 48–56.

Dilworth, R. L. 1998. Action learning in a nutshell. *Performance Improvement Quarterly* 11, no. 1: 28–43.

Dixon, N. M. 1990. Action learning, action science and learning new skills. *Industrial and Commercial Training* 22, no. 4: 1–17.

Dixon, N. M. 1998a. Action learning: More than just a task force. *Performance Improvement Quarterly* 11, no. 1: 44–58.

Dixon, N. M. 1998b. Building global capacity with global task teams. *Performance Improvement Quarterly* 11, no. 1: 108–112.

Egan, G. 1990. *The skilled helper: A systematic approach to effective helping.* Pacific Grove, CA: Brooks-Cole.

Foy, N. 1977. Action learning comes to industry. *Harvard Business Review* 55, no. 5: 158–168.

Froiland, P. 1994. Action learning: Taming real problems in real time. *Training* 31, no. 1: 27–34.

Garratt, R. 1991. The power of action learning. In M. Pedler (Ed.), *Action learning in practice* (2nd ed.). Aldershot, England: Gower.

Gibson, M., and P. Hughes. 1987. The supervisory process in action learning. *Management Education and Development* 18, no. 4: 264–276.

Greenleaf, R. 1977. *Servant leadership.* New York: Paulist Press.

Gregory, M. I. 1994. Accrediting work-based learning: Action learning—A model for empowerment. *Industrial and Commercial Training* 26, no. 4: 41–52.

Hahn, T. N. 1995. *Living Buddha, living Christ.* New York: Riverhead Books.

Hampden-Turner, C., and F. Trompenaars. 1997. *Mastering the infinite game: How East Asian values are transforming business practices.* London: Capstone.

Harries, J. M. 1991. Developing the set advisor. In M. Pedler (Ed.), *Action learning in practice* (2nd ed.). Aldershot, England: Gower.

Heiman, M., and J. Slomianko. 1990. *Learning to learn on the job.* Alexandria, VA: ASTD Press.

Henderson, I. 1993. Action learning: A missing link in management development? *Personnel Review* 22, no. 6: 14–24.

Heron, J. 1989. *The facilitator's handbook.* London: Kogan Page.

Hesse, H. 1932. *Journey to the east.* New York: Noonday Press.

Hofstede, G. 1991. *Cultures and organizations.* London: McGraw-Hill.

Inglis, S. 1994. *Making the most of action learning.* Brookfield, VT: Gower.

Isaacs, W. 1993. Autumn. Taking flight: Dialogue, collective thinking, and organizational learning. *Organizational Dynamics* 24–39.

Jones, M. 1990. Action learning as a new idea. *Journal of Management Development* 9, no. 5: 29–34.

Jubilerer, J. 1991. Action learning for competitive advantage. *Financier* 15, no. 9: 16–19.

Kable, J. 1989. Management development through action learning. *Journal of Management Development* 8, no. 2: 77–80.

Kanter, R. 1985. *The change masters.* New York: Simon & Schuster.

Kanter, R. 1997. *Rosabeth Moss Kanter on the frontiers of management.* Cambridge, MA: Harvard Business School Press.

Kiechel, W. 1990, March 12. The organization that learns. *Fortune* 121, no. 5: 133–136.

Kiechel, W. 1994, April 4. A manager's career in the new economy. *Fortune* 129, no. 7: 68–70.

Keys, L. 1994. Action learning: Executive development of choice for the 1990s. *Journal of Management Development* 12, no. 8: 50–56.

Kolb, D. 1984. *Experiential learning: Experience as the source of learning and development.* Englewood Cliffs, NJ: Prentice-Hall.

Kotter, J. 1995, March–April. Leading change: Why transformation efforts fail. *Harvard Business Review* 73, no. 3: 59–67.

Kotter, J. 1998. 21st century leadership. *Executive Excellence* 15, no. 5: 5–6.

Lanahan, E. E., and L. Maldanado. 1998. Accelerated decision-making via action learning at the federal deposit insurance agency. *Performance Improvement Quarterly* 11, no. 1: 74–85.

Lawlor, A. 1991. The components of action learning. In M. Pedler (Ed.), *Action learning in practice* (2nd ed.). Aldershot, England: Gower.

Lawlor. A., and G. Boulden. 1982. *The application of action learning: A practical guide.* Geneva: International Labor Organization.

Lawrie, J. 1989. Take action to change performance. *Personnel Journal* 68, no. 1: 58–69.

Lewis, A., and W. Marsh. 1997. Action learning: The development of field managers in the Prudential Insurance Company. *Journal of Management Development* 6, no. 2: 45–56.

Limerick, D., R. Passfield, and B. Cunnington. 1994. Transformational change: Towards an action learning organization. *The Learning Organization* 1, no. 2: 29–40.

MacNamara, M., M. Meyler, and A. Arnold. 1990. Management education and the challenge of action learning. *Higher Education* 19, no. 4: 419–433.

MacNamara, M., and W. H. Weeks. 1982. The action learning model of experiential learning for developing managers. *Human Relations* 35, no. 10: 879–901.

Margerison, C. 1988. Action learning and excellence in management development. *Journal of Management Studies* 32, no. 5: 43–53.

Marquardt, M. J. 1984. Working internationally. In L. Nadler (Ed.), *Handbook of human resource development.* New York: Wiley.

Marquardt, M. J. 1993. *Global human resource development.* Englewood Cliffs, NJ: Prentice-Hall.

Marquardt, M. J. 1994. *The global learning organization.* New York: Irwin.

Marquardt, M. J. 1996a, November. Action learning—The cornerstone of building a learning organization. *Training and Development in Australia* 23, no. 4: 7–12.

Marquardt, M. J. 1996b. *Building the learning organization.* New York: McGraw-Hill.

Marquardt, M. J. 1997a. *Action learning.* Alexandria, VA: ASTD Press.

Marquardt, M. J. 1997b. Summer. Action learning in the classroom. *Performance in Practice* 4–5.

Marquardt, M. J. 1998a. *Technology-based learning.* Boca Raton, FL: CRC Press.

Marquardt, M. J. 1998b. Using action learning with multicultural groups. *Performance Improvement Quarterly* 11, no. 1: 113–128.

Marquardt, M. J., and T. Carter. 1998. Action learning and research at George Washington University. *Performance Improvement Quarterly* 11, no. 2: 59–71.

Marquardt, M. J., and A. Reynolds. 1994. *The global learning organization.* Burr Ridges, IL: Irwin.

Marquardt, M. J., and N. Snyder. 1997. How companies go global. *International Journal of Training and Development* 1, no. 2: 104–117.

Marsick, V. 1988. Learning in the workplace: The case for critical reflectivity. *Adult Education Quarterly* 38, no. 4: 187–198.

Marsick, V. 1991. Action learning and reflection in the workplace. In J. Mezirow (Ed.), *Fostering critical reflection in adulthood.* San Francisco: Jossey-Bass.

Marsick, V., and L. Cederholm. 1988. Developing leadership in international managers—an urgent challenge! *Columbia Journal of World Business* 23, no. 4: 3–11.

Marsick, V., et al. 1992, August. Action-reflection learning. *Training and Development* 46, no. 8: 63–66.

McGill, I., and Beaty, L. 1995. *Action learning: A practitioner's guide* (2nd ed.). London: Kogan Page.

McLaughlin, H., and R. Thorpe. 1993. Action learning: A paradigm in emergence. *British Journal of Management* 4, no. 1: 1003.

McNulty, N. 1979, March. Management development by action learning. *Training and Development Journal* 33: 12–18.

McNulty, N. 1983. Action learning around the world. In M. Pedler (Ed.), *Action learning in practice.* Aldershot, England: Gower.

McNulty, N., and G. R. Canty. 1995. Proof of the pudding. *Journal of Management Development* 14, no. 1: 53–66.

Mezirow, J. 1991. *Transformative dimensions of adult learning.* San Francisco: Jossey-Bass.

Moran, R., P. Harris, and W. Stripp. 1993. *Developing the global organization.* Houston: Gulf.

Morgan, G. 1988. *Riding the waves of change.* San Francisco: Jossey-Bass.

Morris, J. 1991. Minding our Ps and Qs. In M. Pedler (Ed.), *Action learning in practice* (2nd ed.). Aldershot, England: Gower.

Mumford, A. (Ed.). 1984. *Insights into action learning.* Bradford: MCB-University Press.

Mumford, A. (Ed.). 1987. Action learning [Special Issue]. *Journal of Management Development* 6, no. 2.

Mumford, A. 1991, July. Learning in action. *Personnel Management* 34–37.

Mumford, A. 1995a. *Learning at the top*. London: McGraw-Hill.

Mumford, A. 1995b. Manager developing others through action learning. *Industrial and Commercial Training* 27, no. 2: 19–27.

Noel, J., and R. Charan. 1988, Winter. Leadership development at GE's Crotonville. *Human Resource Management* 27, no. 4: 433–447.

Noel, J., and R. Charan. 1992, July. GE brings global thinking to light. *Training and Development* 46, no. 7: 29–33.

Noel, J., and R. Dolitch. 1998. *Action learning*. San Francisco: Jossey-Bass.

Nonaka, I. 1991. The knowledge-creating company. *Harvard Business Review* 69, no. 6: 96–104.

Owen, H. 1991. *Riding the tiger*. Potomac, MD: Abbott.

Patrickson, M. 1998. Action learning. In F. Sofo (Ed.), *Human resource development: Paradigm, role and practice choices*. Melbourne: Woodslane.

Pearce, D. 1991. Getting started: An action manual. In M. Pedler (Ed.), *Action learning in practice* (2nd ed.). Aldershot, England: Gower.

Pedler, M. (Ed.). 1991. *Action learning in practice* (2nd ed.). Aldershot, England: Gower.

Pedler, M. 1996. *Action learning for managers*. London: Lemos & Crane.

Peters, T. 1992. *Liberation management*. New York: Knopf.

Raelin, J. A. 1997, Summer. Action learning and action science: Are they different? *Organizational Dynamics* 21–33.

Raelin, J. A. and L. Michele. 1993. Learning by doing. *HR Magazine* 38, no. 2: 61–70.

Redding, J. 1994. *Strategic readiness: The making of the learning organization*. San Francisco: Jossey-Bass.

Revans, R. W. 1965. *Science and management*. London: Macdonald.

Revans, R.W. 1971. *Developing effective managers—A new approach to business education*. London: Longmans.

Revans, R. W. 1980. *Action learning: New techniques for management*. London: Blond & Briggs.

Revans, R.W. 1981. *Management, productivity and risk: The way ahead*. *Omega* 9, no. 2: 127–137.

Revans, R.W. 1982a. *The origins and growth of action learning*. Bromley: Chartwell-Brat.

Revans, R. W. 1982b. What is action learning? *Journal of Management Development* 1, no. 3: 64–75.

Revans, R. W. 1983. *The ABC of action learning*. Bromley: Chartwell-Brat.

Revans, R.W. 1986. Action learning in a developing country. *Management Decision* 24, no. 6: 3–7.

Revans, R. 1998. Sketches in action learning. *Performance Improvement Quarterly* 11, no. 1: 23–27.

Rhinesmith, S. 1996. *A manager's guide to globalization* (2nd ed.). New York: McGraw-Hill.

Schein, E. 1993. Autumn. On dialogue, culture, and organizational learning. *Organizational Dynamics* 40–51.

Schuman, S. 1996. The role of facilitation in collaborative groups. In C. Huxham (Ed.), *The search for collaborative advantage*. London: Sage.

Senge, P. 1990. *The fifth discipline*. New York: Doubleday.

Smith, D. 1992. Company-based projects: Using action learning to develop consultancy skills. *Journal of Management Development* 11, no. 1: 12–24.

Spears, L. 1995. *Reflections on leadership.* New York: Wiley.

Stewart, T. 1991, June 3. Brainpower. *Fortune,* 123, no. 11: 44–60.

Sutton, D. 1990. Action learning in search of P. *Industrial and Commercial Training* 22, no. 1: 9–12.

Sutton, D. 1991. A range of applications. In M. Pedler (Ed.), *Action learning in practice* (2nd ed.). Aldershot, England: Gower.

Tapscott, D. 1995. *The digital economy.* New York: McGraw-Hill.

Toffler, A. 1990. *Powershift.* New York: Bantam.

Trompenaars, F. 1994. *Riding the waves of culture.* Chicago: Irwin.

Tversky, A., and D. Kahneman. 1974. Judgment under uncertainty: Heuristics and biases. *Science* 18, 1124–1131.

Vince, R., and L. Martin. 1993. Inside action learning: An exploration of the psychology and politics of the action learning model. *Management Education and Development* 24, no. 3: 205–215.

Watkins, K. E., and V. Marsick. 1993. *Sculpting the learning organization.* San Francisco: Jossey-Bass.

Weinstein, K. 1995. *Action learning: A journey in discovery and development.* London: HarperCollins.

Weinstein, K. 1998. Action learning in the UK. *Performance Improvement Quarterly* 11, no. 1: 149–167.

Wheatley. M. J. 1992. *Leadership and the new science.* San Francisco: Berrett-Koehler.

Wigglesworth, D. 1987. Is OD basically Anglo-Saxon? In M.J. Marquardt (Ed.), *Corporate cultures: International HRD perspectives.* Alexandria, VA: ASTD Press.

Yiu, L., and R. Saner. 1998. Use of action learning as a vehicle for capacity building in China. *Performance Improvement Quarterly* 11, no. 1: 129–148.

Zhou J. 1991. Self-improvement in Chinese joint venture companies. In M. Pedler (Ed.), *Action learning in practice* (2nd ed.). Aldershot, England: Gower.

Zuboff, S. 1988. *In the age of the smart machine: The future of work and power.* New York: Basic Books.

Index